BERLIN

Directed and designed by Hans Höfer
Produced by Rolf Steinberg
Edited by Dr. Heinz Vestner
Photography by Günter Schneider

APA PUBLICATIONS

BERLIN

Second Edition
© 1990 APA PUBLICATIONS (HK) LTD
All Rights Reserved
Printed in Singapore by Höfer Press Pte. Ltd

ABOUT THIS BOOK

Cityguide: Berlin, like all other books in the *Insight Guides* series, aims at cutting deep into the world's metropolises, to make these accessible to the casual traveller, and to open up new roadways of discovery off the beaten tracks of sightseeing tourism.

The text of *Cityguide: Berlin* has been compiled by 16 writers each with a different background thus reflecting Berlin's melting pot: the same applies to the photographers.

Editor **Rolf Steinberg**, a Berliner by choice, although widely travelled in the USA and Asia and living for a time in Paris, has always returned to the city on the Spree. One of his books on future archaeological sites, *Dead Tech*, stirred public attention in the USA. He has contributed four of the districts chapters and the majority of the boxes in this book.

Jörg Schäfer studied theatre and music in Cologne and Vienna. Since 1972 he has been living in Berlin writing for radio stations. An experienced author of features on cultural history Schäfer took on the task of portraying 650 years of Berlin history.

The Weimar years and the fall of the Imperial capital after 12 years of Nazi dictatorship are described by **Michael Stone** whose life once was directly affected by those events. Stone grew up in a Jewish Berlin family. As a schoolboy he had to flee to relatives in Vienna and thence to England where he became a British citizen. At the start of the 1960s, he visited his birthplace and has since remained.

Post-war Berlin history, the Blockade, the Wall, and the 750th anniversary celebrations are covered by **Ute Frings**. She teaches on this subject at the Freie Universität when not involved in her editorial work with the metropolitan magazine *Zitty*.

Michael Ellsässer is the living proof of what he writes about: "Half the Berliners have been attracted from somewhere else to the Spree." Ellsässer came from Suebia to Berlin and took up residence in the north. He authored a book, *Wonderful Berlin*, and has written a number of articles on the Wall.

When talking about Berliners, Turkish immigrants, now in the third generation, must be included. Holder of a degree in political science and working as a freelance author on the subject of immigrants **Rita Unruh** was recruited to write on this subject. For two years she has been part of a research group at the Freie Universität trying to develop integrational concepts for German and Turkish Berliners.

When it came to the writing of the travel section Steinberg immediately thought of **Arnold Seul** of the metropolitan magazine *Zitty*. Seul, holds a doctorate in theatre science and a teaching assignment at the Freie Universität.

Looking across his shoulder in their shared Charlottenburg attic flat was his girlfriend **Anne Worst**. She might be called the boulevard specialist of this book, and has taken care of the Kurfürstendamm and the Unter den Linden. She also roamed around Alexanderplatz and made several trips to Potsdam. After living for several years in Scandinavia, Worst came to Berlin in 1986 where she has established herself as writer for radio.

Sigrid Hoff also works for radio, and specialises in architectural features. Her programme series has won her a conservationist award and has been published as a book. Hoff was born in Zehlendorf, and now lives with her husband and three children in Spandau—an obvious choice to write on these districts

Steinberg

Vestner

Schneider

Schäfer

including Reinickendorf. Together with historian **Hermann Josef Fohsel**, who provided the scientific and personal background, she compiled the chapter on Charlottenburg.

Udo Meyer studied German, history and political science at the Freie Universität, and for two years was involved in the preparations of the 750th anniversary celebrations. In this capacity he published several features on the Tiergarten district, which made him well qualified to write the chapter on the Tiergarten for this book.

The neighbouring district of Schöneberg has been looked at closely by **Almut Carstens**. She came to Berlin from Kiel and studied sociology at the Freie Universität. The Travel Tips on East Berlin was also compiled under her editorial supervision, while the one on West Berlin profited from her intimate knowledge of the city.

The Travel Tips design came from **Dietrich von Thadden**, Berlin editor of the *PanAm Clipper Magazine* and contributor to the manager magazine *Top-Hotel*. **Annemarie Weber** wrote the section on Berlin gastronomy.

An American from New York, **Michael S. Cullen**, has written about West Berlin's museums. Cullen has been living in the city, with some short interruptions, since 1964.

Hellmut Kotschenreuther is known to many Berliners as the author of the Berlin daily *Tagesspiegel*. He was born in Franconian Nuremberg and has been living in Berlin since 1951 as a concert and theatre critic.

A son of German immigrants **Barry Graves** was born in White Plains, New York. Most of his youth, however, was spent in Germany, as a result of his parents re-immigrating to their homeland. In 1973, he and a friend published a Rock encyclopedia which sold 400,000 copies and which today is regarded as a standard work of reference. In articles for leading West German weeklies such as *Der Spiegel* and *Die Zeit*, Graves has thoroughly dealt with the phenomena of mass culture and on film, music, theatre and design. His television film *24-Hour City* was the basis for the chapter in this book.

Günter Schneider being available to do the photography for the book was a great stroke of luck. Schneider has known Berlin for many years as a reporter and has gathered together a most comprehensive archive of 5,000 slides which he is continuously updating in his Friedenau studio. Since 1980 he has been a freelance photographer and reporter in Berlin. His work has been published in *Stern Paris Match*.

Most box pictures were provided by **Erhard Pansegrau**, a trained electronics engineer and business school graduate. At the end of the 1970s he opted for photography and started as a free-lance travel photographer. He has published a photography book on China and provided the pictorial side of Michael Ellsässer's *Wonderful Berlin*.

Other photographs were contributed by **Jens Schumann**, **Dieter Bechert** and **Gerhard Bersick**. Additional slides came from Joachim Dillinger, the Deutsche Lufthansa airline, the district administration of Spandau, the Kreuzberg arts council and the Haus am Checkpoint Charlie. Thanks to all of them and to the four archives involved **Bildarchiv Stiftung Preussischer Kulturbesitz**, **Landesbildstelle Berlin**, **Archiv für Kunst und Geschichte**, and **Archiv Jürgens** in Cologne. A word of gratitude also to the district administrations which provided maps and brochures and to Michael Broderson of the Berlin Tourist Office.

Ellsasser   *Seul*   *Worst*   *Hoff*

TRAVEL TIPS

WEST BERLIN

EAST BERLIN

A MYTH OF TODAY

Berlin is always a new city, a city where, according to the philosopher Ernst Bloch, "not even the whitewash has time to dry". Compared with other European metropolises, Berlin is still very young, having celebrated its 750th anniversary in 1987.

Nonetheless, Berlin is a place burdened with destiny, where German and European history have been made, and where today the world's superpowers confront each other. Hence, a journey to Berlin will always be an imaginary encounter: with two military blocks, two social and legal systems, two completely different worlds. Looking across from the observation-platforms at the cordoned-off Brandenburger Tor, Berlin's triumphal arch, one does not just see the other side of the city. It is as if the gaze was wandering into another world, extending to the east across the Urals and to the Berings Straits; to the west across the Atlantic as far as the Pacific coast.

Somewhere between Washington and Moscow, its inner city decaying into two unequal halves, Berlin is in search of its identity, forever fluctuating between provincialism and the desire for the cosmopolitan. In the contest of the systems, the eastern part, with its magnificently restored buildings of the Prussian era, has become the self-styled capital of the first socialist state on German soil. The western part, on the other hand, presents itself as "the show-case of the Free World", where freedom often is equated with the freedom to consume and a high standard of living.

In the course of this century, Berlin has become more of a myth than any other European city. Within a few decades, its character has been continually transformed by a series of radical changes: from the swinging city of the "Golden Twenties" to Hitler's megalomanic "world" capital Germania; from the enormous pile of wreckage left by the Third Reich to front-line city in the Cold War; from the centre of protest in '68 to the hub of the alternative sub-culture; from the centre of political unrest in the early 1980s to a tourist attraction displaying cultural splendour and artistic creativity as well as offering a most comprehensive nightlife.

Above all, however, Berlin is the present: both progressive and conservative; a confusing hot-bed of contradictions where everything and nothing seems to be moving at the same time. For Berlin, as a wit once put it, "is always the alternative to itself".

Preceding pages: the Siegessäule on a winter evening; easy-going biker; Kurfürstendamm at Christmas; Prussia's glory at Charlottenburg castle; SED party conference in East Berlin; and sunset at Havel river. **Left**, never at loss for a flash of wit–a Berlin hurdy-gurdy man.

Berlin has been a divided city since 1961. Yet despite—or perhaps because of—the political situation, life, culture, history and literature seem to thrive on every street corner. The Berliners have learnt to think politically; in particular they realise how much their city depends on international support and recognition. Nicosia, the capital of Cyprus is also a divided city, yet the status of Berlin is unique. Richard von Weizsäcker, president of the Federal Republic, describes Berlin as being both centre and boundary: the centre of Europe and the boundary between two systems.

On a map, you can find Berlin east of the Elbe river in the Mark Brandenburg, approximately on the same latitude as London and the same longitude as Naples. Before the partition of Germany in the aftermath of World War II, Berlin was the administrational and geographic centre of the German Reich which was founded in 1871. It is still a focal point of international politics. Nowhere else on the globe have the United States and the Soviet Union been confronting each other so directly while, at the same time, being tied by a singular responsibility.

A drive to Berlin by car gives a definite idea of the peculiarity of the city's situation. Three transit routes, veritable "life arteries" for Berlin, stretch through East German territory, and attach the city to the Federal Republic. The northern route leads to Hamburg, the western to the Helmstedt/Hannover crossing, and the southern one to Nuremberg. In addition, there are three air corridors which were agreed upon by the four Allies after the war.

A green city: Having finally crossed the border, the visitor makes a surprising discovery: Berlin is an oasis of greenery. At first all one sees is a sea of forests and fields. Then comes the urban sea of houses separated by tree-lined alleys, waterways and parks.

Left, Funkturm in autumn. Above, façade painting in Neukölln.

Forty percent of the city surface consists of vegetation and water—42 sq yards (35 sq metres) of forest for every West Berliner. The surrounding area is also full of forests and lakes, once favourite spots for outings for all of Berlin's citizens. Nowadays West Berliners once again have access to their old haunts on the waterside. These three large lakes in Berlin are linked both by the Spree river, which branches out into several tributaries in the middle of the city, and by the Ha-

vel river, which widens into a lake when it reaches Potsdam. Both rivers have always been important waterways. Within the city, they are connected to each other and through a network of canals, provide access to all of Europe's largest rivers.

With an area of 341 sq miles (883 sq km) Berlin is the largest city in Germany, the western part making up 54.5 percent of the total area, or 185 sq miles (480 sq km). Berlin is 24 miles (38 km) long from north to south, and 28 miles (45 km) from east to west. About 3.1 million people live here: 1.9 million in the west and 1.2 million in the east.

Surviving on immigrants: Berlin's isolated situation and repeated political crises—the 1948 blockade, Khrushchev's 1958 ultimatum, and most of all the construction of the Wall in 1961—have affected the city's development, with quite different results for each section. Before the Wall, East Berlin forfeited many of its inhabitants to West Berlin, which served as a convenient stepping-stone to West Germany. Since 1961, when the stream of refugees dwindled, West Berlin has been dependent on immigrants. Because it is the largest industrial city between Moscow and Paris, Berlin requires a constant inflow of labour. Since Berlin is located

employees and the civil service. In all, a workforce of 840,000 Berliners earns a gross total of 63 billion marks.

Berlin's main business partner is West Germany, but there is also a brisk trade over the border to East Germany. More recently Berlin's focus has shifted to a new goal: to become more involved with hi-tech industries. This coincides well with the fact that research is another of Berlin's important "products". It is, after all, one of the largest German university cities, housing about 75,000 students. New knowledge generated by the 180 research institutes can often be directly applied in local industry. This state of

far from sources of raw materials, it has no heavy industries. Instead, processing and refining industries such as electronics, machine-building and chemical processing have flourished. World renowned firms which include Siemens, Borsig and Schering have factories here. Altogether, there are more than 2,200 industrial companies which employ 165,000 workers. They manufacture a wide variety of products ranging from cigarettes and light bulbs to complicated processing machinery. Other important sectors of the economy include the handicraft industry which boasts 11,700 firms and 125,000

affairs is also reflected in the city's eloquent statistics which show a much higher than average number of scientific, technically-oriented people living in Berlin. Retirees were over-represented; until recently, younger families tended to avoid living in Berlin because of the lack of easy accessibility to the countryside.

Generations of children have grown up in dark courtyards. Despite the heavy damage inflicted by bombings during the war the old working-class neighbourhoods have remained much the same as they were in the 19th century: barrack-like housing estates, generally five storeys high, with poorly lit inner courtyards, and lacking in comfort and sanitary facilities.

Berlin is unique in yet another aspect. Unlike other cities which can expand beyond their borders, West Berlin has a limited amount of land and therefore less room for private homes. Berlin has grown into a city of tenements, with many more old buildings than other cities. Of its 1.1 million apartments, 585,000 date from before 1949 and 15 percent were built in the 19th century. More people rent rather than buy.

Living in the "Kiez": Of course there is also the new Berlin—like the "Gropiusstadt" in

ning and disregard for the need to modernise old buildings in the downtown area led to protests, squatting and violent conflicts with the police in the 1970s. The Senate immediately developed programmes to renovate empty buildings and to encourage self-help activities. This eased the pressure on the apartment market and led in turn to changes in building policy generated by the former, at times rather militant, squatters' movement.

The "Internationale Bauausstellung" (IBA) brought a breath of fresh air to city planning which had been caught in the strangle-hold of board of works bureaucrats and speculators. The IBA was originally an

the south, the "Märkisches Viertel" in the north, "Falkenhager Feld" in the west and "Marzahn" in East Berlin. These satellite-towns, soulless cement castles, albeit with parks but otherwise sterile, were built in the 1960s according to Utopian plans. Today, the key-word is "city-repair"—preserving old ground plans and neighbourhoods.

Mistakes in restoration policy, poor plan-

Left, view from Grunewald tower onto Havel river. **Above**, farmer in front of the Märkisches Viertel.

architectural contest organised to solve the problems of the Kreuzberg district. However, the IBA planners went on to develop concepts for a "careful city renewal" and new planning instruments for those neglected areas bordering the Wall and the results of the contest are regarded as exemplary. The IBA houses in Kreuzberg—between Oranien Strasse, Linden Strasse, Hollmann Strasse and Alte Jakob Strasse—with their lush verdant yards blocking out the noise from the omnipresent, pulsating city life are models of modern city planning. Areas which were destroyed and isolated first by the war and then by the erection of the Wall were thus revived. In the same way, in other parts of Berlin, a judicious policy of urban renewal succeeded in resurrecting the "Kiez", that original Berliner feeling of kinship with a certain district.

A small town at heart: Berlin as a metropolis has only existed since 1 October 1920, when seven cities, 59 townships and 27 estates, in fact already part of Berlin, were officially joined with Berlin into one unit by the Prussian government. This measure supplied Berlin with the necessary administrative infrastructure to allow it to rise to a capital of international stature. Suddenly the city was

13 times larger; 3.8 million people lived in 347 sq miles (900 sq km)—at that time an area larger than London or Paris.

The centralised administration of such an agglomeration was impossible and so the new city was divided into 20 districts, each in truth a big town in its own right. Thirteen districts had been part of the original Berlin and retained their names and their stately town halls. They are Mitte, Tiergarten, Wedding, Prenzlauer Berg, Friedrichshain und Hallesches Tor, Kreuzberg, Charlottenburg, Köpenick, Schöneberg, Neukölln (former Rixdorf), Lichtenberg, Spandau and Wilmers-

dorf, until 1920 independent towns. Other rural communities and large estates around Berlin were parcelled out into seven new districts—Pankow, Reinickendorf, Steglitz, Tempelhof, Treptow, Weissensee and Zehlendorf. These names were taken from the community with the greatest population. With its territorial expansion in 1920, Berlin became the second largest city in Europe. In subsequent years, it enjoyed a short-lived golden period, internationally recognised for its cultural and intellectual significance, and often transfigured into a myth. Despite, or perhaps, because of its expansion, Berlin has kept its small-town character which is reflected both in its appearance and in the friendly "Kiez" atmosphere so prized by Berliners. The village churches also testify to the rural past. There are 20 in West Berlin, seven of which were built before the 13th century.

Two centres: Berlin has another peculiar trait which distinguishes it from other European capitals. The political division has created a unique city in that it has two centres. The traditional centre—the island on the Spree and the magnificent boulevard "Unter den Linden"—has become the central district of East Berlin. Most of the Prussian royal monuments are found here. The second downtown, the "new west" around the Kurfürstendamm, was first built during the imperial era. The Ku'damm was celebrated as a boulevard with an international atmosphere during the "Roaring Twenties". After the war it became the heart of West Berlin, especially after the original city centre on the other side of the Tiergarten was finally completely cut off by the Wall.

Doubling seems to be Berlin's fate. In the beginning there were the twin cities of Berlin and Cölln. Today there are two town halls, two official flags, two sets of coats of arms, two social systems. In reality, Berlin is two separate cities with the same name. Following recent dramatic events, Berlin seems to be rejoining itself, and is becoming one city again.

Left, goods-station at the western docks in Moabit.

CITY ON THE SPREE

Berlin's 750-year history began in two distinct locations. The settlements of Berlin and Cölln, situated on two neighbouring islands on the River Spree, were closely united by economic interests. At the beginning of the 14th century they decided to merge under the guidance of a single administrative body.

The settling of the two islands is thought to have taken place some time in the last third of the 12th century. Early chronicles mention Cölln for the first time in 1237, and Berlin seven years later. Both were granted town-rights around 1230.

Trade and shipping: In those days the Havel-Spree lands were inhospitable, only thinly settled, covered partly with sand and partly with thick woods, sprinkled with lakes and streaked with water-courses and bogs. In the clearings the inhabitants of small Slavonic villages eked out a living raising cattle and practising some modest agriculture. The invention of the iron ploughshare finally permitted the cultivation of the loamy soil and this contributed decisively to the flourishing of business settlements in both Cölln and Berlin. Noble vassals and the Knights of Templar summoned by the Askanian rulers founded new villages and provided security with new castles. Farmers, peasants and businessmen from the lower Rhine, from Flanders and from the foothills of the Northern Harz, the homeland of Askanian dynasty, were recruited.

Unlike Spandau and Köpenick, the other two medieval cities on Berlin's territory, the double settlement owes its origin to economic reasons. The ford between the two islands provided the most comfortable crossing for miles for the carts of travelling traders. In addition, the location of the twin towns permitted control of shipping. Soon,

Berlin businessmen and boatmen monopolised not only supplies to the hinterlands but also the export trade of the Brandenburg Marches.

Trade brought money and the demands of the nobility and prosperous businessmen grew. More refined wares and a touch of *savoir-vivre* penetrated the remote March. Craftsmanship flourished in the atmosphere of affluence. Solid housing gradually replaced the straw-covered clay huts. Hospitals and bridges were built, churches and cloisters were erected. The municipal council as well as patricians purchased land around the city and even entire villages.

Berlin's prosperity and brilliance was rather modest in comparison to the old German trade cities on the Rhine and the Danube. It hardly played any role in Germany's medieval cultural and economic life. This was made clear by the fact that law and security and noble power in the land vanished entirely the moment the house of Askania became extinct.

The inhabitants of the March, plagued by knights turned highwaymen and by gangs of brigands, pleaded for help from the Emperor. However he was concerned about his crown and his problems with the Pope. The cities opted for self-help led by Berlin. They organised a territorial militia and fought indecisive battles. More peaceful times returned in the year 1411 when the Baron Frederich of Hohenzollern from Nuremburg first became governor and then Elector of Brandenburg.

The first castle: The arrival of the Hohenzollern dynasty in Brandenburg coincided with the last phase of the medieval power struggle among cities, knights and princes in the German Empire. At the time of the second Hohenzollern Elector, a severe conflict broke out in Berlin between the authoritarian city council and the citizens who strongly demanded greater participation in governmental affairs.

With their appeal for help to the Elector, the citizens instigated the end of their autonomy. The Elector did not need to be asked twice to seize the opportunity to increase his power over the city. Deep cuts in the city's constitution placed communal administration almost entirely in the prince's hands. He now confirmed the election of councillors, dealt personally with legal matters, forbade any ties with other cities and revoked the common administration of the twin city. An attempt by the Berliners to regain some of their civil rights by rebellion failed.

The prince's new position of power was made visually clear by the construction of a city castle in Cölln. His princely predecessors had only possessed a modest *pied-à-*

street cleaning to speak of. Rubbish piled up in the alleys and streets, where misery and wealth still lived side by side. Installation of a water conduit for paying subscribers failed because of high rates. In 1576 the plague claimed 4,000 lives. The former population level of 12,000 was only reached again at the beginning of the Thirty Years' War.

Though the city was never directly involved in the armed conflict, the three war decades from 1618 to 1648 brought hard times. Tribute payments and overall inflation, dwindling trade and pillaging by Swedish and Imperial troops reduced the city to utter poverty. When an Imperial minister

terre in Berlin. Fifty years later Berlin and Cölln finally became residential towns. Knights, officials, businessmen and courtiers moved from the Hohenzollern lands in Franconia to the Spree.

Culture and education among commoners was also progressing at this time. New schools, including a grammar school were founded, a printer and a chemist opened their doors and, Berlin's first stage production was performed. The first weekly periodical was published in 1617.

Hygiene conditions in homes still left much to be desired. There was no public

burnt down the suburbs because of a suspected Swedish attack, thousands were made homeless. A magistrate's report of those years noted the staggering rate of suicide. Since the beginning of the war the population had shrunk to 6,000.

When the war ended Frederick William, later surnamed the "Great Elector", energetically pressed for the rebuilding of his inchoate capital. A series of fortifications were constructed to defend against possible attacks and by the end of his 50-year reign Berlin's outward appearance had totally changed. The city had become more beautiful, more splendid and somewhat larger. With its 20,000 inhabitants, however, it was still just a provincial town compared to Paris or Vienna.

Arrival of the Huguenots: The Elector took wise measures to revive the region's shattered economy. A tax reform spurred trade and industry, and the construction of the Oder-Spree canal linking Breslau with Hamburg contributed decisively to Berlin becoming a key centre of trade and traffic.

The Great Elector's astute refugee policies with regard to Jews and Protestants who were being persecuted in France at the time, had an extraordinary propitious effect on the enmity of their Christian competitors. The privileges granted the Jews—who incidentally were not allowed to build a synagogue at first—were later to be gradually cut back. They were saddled with a special tax system which was equivalent to financial pillage, and during the 18th century, various restrictive orders of a similar nature meant that only the richest Jews could remain in the region.

About 5,000 French Huguenots also found refuge in Berlin after the revocation of the Edict of Nantes in 1685, and they too brought along money and economic experience. The city benefited from their technical abilities and craftsmanship—and adopted

economic and cultural evolution of the city. Frederick William granted protection warrants and almost unlimited freedom of trade to 50 wealthy Austrian Jewish families who had been expelled from Austria. Their capital, knowledge and international connections soon made them virtually indispensable to the economic life. This protected them to a certain extent from the envy and

Left, the Great Elector welcomes the French refugees. **Above**, general view of Berlin-Cölln about 1729 (from a copperplate engraving by Pieter van der Aa).

something of the refined lifestyle of France. The Huguenots founded a number of new manufacturing plants: silk mills, paper and glassworks and they also introduced tobacco farming into the March.

During the following decades further groups of persecuted Protestants arrived in great numbers from the Palatinate, and from Switzerland, Salzburg and Bohemia. Living together with peoples of varying backgrounds gave Berliners, even in that early period of their history, an attitude of tolerance and cosmopolitan openness.

The economic boom of the last 30 years of

the 17th century benefited the arts and sciences. A daily newspaper was founded; a medical board supervised the healing trades; the alchemist Johann Kunckel discovered a way to manufacture ruby glass. An arts academy was founded in 1669 to be followed a few years later by an academy of sciences in 1700. Its first president was philosopher Gottfried Wilhelm Leibniz.

With cunning and with violence, and by marriage and by inheritance the Hohenzollerns managed to increase their possessions. With the acquisition of the Polish Duchy of Prussia their territory eventually extended as far as the Russian border. In

there was nothing but "Armee und Menage"—the army and thriftiness. The spending of the royal household was cut down to one-fifth of what it had been, salaries were reduced, servants discharged. Cabbage was grown in Charlottenburg park, and the Lustgarten with its exotic greenery was turned into a drill ground. The king scorned the arts and sciences as useless, with the exception of medicine. He founded the famous Charité which was both a hospital and a research centre, and something of a novelty. And Prussia owed the introduction of compulsive schooling to this "father of militarism".

1701, the successor of the Great Elector crowned himself "King in Prussia". Berlin had become a royal residence.

The master builders Schlüter, Nering and Eosander created masterpieces of baroque architecture. However, the exaggerated extension to the city castle, the construction of the castles Charlottenburg and Monbijou, of the arsenal, of the academy and of the two cathedrals on the Gendarmenmarkt bankrupted the treasury of the young kingdom.

Drill and thrift: Royal prodigality ended with the accession to the throne of Frederick William I in 1713. For the "Soldier King"

The main purpose of the king's concern for a smooth economic development was to raise funds for his smartly drilled army. At the beginning, Berlin suffered under the compulsory military service. Within two years, in spite of the threat of capital punishment, 17,000 men, about one half of them craftsmen, had fled the city. Compulsory service for those in the city was then abolished. After that, new factories, most of them supplying the military, started to attract qualified workmen again.

Courtly culture and pleasure resumed after Frederick II succeeded the spartan "Soldier King" in 1740. An opera house was immediately built. Festivities, music and comedies once again became part of Berlin's life. However, militarism remained. Frederick's wars earned him the title "the Great", and his conquests resulted in a considerable increase in territory. Prussia quickly rose to the rank of a European power but at the cost of entire regions being reduced to utter poverty.

Age of enlightenment: The royal measures to subsidise industries bore fruit. In the next two decades the city's population grew by 50 percent. Knobelsdorff, Gontard and others redesigned the city centre with the Gen-

such critics as Lessing, Nicolai and Mendelssohn were unfolding the thinking of Enlightenment in Berlin. Their presence caused Berlin to develop its reputation as the capital of German intellectualism. A generation after the first Jew was granted full civil rights, the Jewish salons became the centre of "intellectual Berlin" and of the budding Romantic movement. Nobility and intellect was engaged in a new type of liberal, egalitarian social life, which was currently in vogue in France.

The who's-who of Germany's intellectuals met at the homes of Henriette Herz, Rahel Levin-Varnhagen and Dorothea Schlegel.

darmenmarkt constructions, integrating the opera house, the cathedral and St. Hedwigs-Kathedrale, which had already been built before the war and topping it all with the enlargement of the "Lindenallee" into a glorious royal avenue. Under Frederick's successor, the neo-classic Brandenburger Tor designed by Langhans provided the splendid finish to the plans.

At the same time literature flourished and

Left, Frederick the Great inspects the 1st Battalion (by D. Chodowiecki, 1778). Above, Berlin Potsdam railway about 1850.

The Humboldt brothers, Schlegel, Tieck, Fichte, Schelling, Schleiermacher, Hegel, Chodowiecki, Schadow, Kleist, E.T.A. Hoffmann, Chamisso, Bettina and Achim von Arnim, Börne, Heine, Ranke, all lived, worked or taught in Berlin during the first quarter of the 19th century. Jean Paul wrote: "Berlin is more a part of the world rather than just a city."

In 1806, when the battles of Jena and Auerstädt were lost to Napoleon the government collapsed, and some time later, the French emperor, at the head of his troops, marched into Berlin through the Brandenburger Tor. Two years of occupation followed to be succeeded by nearly a decade of French rule. Patriotic feeling seethed, fired by the preachings of Schleiermacher and the "Speeches to the Nation" by Fichte. "Turnvater" Jahn, the personification of German gymnastics, trained Berlin's male youth for the struggle against the oppressor which was waged victoriously in the "liberation wars" of 1813-1815.

The idea of liberty spread by the French Revolution found a strong echo in Berlin. The victories of Napoleon had weakened the absolutist state which was now forced to make concessions to the bourgeoisie striving for emancipation. But, the political restoration after the 1815 Vienna Congress soon led again to oppression, denunciation, police terror, arbitrary condemnations and deportation. The disappointed bourgeoisie retreated to its business and enjoyed its private pleasures. New forms of entertainment became fashionable. Cafés and bakeries with seats for customers and, for the working classes, beerhalls and coffee-gardens with music in Hasenheide and Tiergarten.

Since 1810 Berlin has had a university. Important scholars established it and ensured its growing reputation. Among them were Wilhelm von Humboldt (who founded the Humboldt Universität zu Berline), Fichte, Schelling and Hegel, Niebuhr, Savigny and Ranke. Within a few decades it would grow to become Germany's largest university with 2,000 students.

The first tenements: Economically and socially, the long reign of Frederick William III (1797-1840) was marked by the final emancipation of the bourgeoisie and by the beginning of the Industrial Revolution with pauperisation of the masses and the rise of the proletariat.

The steam engine first began to operate in Germany in the royal porcelain factory shortly after the king's accession to the throne. Twenty years later the first steamboat was travelling on the Spree and a factory district sprang up in the north near the "Neues Tor". Towards the end of William III's reign it was possible to ride from Berlin to Potsdam by train. While Langhans, Schinkel and their disciples were adding to the splendour of the residence city with churches, palaces, museums and theatres in neo-classic style, the age of housing estates and dark backyards had already begun in the suburbs.

The coronation of Frederick William IV was at first accompanied by great hopes. Yet, the long-expected political and social reforms in the wake of the new constitution never materialised. There was hardly any loosening of censorship. The new king sketched grandiose plans for the embellishment of the capital, and with money brought some aged celebrities to Berlin: the poets Rückert and Tieck, the philosopher Schelling and the painter Cornelius. The Grimm brothers, who had been exiled from Göttingen, were given asylum and work. Meyerbeer was invited to direct the opera in addition to his engagements in Paris. Kroll's entertainment gallery in the Tiergarten was the popular attraction. In 1844 Germany's first zoo was opened to the public.

In the meantime, social misery was growing. Half of Berlin's 400,000 inhabitants were proletarians. In 1847, the city spent up to 40 percent of its budget to take care of the poor. Social risings were not uncommon in Prussia. A notable case was the Silesian weavers' strike. In 1848, Berliners, middle and working class, took to the streets following the examples of Vienna and Paris where revolution had broken out. The fighting cost 200 lives but the revolution won. The king had to bow publicly to the dead lying in state on the square before the castle.

The dream of a free and better future did not last for long although it was discussed in countless democratic clubs and in the 150 newspapers—there was freedom of press and assembly. However, Nationalists and Democrats paralysed each other, and by November 1848 General Wrangel was able to occupy Berlin with royal troops. Again, a period of repression began. The constitution, finally proclaimed, essentially reconfirmed the political power of the ruling house.

Right, William I, Reception in the White Hall of the Berlin Castle (paintng by A. von Menzel 1897).

In the second half of the 19th century, Berlin grew to become the second largest industrial city in Europe. Karl Marx who, two decades before, had been studying on the Spree, wrote as early as 1859: "Anyone who has seen Berlin ten years ago would not recognise it today. It has developed from a rigid parade-ground to the busy centre of Germany's machine manufacturing." The biggest company was owned by "locomotive tycoon" Borsig. Corporate giants such as Siemens and Halske founded the "Telegraphen-Bauanstalt" which, when it invented the dynamo, became a major factor in Berlin's economic life.

At the other end of the economy the workers' movement gathered. With workdays lasting up to 16 hours, the proletariat often earned just enough to insure survival in desolate tenements. Socialist thought found increasingly fertile ground in the slums of eastern and northern Berlin. In 1863 Ferdinand Lassalle (1825-1864) founded the first German workers' organisation, the "Allgemeiner Deutscher Arbeiterverein". The city became the centre of trade unionism and increasingly a bastion of the social democratic movement—only slowed by Bismarck's suppression of the Socialists. In 1875 the "Allgemeiner Deutscher Arbeiterverein" joined forces with the "Sozialdemokratische Arbeiterpartei" (Social Democratic Labour Party) which had been founded in 1869 in Eisenach by Wilhelm Liebknecht (1826-1900) and August Bebel (1840-1913).

Germany's first capital: In the meantime, Prussia had harvested new territories as a result of her wars against Denmark and Austria. She now ruled over most of Germany north of the Main, from the French to the Russian border. After the dissolution of the German Confederation ("Deutscher Bund") in 1866, Austria dropped out of the

century-old struggle for political supremacy within Germany.

Frederick the Great's dream had become reality: Prussia had finally gained the upper hand. In the same year Berlin was declared capital of the North German Confederation ("Norddeutscher Bund") which, together with its allied German states in the south, formed the first step toward a unification of Germany without Austria.

Five years later, after the victory in the war

against France (1870-1871), the German princes crowned the king of Prussia as their emperor. Their motives were not idealistic. They had to comply with the forces of political and economic reality which called for a unified national state. On 18 January 1871, immediately after the French defeat, the Second German "Reich" was proclaimed in the Hall of Mirrors in the Palace of Versailles. William I (1797-1888) was declared emperor. Otto von Bismarck (1815-1898), the actual driving force behind the unification of Germany under Prussian dominance, became the first chancellor of the empire.

Left, lunch at Borsig factory (painting by Hans Baluschek, 1912). **Right**, miserable dwellings at Prenzlauer Berg.

From Berlin he was to decisively shape the direction of European politics. Berlin, the old residence of Prussia and Brandenburg rose to become capital of the new empire.

The founding years: With its 826,000 inhabitants the empire's new capital was by far Germany's largest city. However, compared to Paris with twice that number and cosmopolitan London which already had a population of 3.2 million, Berlin cut a rather provincial figure. But, after the founding of the Reich in 1871, provincialism no longer inhibited Germany's economic and industrial development. Nourished by French war indemnity payments, the past was quickly

not downright fraudulent. Construction and real estate speculation was particularly liable to financial crashes and scandals. While expanding industry sought land for its new factories, the affluent bourgeoisie was also looking for lots on which to build villas and country houses. From all corners of the Reich workers flooded into Berlin. They too needed housing: great numbers of tenements shot up. In the rural suburbs the price of land rose to 50 times its pre-war value: farmers in Wilmersdorf, Schöneberg and Tempelhof could retire as millionaires.

Even after the stock market crash in 1873 and during the ensuing depression, real es-

recouped. The years 1871-1873 witnessed the roaring boom of the "founding years", a period during which the historically "come late" German Empire waged an economic and technical battle to catch up with the Industrial Revolution. Under the guidance of the German monopoly capital, residing in Berlin, the flourishing natural sciences were put to practical, economic use. Large-scale government contracts and the repayment of war loans pumped great sums of money into the economy. Joint-stock companies shot up like mushrooms—174 in Berlin in a single year. Many turned out to be rather shaky if

tate speculation remained a profitable business. The demand for living quarters was high. Factory suburbs, villages and settlements of villas coalesced to form an urban area. The idea of Greater Berlin was a reality long before the numerous rural and urban communities with almost 4 million inhabitants finally formed one political and administrational unit in 1920.

Berlin's swift rise in the last decade of the 19th century to become Germany's first modern metropolis reflected the German Reich's economic prosperity and its ascension to a world power—albeit with all its dark and bright aspects. Some things were impressive indeed.

The installation of a sewage system considerably reduced the spread of infectious diseases. A market and a central slaughterhouse improved the supply of food. Even the traffic problems in the sprawling city were satisfactorily solved by creating an urban and suburban train system, laying out generous avenues, and establishing a network of horse-drawn street-cars. In 1879, the founding year of a technical academy which is now the Technische Universität, Siemens and Halske unveiled the world's first electrical train. Two years later it was already used as a

The "Wilhelminian age": On 18 January 1888, the aged Kaiser William I died. He had given Bismarck, the "Iron Chancellor", a fairly free reign in shaping the young German Reich. The year was to become known as the "year of three Kaisers," as his successor, Frederick III, died after 99 days. Then it was the turn of the latter's son, the ambitious and thoroughly "Prussian" William II, for whom a powerful chancellor such as Bismarck could only be an obstacle. By March 1890, with bitterness of heart, Bismarck had to go. The "pilot of German politics" disembarked and now the "Wilhelminian age" began, an epoch during which Germany,

means of public transport in Lichterfelde.

The first electric streetlamps appeared, and a telephone network with a mere 50 subscribers initially followed. Around the turn of the century horse-drawn carriages began to give way to automobile cabs and buses. In 1902 Berlin's first surface and underground train line connected the Warschauer Brücke and the zoo.

Left, parade with Kaiser William II on occasion of the inauguration of the national memorial in 1897. **Above**, demonstration for women's suffrage in 1912.

from its centre in Berlin, achieved the final transition from an agrarian to an industrial state, and became one of the leading imperialist nations.

Berlin's swift economic development and its tempestuous population growth gave rise to a dynamic and modern spirit which, in spite of Wilhelminian conservatism, would pervade life and culture for the following decades. Poets, radicals and "culture gypsies", all dreamt of rejuvenating life and the world through art. The premières of the scandalous naturalistic plays of Gerhart Hauptmann opened a new chapter in the history of German theatre. More and more Berlin became the gathering spot for the new, the modern, the exciting. The list of literary women and men who, since the 1890s, lived and worked there at least for a time is illustrious. Hardly an important name is missing: Gerhart Hauptmann and Heinrich Mann, Frank Wedekind, Rainer Maria Rilke, Stefan George and Robert Musil, not to mention the poets of the expressionist generation, Else Lasker-Schüler, Georg Heym and Gottfried Benn. Strindberg also spent some time in Berlin as did the Norwegian painter Edvard Munch. The scandal caused by an exhibition of the latter's paintings led to the founding of the artists' association "Sezession" shortly before the turn of the century. Its members, with Max Liebermann in the lead, in impressionistic-realistic style opposed the solemn Historicism of the official Wilhelminian "court and state art".

A decade later, following the arrival from Dresden of the "Brücke" group—painters Kirchner, Heckel, Pechstein and Schmidt-Rottluff—Berlin also became the hub of expressionist painting.

From the turn of the century, the Imperial capital occupied a leading position in almost all fields of art and science. Berlin's press and critics set the Reich's journalistic standards. The theatres, under the leading influence of Max Reinhardt, established standards for all of Germany's stages. Richard Strauss was the conductor and composer of the Imperial court opera and Hans Pfitzner conducted at the "Theater des Westens", where Enrico Caruso, on his way to stardom, made his first Berlin appearances. The "Berliner Philharmoniker" became internationally acclaimed under Hans von Bülow and Arthur Nikisch. The next generation was well cared for in excellent schools, notably Joseph Joachim's "Musikhochschule" and the Stern conservatory where Arnold Schönberg taught for many years.

The significance of Wilhelminian Berlin as a centre for research and for instruction in the fields of philosophy and increasingly in the sciences is documented by many famous names such as Theodor Mommsen, Wilhelm Dilthey, Robert Virchow, Paul Ehrlich, Robert Koch, Hermann Helmholtz, Max Planck and Albert Einstein. Half-a-dozen future Nobel Prize winners lived and worked in Berlin around the turn of the century.

The Kaiser goes: After the turn of the century political tensions in Europe intensified. Mutual mistrust between nations grew: the arms race was on. In 1914 the crisis reached its climax. On 28 June, the Austrian heir to the throne and his wife were assassinated in Sarajevo. Six weeks later most of Europe was in a state of war. German youth rallied enthusiastically to the front and, even the Social Democrats voted for war credits. The German military estimated six months would suffice for victory. They were thoroughly mistaken. Germany was blockaded at sea, the war flared up to a global conflict. Its side-effects were soon felt in daily civilian life. Prices rose and the black market flourished. A "bread card" appeared in Berlin in February 1915, and other foodstuffs were either rationed or disappeared from the shops altogether. Famine broke out after the poor potato harvest of 1917-1918. Bakers and butchers in Berlin were stormed. Dogs and cats became a delicacy.

In the meantime, led by Karl Liebknecht and Rosa Luxemburg, parts of the Social Democrats broke away, and began agitating for peace. The successful revolution in Russia in 1917 ignited the hope that a political overthrow could also be brought about in Germany. The working class, and later also parts of the middle class, exerted growing pressure for a negotiated peace. In January 1918, 300,000 working men and women went on strike. It was brutally suppressed by the military.

Over the years, the fronts of the Reich collapsed. In November 1918 thousands of sailors in Wilhelmshaven and Kiel mutinied. The rebellion spread quickly. In Berlin, a committee of workers and soldiers called for a general strike. The Kaiser abdicated. From a window in the Reichstag, on 9 November the Social Democrat Philipp Scheidemann proclaimed the first democratic German Republic.

Right, public proclamation of the order to mobilize at Unter den Linden on 31 July 1914.

FROM CAPITAL TO RUBBLE FIELD

What began as a revolution in November 1918 certainly did not deserve that title. "The Kaiser has gone, the generals have stayed on", is how Theodor Plivier described the dilemma of the rebellious sailors of Kiel in his novel of that name. The period between 1918-1933 was a time of political turmoil and the rise of Adolf Hitler.

Indeed, at first revolutionary fever spread throughout Germany, and the old order started reeling. Workers' and soldiers' committees were formed across the empire, and in many places the red flag waved over town halls and military barracks. The "Volksmarinedivision", consisting of 3,000 sailors who had mutineered in Kiel, marched into Berlin. They occupied the Imperial castle and the royal stables. Some of the members of the local garrison, including the Emperor Alexander Regiment, fraternised with the workers. The war-weary people marched through the streets calling for "Peace, Freedom, Bread!"

In view of the threat of revolution, chancellor and prince Max of Baden decided to transfer governmental authority to the chairman of the Social Democratic Party, Friedrich Ebert. The Social Democrats had the largest share of seats in the Reichstag. Suddenly, the Socialist labour movement had become the most important political force in the power vacuum.

It was unprepared, however, for this sudden access to power and split into at least three factions. The majority of Socialists under the direction of Ebert and Scheidemann opted for parliamentary democracy, while the group of independent Socialists that had broken away agitated for a revolutionary transformation of the state. On the far left of the political spectrum, the militant "Spartakusbund" thought that the time had come to set up a Soviet ruled state, as the October Revolution had done in Russia.

No sooner had Scheidemann proclaimed the founding of the "German Republic" at the Reichstag in front of cheering crowds, than Karl Liebknecht proclaimed the "Free Socialist Republic of Germany" from the balcony of the Berlin castle. It was on this fateful 9 November 1918, that an unbridgeable schism appeared in the German left. It marked the doom of Weimar democracy 14 years later.

Barricades in the newspaper district: Back to 1918…when he fled, the Kaiser left the empire in utter chaos. Throngs of hungry people ploughed through the streets of the industrial centres; strikes paralyzed the economy and traffic. Over two million soldiers of the western army crossed back over the Rhine. Many disgruntled lay idling in their barracks. Among them was a failed painter, corporal Adolf Hitler. Civil war was in the air. In order to re-establish state authority Berlin's provisional government was forced to adopt drastic measures. It re-enlisted some of the troops of the old army which had been organised into the so-called "Freikorps" after demobilisation.

In the winter of 1918, Berlin's historic centre was a revolutionary bivouac. Sailors of the "Volksmarinedivision" patrolled the streets along with the workers defence militia. At the end of December, defence minister Noske ordered the Berlin castle to be stormed by regular troops—67 dead. The bloody clashes ultimately escalated to an open struggle for power on 5 January 1919, when the army broke up a massive demonstration protesting the dismissal of the revolutionary superintendent of police Eichhorn. The Spartakusbund, now renamed Communist Party of Germany (KPD), called for a general strike. Armed red front fighters set up barricades at the Brandenburger Tor. The press district, not far from today's Checkpoint Charlie was converted into a fortress. More than 3,000 government troops were needed to drive the revolutionaries out of their strongholds; the rebellion collapsed.

Left, November Revolution 1918–machine-gun flighters of the "Volksmarinedivision" in the occupied Berlin castle, in the background the Begas fountain.

There were no prisoners.

Karl Liebknecht and Rosa Luxemburg, the leaders of the November Revolution, went into hiding. They were discovered on 15 January in a Wilhelmsdorf flat and taken to the staff of the Guards Regiment residing in the Hotel Eden. After interrogation, they were to be transferred to the criminal court in Moabit. On the way they were abused by their guards and then murdered in the Tiergarten. The body of Rosa Luxemburg was tossed into the Landwehr canal. The murderers were merely reprimanded.

General strike versus *coup d'état*: In the same week general elections for the Constitutional

military refused to face the fact of their own debacle. Brandishing the slogan "undefeated in the field", they spread the fallacious word that "unpatriotic scamps" at home had stabbed the fighters at the front in the back in 1918. The myth of the "stab in the back" poisoned the climate, and in view of the treaty's unbearable conditions, the agitation from the right found fertile soil in conservative middle class circles.

The "Kapp" *coup d'état* on 13 March 1920 made it clear, that the young republic could least of all count on the military. The "Freikorps" soldiers returned to the city from their Döberitz camp, but this time with

Assembly were held. The Social Democrats became the strongest party. To confer in quiet about the new constitution, the deputies moved out of the unruly city to the town of Weimar. On 11 August 1919, they passed the so-called "Weimar Constitution". Ebert became president.

In the meantime, under the pressure of an ultimatum, the German negotiators in Versailles signed a peace treaty. The victorious powers could not have chosen a worse burden to heap onto the fragile republic. The nationalist right raised a storm against the "infamous dictate"; monarchists and the

the black-white-red war banner and swastikas on their helmets. Over 6,000 men occupied the government district and other strategic points. The instigator of the act, one Baron Walter von Lüttwitz, declared the constitutional government to be deposed. His man was the chief landscape director Wolfgang Kapp, an arch-reactionary civil servant from East Prussia who, until then, was unheard of in Berlin.

It was not the "Reichswehr", the army, however, who rushed to the support of the republic but the workers. Both government and unions called for a general strike. Berlin was without water, gas, electricity and telephone. Post offices and banks stayed closed. Four days sufficed to dispel the military spook. Extreme right-wingers from the ranks of the Freikorps were also responsible for a series of political murders such as the assassination of secretary of state Walter Rathenau, who was shot in broad daylight on 24 June 1922.

The "Golden Twenties": This is how the years before the collapse of the banks in Wall Street on 25 October 1929, were called. In reality the beginning was not golden. The war indemnity payments resulted in a rapid loss of currency value. The costs of living rose astronomically.

In 1914 the U.S. dollar traded at 4.20 Reichsmark. In 1922, it stood at 7,500 and one year later, at the acme of the inflation, at 4.2 billion marks. In that year millions suffered but profiteering and speculation flourished. Finally, the introduction of the "Rentenmark" at the end of 1923 ushered in a period of economic stability.

Light and shadow lay seamlessly alongside one another in the Berlin of the Weimar years. Old Imperial Berlin had turned into a cosmopolitan city comparable to London, Paris or New York. Its population rose from 3.8 million to 4.3 million between the wars. The basis for the rapid growth was laid by the then highly controversial territorial reform of 1 October 1920, which, with a stroke of a pen, increased the surface area of the nation's capital 13 times. Industry expanded into the outer districts. The population tended to leave the dismal tenements and settle in the pastoral communities beyond the city's limits. Charitable organisations set

up model suburban settlements like the *Hufeisensiedlung* in Britz.

On the whole, the capital of Weimar Republic came up with exemplary communal services. Thanks to the indefatigable efforts of the city's traffic councillor, Ernst Reuter, the public transport company Berliner Verkehrs AG (BVG) was founded on 1 January 1929. The company ran 92 tram lines, 30 bus lines and four subway lines. For a flat rate of 20 pfennigs one could ride all around Berlin.

Left, the "Golden Twenties": revue at the Admiralspalast near Friedrichstrasse station; the girls posing with "Roman Quadriga". **Above**, *Graf Zeppelin* airship above Berlin in 1928.

Modern-day Babylon: Republican Berlin was characterised by a hitherto unknown freedom and openness, but also by sharp social contrasts. Added to this was Berlin's proverbial rush and the political clashes on the streets. The overall result was an electrifying atmosphere that sharpened the senses and consciousness at all levels of life.

With this background, Berlin became Europe's cultural capital, a Babylon of modernism that attracted intellectuals, artists, architects, musicians, the film crowd and journalists from all across the continent. In this respect the term "Golden Twenties" was certainly appropriate. It was the era of the Charleston and the Shimmy, the era of Jazz, of great revues and of literary cabaret.

The new West End around the Kurfürstendamm became the centre of cosmopolitan night life, the focal point of *demi-monde* and bohemians. This is where cinemas, nightclubs and the popular artists' cafés were concentrated. The "Romanisches Café" was, according to Günther Birkenfeld, the focal point for everyone "between Reykjavik and Tahiti related to the muses either professionally or for love's sake."

Just outside the city, in Babelsberg, the Universum Film AG (UFA) built Europe's largest film studios. This is where films of world repute such as *The Cabinet of Doctor Caligari*, Murnau's *Nosferatu* and Fritz Lang's *Metropolis* were shot. The Polish actress Pola Negri became the silent movie star of Germany. Directors like G. W. Pabst, Ernst Lubitsch and Erich Pommer worked here. Billy Wilder was still a reporter when Greta Garbo and Marlene Dietrich used Berlin as a stepping stone to Hollywood. Werner Krauss, Emil Jannings, Conradt Veidt and Peter Lorre were to become some of the first great actors of the talkies.

In terms of theatre Berlin experienced an undreamt flourishing under the leadership of Max Reinhardt, Erwin Piscator, Leopold Jessner and Jürgen Fehling. For the first time Reinhardt, the "magician", produced Bernard Shaw in Berlin. The theatre of Piscator at Nollendorfplatz became a laboratory of drama—with films interacting with plays, and two moving walkways taking the actors and scenes across the stage.

Postwar Berlin grew into a newspaper and publishing capital ruled by Ullstein, Scherl and Mosse. About 150 weeklies and dailies covered politics, culture and other events from every possible angle. Ten out of 19 German Nobel Prize winners in the Weimar years were Berliners, including Max Planck and Albert Einstein.

A "peculiar fellow": In the beginning the Nazis went almost unnoticed in this gigantic city. Hitler's planned march on Berlin failed miserably along with his attempted *coup d'état* in the Munich "Bürgerbräukeller" in November 1923. At a non-public party conference in Berlin in 1927, only 680 members were present. In 1928 he spoke for the first time in the "Sportpalast". Mainly out of

curiosity Berliners attended to have a "look at this fellow."

Undoubtedly Berlin was a tough nut to crack for the Nazis. Hitler disliked this hectic, sharp-tongued city and preferred his headquarters to remain in Munich where he was socially accepted. On the other hand, he knew quite well that Berlin lay on the road to power. At the end of 1926 he sent his best agitator as "Gauleiter", or district leader, to the Spree. Joseph Goebbels fought his own "battle of Berlin" according to the motto: "the one who rules the streets will conquer the city". He concentrated his propaganda efforts on the "red" working class districts of Wedding, Kreuzberg, Neukölln and Friedrichshain. Brown-shirted raiding parties attacked political opponents, and at the great party conferences SA squads started bloody fights. On the other hand, the elections for the city council on 17 November 1929, saw the Nazis win only 13 out of 225 seats. In the meantime, however, the Wall Street crash had set other forces in motion.

Hitler's take-over: The literature of the Weimar years reflected the social consequences of the lost war and the inflation. In their stageworks, playwrights Carl Sternheim, Ödon von Horvath and Georg

Kaiser described the extent of the moral decline in middle-class circles. This was also written about in numerous novels such as Erich Kästner's *Fabian* and, above all, Alfred Döblin's *Berlin Alexanderplatz*.

George Grosz railed at the spirit of the age in his virulently satirical drawings depicting the brutality and greed of the ruling classes. Heinrich Zille showed the urban proletariat

Left, communist demonstrations before the Berlin cathedral in 1932. **Above**, Nazi propaganda minister Joseph Goebbels during a public speech in 1931.

in its tenements and backyards and Käthe Kollwitz portrayed blatantly the misery of the poor. The atmosphere of hopelessness made the plight of the less fortunate particularly susceptible to nationalistic and anti-Semitic feelings.

At the end of 1929 there were 2.8 million unemployed in Germany. A year later, on 14 September 1930, in the national elections, 6.38 million voters cast their ballots for the presumptive "saviour" Adolf Hitler. In Berlin the Communists received a majority. By the beginning of 1932, six million unemployed, 600,000 of whom alone lived in the industralized capital, were counted. The polarisation of the right and the left blocked parliamentary co-operation in the Reichstag. The Reich had to be governed by Presidents' rule according to article 48 of the Weimar constitution.

After the quick succession of the chancellors Brüning, von Papen and von Schleicher, it was Adolf Hitler's turn, as leader of the strongest party in the Reichstag, to try his hand at governing. President Paul von Hindenburg ordered him to form a "cabinet of national concentration". On 30 January 1930 he was appointed the new chancellor. That night a huge torchlight procession swarmed through the Brandenburger Tor, and down into Wilhelmstrasse under the balcony of the chancellery. Because no photographer was present, the show was repeated on the following evening for the weekly cinema newscast.

The way to dictatorship: New elections for the Reichstag were set for 5 March 1933. A week before, on 27 February flames roared through the parliamentary buildings on the Spree. Were the Nazis responsible for setting the fire or was it the anarchist loner Martinus van der Lubbe? The question has never quite been resolved. In any event the burning of the Reichstag provided the National Socialists with a ready excuse to unleash a wave of terror against the left-wing opposition and the trade unions.

The Communist Party was outlawed and Ernst Thälmann, its leader, arrested and put in a concentration camp where he was murdered toward the end of the war. Yet, inspite of a massive intimidation campaign and control of practically all media, in particular the radio, the Nazis did not win an absolute majority at the elections for the Reichstag. To achieve this, they first had to declare the 81 Communist mandates null and void. The Social Democrats, the last opposition party remaining, refused to consent to the so-called "Enabling Act" which allowed Hitler to suspend the constitution and to attain dictatorial powers on 23 March 1933.

What it really meant was made clear on 1 April 1933 in Berlin, when SA and SS squads marched through the streets calling for a boycott of Jewish shops and department stores. May 1, renamed "day of national

the main court of the Humboldt university a symbolic burning of 20,000 books written by authors branded as "un-German" such as Heinrich Heine, Thomas Mann and Kurt Tucholsky was organised. This *auto-da-fé* on 10 May 1933 signalled the beginning of a general bringing into line of artistic and intellectual life within the postulates of Nazi ideology. The supervisor was the new minister for "public information and propaganda", Joseph Goebbels.

The Third Reich: With the passage of the Nuremburg Laws in September 1935 those who had thought that police terror, book-burnings and persecution of Jews were ini-

work", was celebrated with a massive rally on the Tempelhof field. A day later SA commandos stormed the headquarters of the unions. On 22 June 1933 the Social Democrats were outlawed and the other parties dissolved themselves. The Nazis set up concentration camps in the notorious Columbiahaus in Tempelhof and outside Berlin in Oranienburg. In the first year of Adolf Hitler's rule about 150,000 people were arrested for political reasons and about 100 concentration camps were built. Many Nazi opponents, including prominent artists and intellectuals, were forced to flee abroad. At

tial excesses were rudely awakened. Now Jews were publicly and privately segregated from "Aryans with German blood" and were branded as of an inferior race and deprived of their civic and human rights.

In the following year the youth of the world came to attend the 11th Olympic Summer Games in a festively decorated city. With perfect organisation and splendid celebrations, the Nazi regime hoped to influence world opinion. In the Olympic summer of 1936 Berlin offered her guests a spirited nightlife. Even jazz was allowed. For a few weeks signs announcing "Forbidden for

Jews" and display boxes with the infamous slanderous anti-semitic *Der Stürmer* magazine dropped from sight.

On 9 November 1938 Goebbels unleashed an anti-semitic orgy of destruction when Herschel Grynszpan, a young Jew from Hannover shot a German diplomat to death in Paris. In what came to be known as "Reichskristallnacht" SA and SS hordes devastated Jewish shops, houses and synagogues. The main synagogues in Berlin on the Fasanen Strasse and on the Oranienburger Strasse were burned down. A sea of glass was strewn on Kurfürstendamm and Tauentzien.

ries in Poland, Scandinavia and in the West filled mainstream Germans with enthusiasm that made resistance to Hitler and his regime difficult if not, at times, hopeless.

The sound of drums and fanfares broke the Sunday peace of Berliners on 22 June 1941. A proclamation by the "Führer" was about to be broadcast: the attack on the Soviet Union had begun. The news was received with an overall sense of anxiety. In the first place there was the non-aggression pact, and Hitler had just received the Soviet Foreign Minister Vyacheslav Molotov the previous November. Thoughts of Napoleon's defeat at the gates of Moscow inevitably cropped

World War Two: This time, as opposed to August 1914, no jubilant crowds filled the streets of Berlin or other European capitals. "I can only say that the overall mood was one of apparent depression and gloom," wrote Ambassador Neville Henderson, who delivered the British ultimatum at the Foreign Ministry at 9 a.m., 3 September 1939.

The series of surprising and quick victo-

Left, the second torchlight procession on 30 January 1933 at Brandenburger Tor. Above, first boycott of Jewish shops in 1933–SA men in the streets of Berlin.

up. At that point, however, no-one ever thought that in less than five years the Red Army would hoist its flag over the Reichstag which marked the end of an era.

The Royal Air Force started its night raids on Berlin as early as summer 1940 during the Battle of Britain. In 1941 the British used four-engine bombers for the first time. In 1942 they began the carpet bombing of Germany's major cities. In winter 1943-44 it was Berlin's turn. In all, the RAF carried out 16 devastating raids using a total of 9,111 planes. The Americans participated in the final phase of the Battle of Berlin by flying the first daytime raids. The air war against Berlin turned into a continuous offensive. Hardly a day went by until mid-April 1945 without an air-raid alarm.

On 18 February 1943, after the military catastrophe of Stalingrad, Goebbels proclaimed "total war" to a fanatical crowd in Berlin's Sportpalast. All men between 16 and 65 and women between 17 and 45 were to be conscripted for war service. At the same time an evacuation was in progress: by the end of the year about a million children, mothers and senior citizens had left the city.

Another kind of transport was leaving Berlin at night from the Grunewald train station. At the Wannsee Conference in January 1942 representatives of the SS and other governmental institutions had agreed upon the "final solution to the question of European Jewry", which meant in real terms the physical extermination of all Jews on the continent.

In 1933, 160,000 so-called religous Jews had lived in Berlin. By 1942, the number was 60,000 who, from then on, were deported to the extermination camps to be murdered. About 3,000 Jews succeeded in surviving in the expanse of the ruins of bombed Berlin until the end of the war.

In May 1942 a group of Jewish anti-fascists led by Herbert Baum set fire to the anti-Soviet exhibit in the Lustgarten. Scientists, officials, officers and artists met in the "Rote Kapelle" to pursue the struggle against the Nazi dictatorship. The supreme army command in the Bendler Strasse housed the leaders of the military resistance and of the 20 July 1944 conspiracy. A total of 2,400 men, women and youths were executed in Plötzensee prison between 1933 and 1934 because of so-called subversive activities.

In January 1945 the Soviet troops reached the Oder river at Küstrin and established a bridgehead on the western bank. A mere 44 miles (70 km) separated their front line tanks from the city limits. It was an eerie spring in Berlin in the shadow of the Red Army. In February and March the city suffered its most destructive air-raids of the war, in which the Americans flattened almost the entire inner city including the historic castle and the newspaper district. Theatres and

recreational facilities fell victim to total warfare. Only a few cinemas still ran comedies, and Veit Harlan's *Kolberg*, a cinematic call for endurance portraying the defence of the fortress Kolberg against Napoleon as a heroic example. Berlin too, should be "defended to the last man and cartridge."

Shortly after three in the morning of 16 April 1945, the windows in the eastern sectors of the city began to tremble. The main Soviet offensive had begun on the Oder front with fire from 20,000 cannons. Ten days later Berlin was surrounded by Soviet troops. The battle reached the streets in the suburbs. On 29 April the Soviets concentrated their attacks on the inner defence circle, the "citadel" from three directions. That was the location of the most important target, "Objective Nr. 153". This was Hitler's bunker under the chancellery.

Down in the bunker, hoping for some intervention from the outside, Hitler had played commander-in-chief using fictitious situation maps and without the slightest regard for the sufferings of the civilian population. But the "twilight of the gods" was at hand. Seeing the end in sight he dictated his political testament. On April 30 he committed suicide with his lover Eva Braun whom he had recently wed.

A week later Field Marshall General Wilhelm Keitel, chief of the German supreme command and now prisoner of the Allies, was transferred to Berlin-Karlshorst. In Marshall Zhukov's headquarters, before the hum of the cameras, he signed the unconditional surrender of the German Reich.

During the war the Allies dropped about 45,000 tons of bombs on Berlin, and in the last battle alone, the Russians fired more than 1.1 million shells. The city that a megalomaniac dictator and his accomplices planned to turn into the power centre of a world empire now resembled a lunar landscape. "It's a second Carthage", commented Harry Hopkins, American presidential advisor, as his plane flew over the endless ruins on the Spree on its way to Moscow, 25 May 1945.

Right, May 1945–Red Army soldiers shooting salute on the roof of the conquered Reichstag.

The "Battle of Berlin" raged for 10 days. In the course of their senseless, fanatical last-ditch defence, the Nazis sent children and old men into battle with bazookas. Thousands were killed in air-raids and street-fighting, and others by "mobile court-martials". SS-squads went hunting for presumed deserters right up until the last moment. The victims were condemned on the spot and hanged from street-lamps as a general deterrent.

The costs of the Nazi dictatorship for Berlin were 80,000 dead and 98 million cubic yards (75 million cubic metres) of wreckage, making up one-seventh of the debris in all Germany. The inner city was strewn with corpses and burnt-out tanks. Of the 4.3 million inhabitants there remained, at the most, 2.8 million, while some sources put the figure at only two million. The survivors were mostly women, children and old men barely eking out a living in the ruins and cellars. "There was something frightening about the emptiness of this huge city, in which even the inhabitants moved about furtively", noted a Soviet war-correspondent. "Behind the half-alive, inhabited city hovered the monstrous city of the dead. The third Berlin, bombed and torn up."

Experts seriously considered abandoning this ghost town and rebuilding Berlin elsewhere. Of the 245,000 buildings, 50,000 were completely, and 23,000 partially destroyed. There was no electricity and no gas, with water available only in the outer districts. One-third of all subway stations were under water, whilst more than half of the bridges were unpassable. A plague of rats and insects, the destruction of the sewage system and shortage of soap all increased the danger of typhoid. Other epidemics like dysentery were widespread. Catastrophic famine seemed inevitable.

Left, Berlin "wreckage women" clearing up 75 million cubic metres of ruin left behind after the war.

At best, daily food rations met half of the necessary calorie intake. In order to survive, people resorted to bartering, to foraging in the countryside or to the black market. They traded everything, particularly on Potsdamer Platz, in front of the ruins of the Reichstag and at the bombed Zoo station.

The occupying armies, eastern and western, were heavily involved. A Leica or some Meissen porcelain could buy a couple of cartons of "Yank cigarettes". Competition between East and West began on the black market earlier than anywhere else. The sought-after *Chesterfield* and *Lucky Strike* rose to the status of unofficial reserve currency. At 12 Reichsmarks per packet, they were three times as costly as Russian ones.

One activity, described simply as "organising", dominated the daily lives of most Berliners. It involved getting hold of food, building material and other rare goods. Everything was scarce and winter was coming: it was a struggle for bare survival. In addition, the city had to be cleaned up. The legendary "wreckage women" made the start, knocking down stones—125 per hour, 1,000 per day—for a weekly wage of 28 marks and a ration card. At that time politics were of little interest to the Berliners who, anyhow, had no influence.

The four-sector city: As far as the three western sectors were concerned, the occupation of Berlin by the Red Army was of a purely trustee nature. The same applied to the large parts of central Germany occupied by General Eisenhower's troops. In April 1945, they had advanced far beyond the agreed demarcation line, to the Wismar-Magdeburg-Leipzig line. By the end of June the Anglo-Americans withdrew from Mecklenburg, Saxony and Thuringia to take over their sectors in Berlin. The French followed in August, moving into parts of the British sector districts of Wedding and Reinickendorf which Churchill had conceded to them.

The London Protocol of 12 September 1944 provided the basis for the exchange of troops between East and West. In this document, the "Big Three" had resolved on the division of Germany and the occupied status of Greater Berlin. The Western Allies now moved, without clear agreement on approach routes, toward a heap of ruins which lay 63 miles (100 km) east of the Elbe, in the middle of the Soviet-occupied zone.

In the summer of 1945, US President Truman, Generalissimo Stalin and the British Prime Minister Churchill (later succeeded by Attlee) met at the Potsdam Conference to discuss the fate of Germany. They agreed on the complete demilitarization and denazification of the country, payment of reparations and the creation of new adminis-

the Western Allies. The sector limits, however, were irrelevant to the daily lives of the people. Food-rationing was the same everywhere, and one could move about freely in all of Berlin.

The first—and last—election for an all Berlin city council took place under Allied supervision on 10 October 1946. Four parties competed: Social Democrats (SPD), Conservatives (CDU), Liberal Democrats (LPD) and the new Socialist Unity Party (SED), a union of Social Democrats and Communists, which was passionately rejected by the Western-sector SPD. The latter received the majority of the votes cast, while

trative structures based on democratic principles. None of the "Big Three" questioned either the unity of Germany or the retention of Berlin as its capital.

Berlin was now ruled by the four powers. Their commanding officers formed the Allied High Command which still meets today, although without the Soviet representative. They passed their resolutions unanimously, or not at all. These were then transmitted to the city mayor Arthur Werner to be put into practice: he had already been named head of the first post-war municipal authority by the Soviet general Bersarin, before the arrival of

the Soviet-supported SED garnered almost 20 percent of the votes. This was seen as a sort of referendum on the integration of Berlin in the West or the East.

Ignoring the election results, the Soviets intensified the building of a socialist system in their sector. A change of personnel in public administration, half of whom had been chosen from trusted German Communists of old before the election by the Soviets, did not occur. In June 1947, the Soviet commanding officer blocked the election of Ernst Reuter (SPD) to the office of city mayor. Thereupon Louise Schröder,

Reuter's courageous deputy, became the first woman to head a Berlin government.

Stalin's blockade: The differing interests of the victorious powers in Germany climaxed at the London Conference of the Western Allies in February 1948 when collective measures for economic revival in their three sectors were agreed upon. Moscow regarded this as a violation of the four-power agreement and left the Allied Control Commission in protest. The resignation of Marshal Sokolowski on 20 March ended the collective government of Germany, and in turn affected Berlin. The inclusion of the three western sectors in the West German cur-

rency reform programme provided the excuse for the Berlin Blockade.

On 24 June, the Soviet military authorities closed the roads, waterways and railroads to the West. Two-and-a-half million Berliners were confined to the city without electricity and food supplies for 36 days and coal for 45 days. "It was one of the cruellest attempts in modern Russian history to use mass starva-

Left, airlift in action—US Skymaster transport planes at Tempelhof airfield. **Above**, Mayor Ernst Reuter at the freedom rally front of the Reichtstag building.

tion as a means of exerting political pressure", American military governor, Lucius D. Clay, described the situation.

Clay accepted the challenge. He found an ally in mayor Reuter who was certain that "the Berliners will stand up for their freedom." An airlift was hastily organised to prevent all attempts to cut off important supplies to the city. The first American transporter, a Douglas Dakota with three tons of freight on board, landed on 25 June at Tempelhof airport. In the following 11 months Americans and British flew 277,264 times to Berlin. They brought a total of 1.8 million tons of essential goods into the city. For almost a year, the Berliners lived without fresh fruit and vegetables. Eggs and milk were only to be had in powdered form, and electricity came on for only a few hours a day. In autumn, the Soviets offered the besieged West Berliners food ration cards for the eastern sector: only 100,000 people accepted this offer.

Following secret diplomatic negotiations in New York, the USSR lifted the blockade on 12 May 1949. Stalin had not attained his goal of driving the Allies out of Berlin, but the city was a step closer to division. In September 1948, the elected city council had transferred its seat to West Berlin. In the eastern sector, the remaining SED summoned an "extraordinary city council meeting" and, on 30 November nominated a municipal authority acceptable to the Soviet officials. The reaction was the nomination of a magistrate for the western half of the city, later called Senate, with Ernst Reuter as its first mayor.

The division of Germany and Berlin deepened when, on 7 September 1949 the Federal Republic of Germany with Bonn as provisional capital was constituted. Two months later, East Berlin witnessed the constitution of the German Democratic Republic. The Four-Power Status arrangement remained valid for both parts of the city. While the constitution of the FRG declared Berlin a state ("Land") of the Federal Republic, the Allies insisted that the city "will not be governed by Federal authority". Supreme authority continued to reside with the Allies. Formally, this situation was not questioned by the Soviet authorities, yet in practice it was undermined from the beginning by the choice of East Berlin as the governmental seat of the GDR.

Showcase of the West: The economy of West Berlin had a slow start. The uncertain political situation, the blockade, its isolated position and resulting lengthy transport routes all had an inhibiting effect. In order to compensate for geographical disadvantages and to create a "Showcase of the Free West" at this exposed position, the United States, and increasingly the Federal Republic, provided enormous financial assistance. Political and economic ties with the Federal Re-

boasted full warehouses and shops. Construction of flats was flourishing and the chimneys were smoking again. In East Berlin on the other hand, shortages of every kind were the order of the day: a situation determined for the most part by the high GDR war indemnity payments to the Soviet Union. Dissatisfaction with the living conditions in the so-called "Workers' and Peasants' State" became widespread. It finally exploded in the uprising of 17 June 1953. The cause was a decree of the SED government which stipulated that work-norms were to be raised. The day before, 5,000 construction workers had stopped work in the Stalin-

public strengthened, but as a result, West Berlin drifted away from the eastern part of the city and the surrounding GDR.

In May 1952, the SED authorities cut the telephone network and, in January 1953, they disconnected the inter-city tram and bus routes. West Berliners were now only allowed to travel into the surrounding GDR with an official permit. This regulation did not apply to public transport by subway and S-Bahn within Berlin. About 500,000 people crossed the sector borders daily in both directions.

Since the currency reform, West Berlin

Allee in protest. They were supposed to be building the "first socialist street in Germany", with houses in the typical "confectionary" style of the Stalin era. Instead, they marched together to the ministerial buildings in Leipziger Strasse and demanded the revocation of the decree. On the morning of 17 June, the rebellion spread to other towns in Eastern Germany. The workers took to the

Above, Potsdamer Platz on 17 June 1953: Soviet T34 tanks suppress the uprising. Right, "Four-power" souvenirs in a gift-shop.

THE FOUR-POWER STATUS

Berlin is the last remaining place in Germany where the fact of the unconditional surrender of Nazi Germany cannot be evaded. The old capital of the German empire is but a shadow of pre-war times; paradoxically, the freedom of West Berlin depends on the fact that it is under military occupation. The treaties and decisions of the Four Allies after 1945 constitute the basis for the presence of the three Western Powers and their 12,000 soldiers.

On 12 Sept 1944, an Interallied conference in London decided that Germany was to be divided into four different zones and that Berlin should become a "special area" to be administered jointly. The East-West co-operation in the Interallied headquarters, however, only lasted until 1948. Nevertheless, in some aspects, the Four-Power Status is still in operation. Military personnel of any of the Four Powers can move about the city at will. Every day, the three Western Powers send officers' limousines across Checkpoint Charlie on so-called "flag tours" to emphasise their rights based on the Four-Power Status. In return, the Soviets send military patrols to West Berlin.

Access to the three air routes to Berlin and the 20-mile (32-km) control zone over Berlin is strictly under the jurisdiction of the Four Powers. Even the West German airline, *Lufthansa*, is not allowed to make a stop-over landing at Berlin-Tegel. The Soviet Union demonstrates its share of responsibility for the co-ordination of air traffic by sending a delegate to the Interallied air-traffic control centre.

Ten foreign military missions, admitted by the Allied Control Assembly, conduct their affairs in the western part of the city. The three Western Powers have accepted *de facto* that East Berlin is now the capital of the GDR. However, they maintain their legal position that Berlin, as a whole, is something different from the halves incorporated into the former occupied zones. Parades of the GDR people's

army regularly result in protest notes to the Soviet ambassador in East Berlin, because Berlin, according to the Four-Power Status, is supposed to be a demilitarized zone.

On 3 Sept 1971, in an additional note to the Four-Power Agreement, the three Western Powers re-emphasised their sovereign rights in West Berlin which, due to legal reservations of the Allies, is not part of the territory of the Federal Republic of Germany. The laws passed by parliament in Bonn are not valid in the Western Sectors; these laws have to be accepted by the Berlin parliament and authorised by the Allied city commanders. West Berlin has its own stamps and its citizens still have to carry a special "temporary" identity card at all times. Hundreds of such decrees from the early years after the war are still binding, sometimes enforced by the threat of the death penalty, which is banned in West Germany. Now, however, there are plans for the Allied penal code to be modernised. However, in daily practice, the Western Allies limit the employment of their rights to certain areas such as the claim of the annual costs of their presence (in 1986 this was 1.4 billion marks) from the city. Berlin, in turn, is refunded the same amount by the West German government.

All questions concerning security interests and immunity of the Allied Forces are decided upon by the three city commanders who can issue direct orders to the Berlin police. Whenever they deem it necessary, they can control the mail and telephone services, and also rescind basic rights without judicial proceedings. Thus Heinrich Albertz, mayor in 1966-67, speaks from experience when he says: "In the case of an emergency there is no mayor in any city in the world who can govern as little as the governing mayor of Berlin...." A paradoxical situation, but no less a paradox than the entire political status of the former capital of the Reich.

streets demonstrating for higher wages, free elections and the abolition of the zonal borders. In East Berlin, SED offices were stormed and state shops emptied. Demonstrators took the red flag down from the Brandenburger Tor. At about 1.00 p.m. the Soviet commanding officer declared a state of emergency. The GDR "People's Police" sealed off the sector borders. Russian T-34 tanks rolled through the streets and crushed the rebellion. According to official GDR figures, 23 people were killed. Although the exact occasion is known only to a minority of today's Germans, 17 June is still considered a "national holiday" of the Federal Republic.

Western Allies declaring the Four-Power Status as being terminated. Within six months the Western armies were to leave West Berlin which was to be converted into a "free, demilitarized city." If the Allies did not comply he would sign a separate peace treaty with the GDR and pass sovereignty of the air-corridors over to the Ulbricht regime. The Western Powers refused. The crisis worsened. By the middle of 1961, the GDR had already lost one-ninth of its citizens.

Due to shortage of labour the harvest could not be completed and delivery deadlines could not be met. Import-export contracts were lost, worsening the GDR's for-

Fleeing to Berlin: Tanks could repress protest in the Soviet sector but West Berlin remained, to which residents of the Soviet sector had unrestricted access. In the 1950s, the "economic miracle" of the West and the freer life spawned a veritable mass migration from East to West. The GDR risked being drained of its young skilled workers. Nine years after the founding of the first "Socialist state on German soil", it was apparent that the "desertion from the Republic" could not go on indefinitely.

In November 1958 Nikita Khrushchev took the initiative and sent a note to the three

eign currency deficit. In addition, East Berlin's 55,000 so-called international commuters crossed daily into the Western sector while there were 45,000 job vacancies in East Berlin. Fugitives and commuters cost the GDR economy some three billion marks per year which could be saved if the Berlin escape hatch was closed for good.

The tension grew when Khrushchev and US President John F. Kennedy left their

Above, Kurfürstendamm 1968–youth protesting against the Vietnam war.

summit meeting in June 1961 as irreconcilable opponents. Khrushchev's war threats made the US boost their military budget by 3.2 billion dollars. The West Berlin newspaper *Tagesspiegel* reported extensive manoeuvers in the USA. Berlin knew which emergency situation was being rehearsed.

By this time, up to 30,000 refugees were streaming into the West each month. On 25 July President Kennedy defined the American guarantees for Berlin. These contained "Three Essentials": the presence of the Western Powers, free access to the city, and freedom for the inhabitants of West Berlin. Free movement within all of Berlin was not mentioned. For his part, Khrushchev suggested altering the sector border in Berlin into a "state border of the GDR...so that a reliable guard and effective check could be maintained." Ten days later, the SED leadership put the suggestion into practice. On 13 August at 3.25 in the morning UPI reported: "Units of the communist People's Police have sealed off the sector border between East and West Berlin in the night from Saturday to Sunday."

The Western Allies scarcely reacted. Only when Mayor Willy Brandt personally appealed to President Kennedy did signs of encouragement come from Washington. Vice-president Lyndon B. Johnson flew to Berlin on 19 August. A 1,500-man task-force was sent to reinforce the US garrison. They were received jubilantly following their march across GDR territory on the inter-zones motorway. This was decisive: there would be no war because of Berlin.

The "dying city": In the 1960s, Soviets and GDR bureaucracy applied a policy of pin-pricks to disturb Berlin's ties with West Germany. In June 1968, the GDR passed laws stating that Berlin travellers coming overland were to carry passports and to apply for a visa.

Over the years, the communist threat had welded the West Berliners together. When President Kennedy made a 33-mile (52-km) round-tour through the city on 23 June 1963, it became a triumphal procession. The Berlin view of the world appeared to be unshakeable: all evil comes from the East, all good from the Western protective powers.

In day to day life, however, the effects of the Wall weighed heavily upon the pressured metropolis. Now that all the dreams of a united German capital had evaporated, the uncertainty of the approach roads and the oppressive constriction of the enclave were all the more apparent. As a bastion of the Cold War, the city-of-the-Wall scarcely offered opportunities for the future. The fashion business emigrated to Munich and Düsseldorf; the film studios were empty. Many businesses moved completely to Federal territory, while others relocated their headquarters and research departments in West Germany. Skilled workers and entrepreneurs packed their bags. At all levels, Berlin was becoming provincial.

Youth rebels: Already the term "dying city" did the rounds when the new protest generation shook up the city's barricade mentality. The years 1967-68 were marked by a worldwide youth rebellion. This was the period of turbulent assemblies and sit-ins at the "Freie Universität" and of anti-Vietnam demonstrations and water-cannons on the Kurfürstendamm. Berlin became the capital of the anti-authoritarian movement which produced the political openings for the social reforms of the 1970s. Out of the many groups, projects and initiatives grew the dazzling kaleidoscope of the "alternative scene". Berlin once again became the market-place of exciting new ideas.

Toward the end of the 1960s, the international *status quo* in Berlin was also set in motion. Both superpowers pursued a course of detente, and in Bonn the social-liberal coalition headed by chancellor Willy Brandt, the Berlin mayor of 1961, developed a new policy towards the East. It was based on relinquishing violence and a recognition of the territorial changes following World War II, *i.e.* including the recognition of the GDR as a second German state. It was obvious that a joint European policy of detente could not ignore Berlin. On a visit to the city on 27 February 1969 President Nixon invited the Soviet Union to take up negotiations on Berlin: "We ought to abandon the slogan of the 'provocation Berlin'."

On 10 July Moscow declared, through Foreign Minister Andrei Gromyko, that it was ready to exchange views on "how complications about Berlin now and in the future can be prevented." Talks began on 26 March at the offices of the former Control Commission. On 3 September 1971, the ambassadors of the Four Powers paraphrased the results. The new Berlin Agreement, in effect since 3 June 1972, included no new regulations, but simply confirmed the *status quo* of 13 August 1961. That is to say, the Wall and barbed wire were to remain. In exchange, the Soviets were no longer to question the presence of the Western Allies. Berlin had to coexist with a new *status quo*.

For the West Berliners, the most important

aspects of the Four-Power Agreement were the practical inner German provisions, particularly the improvements on the transit routes. The GDR authorities renounced the right to check vehicles and baggage. Telephone communication between the two halves of Berlin was resumed. In addition, there were humanitarian improvements in the form of an agreement on permits, entitling West Berliners to spend up to 45 single days visiting East Berlin or the GDR. With the exchange of "permanent representatives" at the respective seats of government, contacts between Bonn and the GDR were

normalized. Berlin disappeared from the headlines as a dangerous focal point of international crises.

The next 750 years: External pressure on Berlin was lifted, but financial assistance through Federal taxes was still required to cope with numerous problems. Half of the current Berlin budget, in 1986 a sum of 11.6 billion marks, was paid for by the West German government. Following the political crises of the 1950s and the 1960s a new existential danger now appeared. Economic decline going hand-in-hand with the dramatic disappearance of about 100,000 industrial jobs. While in 1975 only 3.7 percent of the working population was looking for a job, unemployment has remained at around 10 percent since the beginning of the 1980s.

Nobody, however, talks about a "dying city" anymore. The resident German population is growing again and the image of the city has become noticeably younger. More than 15 percent of all inhabitants are between 20 and 30 years of age. This is where the hopes, but also the problems, of the future lie. Where are the necessary educational vacancies and jobs to come from?

The Senate expects a change for the better with a long-term plan aiming at attracting hi-tech and environmental technology companies to Berlin. Those responsible picture a sort of Silicon Valley on the Spree, extolling the enormous local research capacity as a particular attraction to foreign investors. With its numerous festivals and exhibitions, as well as extensive subsidies for the concert and theatre worlds, Berlin is trying to promote itself as, if not the leading cultural metropolis in Europe, at least as one of the German-speaking part. Thanks to many attractive events which included the biennial international radio and television exhibition, 1985 saw the largest number of tourists to date, a total of 1,682,770 visitors. But this record will be broken, as the attraction of Berlin has grown immensely since the changes in the GDR.

Left, signing of the Four-Power Agreement on 3 September 1971 in the former Allied Control Commission building. **Right**, GDR border guard in his watch-tower at the Wall.

THE BERLINERS

Who should be considered a "true Berliner" or a "thoroughly Berlin woman"? This subject has long been a much-loved topic of discussion. Heinrich Heine concluded in 1822: "Berlin is not really a city at all, but a place where large quantities of people gather, among them many people of intellect, to whom the place is a matter of complete indifference." Another chronicler wrote in 1880: "True Berliners are hard to find, and this city is filled for the greater part with foreigners who make up a colourful mixture."

A look at the statistics appears to confirm such observations. Cautious estimates show that only slightly less than half of the 1.9 million inhabitants of West Berlin are native Berliners. About 130,000 of these merely have a secondary residence on the Spree river, *i.e.* they have one foot in the Federal Republic just to be on the safe side.

Home of the homeless: The first settlers arriving in the Berlin region in the 13th and 14th centuries originated from the area between the Harz and the Thuringian Forests, ancestral home of the Askanian ruler around Ballenstedt and Bernburg. Others arrived from the lower Rhine and Flemish lands.

At the end of the 16th century the population grew considerably when Dutch settlers were invited by Elector Johann Georg to boost the principality's declining number of subjects. However, the plague killed 3,000 of the 12,000 Berliners. The Thirty Years' War contributed its part to the decimation and had new blood not poured in from everywhere Berlin today would be a provincial town.

In the 17th and 18th centuries, the immigrants were mainly refugees: Huguenots and Waldensians came from France; from Bohemia the Herrnhuter Brothers; and from Austria 20,000 Salzburg Protestants. Under

Frederick the Great, Swiss colonists and Jews poured in. In Imperial times and after, mainly Poles, Silesians, East Prussians and Pommeranians migrated to the rising industrial metropolis. After World War II came the influx of refugees from the East and foreign workers. Thus, there is no truly clearcut Berliner.

A "reckless breed"—this is how the much-travelled Goethe characterised Berliners. Indeed, Berlin was a sort of America in the midst of the "Wild East" of Germany, lacking both favourable climatic and geographical conditions. Whoever came here had undoubtedly suffered some injustice, or had been driven or drawn here by circumstance. Berlin offered the chance to begin anew, the attraction of the unknown, the "…big deal of a lifetime. The city was a broker of existential options; this was where the future was being had as a chance bargain; where one could enjoy views without climbing towers, where there was something pleasing for those who knew how to make use of it"— according to the writer Dieter Hildebrandt in *Germany, your Berliners*. In order to get by in this place, one had to be "brazen-faced as well as occasionally a bit rude", to quote Berlin-visitor Goethe again.

"Mother's den of stations": One example of how Berliners came into being made literary history. A father from Stettin, which before the war was one-and-a-half hour's train journey away, ran off to America leaving his wife and five children behind. His wife pursued him but only got as far as Berlin. One of her sons later described his arrival as a 10-year-old in Berlin as a kind of after-birth: he had only been pre-born in Stettin to prepare for this event.

"In the train my mother chatted with people who knew the city. Our area, the Blumen Strasse, was described as a very bad one, there are lots of factories and smoke, the talk was very lively, an incessant flow. I didn't dare say or, to be more exact, ask anything. I sat in labour. I was getting more and more scared. It hit my stomach. The

Preceding pages: parade of the Western Allies on the Strasse des 17. Juni; start of the Berlin marathon in Tiergarten. **Left**, a Berlin physiognomy.

labour-pains increased in intensity. And as we neared the houses of Berlin, my strength was at an end. I stood at the window; it was dark, late evening, I gave way. The child had arrived, it ran down my trousers, I felt better, I stood in a puddle. Then I sat down quietened. Afterwards, we drove through the strange city and then the second miracle occurred. We sat down in a train in a bright station. It set off into the night, travelled for a few minutes and then stopped—at the same station again…Had we travelled in a circle? But why and to what purpose, and, for all that, we arrived in the end. It was not until adulthood that I comprehended this puzzling

Turks and "Wessies": Today, most of these main-line stations have been torn down or are melancholy ruins dying slow deaths. At the "Anhalter" goods station, birches have grown to veritable trees between rusting rails. The Berliners of today mostly come into the city by car along the transit route. Once they pass the depressing border control buildings, they race along the avenues towards the "Funkturm", the vibrant city.

Until the building of the Wall, West Berlin absorbed the influx of GDR citizens. Later, with the help of the Federal Employment Office, 370,000 West German workers were recruited. About two-thirds of these "Wes-

occurrence. It became more and more apparent to me: We had taken the city-train. The stations look similar in the evenings in Berlin, particularly when you come from Stettin." The boy experiencing his second birth was the doctor and writer Alfred Döblin.

No wonder Berlin's stations played such a particular role; weren't they something like delivery rooms? This is why Berliners look on them with a touch of intimacy: the "Lehrter", "Potsdamer", "Görlitzer", "Stettiner", "Schlesischer" and the "Anhalter"— which literary historian Walter Benjamin called the "mother's den of stations".

sies" became residents. By now, they consider themselves "real Berliners". Berlin's astonishing powers of assimilation worked miracles even with Suebians and Frisians, the most stubborn of Germans.

Since the end of the 1960s, Italians, Yugoslavs, Greeks and Turks have been arriving in large numbers. Today, every tenth inhabitant is a foreigner and every fourth child under six has foreign parents. Workers from the GDR and other socialist countries have also been immigrating in increasing numbers to East Berlin.

Dry humour: And so it is impossible to

speak of *the* character of the "real" Berliner. Yet, there are certain idiosyncrasies which residents of this city have long cultivated. The most important of these is a tolerance toward strangers. It does not matter where someone comes from; in the final analysis, nearly half the population are Berliners by choice or are "trained Berliners". So, naturally, terms of abuse for newcomers and foreign residents scarcely exist.

Hardly any of the mayors, or at least none of those of international repute, were native Berliners. Anyone who stays here and likes the city can become a Berliner. But, he must come to terms with the prevailing mentality

After following her for a while, he went past and, stopping her, said: "Dear lady, if you are as lovely from the front as you are from behind, then I cannot resist the temptation of kissing you!" Her reply: "Why not simply kiss me where I am loveliest?"

This exchange goes to show that the female Berliner is not backward in being forward. She likes to play-act a naive role. The prototype of the saucy "Berlin plant", well capable of showing her spines if necessary, which best describes the chanson singer Claire Waldoff. Dry and voluminous, she was born and bred in Gelsenkirchen. Blandine Ebinger, acting with sophisticated

which expresses itself with a quick tongue and a dry humour. Berliners call a spade a spade. They are not bothered about appearing rude or putting their foot into everything.

Painter Franz Krüger once decided to get to know the popular opera soubrette, Johanna Eunicke. He attempted this, as was the 19th-century custom, while taking a stroll down the Unter den Linden boulevard.

Left, the "Popper" generation lives in the better parts of town. **Above**, with "mother green" in a Wedding backyard.

naivéty, embodied the erotically emancipated Berlin woman of the 1920s, most particularly in the literary chansons of her one-time husband, Friedrich Holländer.

The Berliners' much-vaunted addiction to pleasure is also worthy of mention. In the last century it gave rise to the culture of ballrooms like "Resi" or "Little Walter, the Comforter." Even before this, popular establishments on the outskirts of the city such as the "Neue Welt" in the Hasenheide and "Krolls" in the Tiergarten were blossoming. These provided lively entertainment in the form of music, dance, theatre and acrobatics.

BERLINERISCH

Whether *Berlinerisch* is a dialect or just slang is for linguists to decide. Together with other idiosyncrasies, the Berliner's language is a part of him. Berliners are easily recognisable as soon as they open their mouths. Their gift of the gab, their insolent way of talking, and their colourful use of language immediately announces their origin.

Berlinerisch is full of ambiguous expressions and funny puns. Several publishers live off these anecdotes, the odd humour and quick tongue of the Berliners. To the outsider, their talk seems more acidic than it really is. The point which is frequently overlooked is that the Berliners often use their picturesque speech more to show off their lingual proficiency than to hurt .

Sobriety, is said to be a characteristic of this city. This could as well refer to the Berliners' manner of speaking and their drinking habits. Berliners do not fuss around with formalities and fancy talk: they always get directly to the point. Harsh consonants are changed to softer ones and, in certain instances, consonants are entirely omitted, as in the common question "*Wa?*" which originates from "*Was?*" (what?). All this allows the Berliner to talk quickly and more economically, which is a clue to the fact that Berliners love to discuss and are very argumentative.

Because the peculiarities of Berlin grammar are practically impossible to explain and because they are boring in the extreme, they will not be considered in this essay.

Berlinerisch originated from the Lower German family of languages. It was brought to Berlin by merchants and colonists who had left the area between the Harz Mountains and the river Elbe where, during the Middle Ages, pure *Platt*-German (a dialect) was spoken.

During the 16th century Berlin underwent a major change in its language. This is because the hub of its trading activities was moved from the Hanse (Hamburg, Bremen, Lübeck) to Frankfurt/Oder and Leipzig, where "High Saxon", a language similar to the later German writings of Martin Luther prevailed. In 1504, Johann Rether from Meissen became the City Clerk and introduced "Meissener" High Saxon as the new official language. Naturally, the Berliners did not adapt immediately to the Saxon sing-song. They merely adopted some sounds and added them to their language. Thus, the original *Berlinerisch* came to occupy a position between Lower German and Lutheran High German.

It is possible to discern many words that stem from the old *Platt*-German, especially the classic "*Ick*" or "*Icke*" (I) of the Berliner. *Berlinerisch* also borrowed colloquialisms from Huguenot immigrants. The gastronomical vocabulary has been especially enriched with many expressions such as *Boulette, Destille,* and *Roulade.* Some words have become so distorted by common use that it is often difficult to trace their origins. Such words are "*Botton*" (french: *bottes* = boots), "*Kinkerlitzchen*" (french: *quincaillerie* = kitchen equipment) and the French expression "*mocca faux*" for artificial coffee which has become "*Muckefuck*".

More recently, however, there have been influences from underworld slang which, interspersed with Yiddish and Hebrew expressions, thrived in the quarter which was inhabited by poor Jews from Galicia. Here, "*Baal emoch*" meaning "coward" was transformed to "*einer, der Bammel hat*" (one being anxious) in Berlinerisch. And who would suspect the Berlinerisch "dufte" which means "wonderful" is derived from the Yiddish "*tov*" which means "good"? Such contributions have added to the colour of Berlinerisch, as well as to its bad reputation.

Out into the "Green": Something which is seen as being typical of Berliners is their touching soft spot for nature, not least because greenery is rare in tenements and backyards. They grow flowers on their balconies, or have a few plants on the windowsills. The Sunday trip out to the country has a long tradition. The pre-requisites for a picnic on the Havel are meatballs, homemade potato salad, an appropriate supply of beer and perhaps a pack of playing cards. Berliners then sit back and imagine they are on a sunny beach under swaying palms, rather than amidst tattered pines.

On Sundays, everyone seems to have a regular spot somewhere in the country. Some fathers, however, are overcome by thirst as soon as they set out for the country, and the trip ends up at the first pub they see. And so, beyond the former city wall, a belt of tourist cafés came to life, advertising: "Families can make their coffee here!" Clients need only pay for the hot water and unwrap the cake that they brought along. The proprietors still manage to do good business because the fathers buy a glass of beer and, of course, Berlin wheat-beer with a touch of syrup is just the thing for mother and the children.

Dogs' capital: The Berliner's love for animals, bordering on the pathological, is proverbial. It is especially apparent in the number of dogs to be found in the city. In proportion to its population, there are more dogs around the Spree than anywhere else in Germany: five per 100 inhabitants. One reason for this is the age and social structure of West Berlin. More than a quarter of its population is over 60 years old. For many of the widowed and the lonely in their anonymous council flats, a barking housemate is their sole companion. A study by the Technische Fachhochschule has described the many "dogs of comfort" in Berlin as one of "high social functional value".

However, these dogs do need to be taken out three or four times a day for a walk. Their deposits are impressive and the total daily business adds up to a colossal 16 tons of dog excrement on streets and squares alone. As the senator for the environment proclaimed in a well-meaning information campaign: "Goodwill can dispose of those little piles!" Until then, commented the metropolitan magazine *Zitty*, "the problem can only be avoided by following a sharp zig-zag course, eyes fixed on the street".

Wit as safety-valve: Taking pleasure in mockery and drastic jokes is a typical characteristic of the Berliners who are both renowned and feared for their ready wit. They like to grouse about any- and everything which opposes their desire for indepen-

dence, in particular about the powers-that-be. These have always had difficulty in trying to make faithful, submissive subjects of the Berliners. Frederick the Great, well aware of this even exempted them from military service, and intentionally ignored the pointed jokes about his sexual orientation. "Then get drunk yourself!" he wrote on the margin of a letter from an informer reporting the treasonable statements of a drunkard.

Adolf Glassbrenner 150 years ago described the safety-valve function of grousing in the new coffee-houses: "Only the lieuten-

Left and right, whether young or old–the female Berliner has a ready tongue.

ants eat cake for the sake of eating cake. Other Berliners eat cake in order to read the newspapers, and most people only go into the pub for the lack of any other forum in Berlin. The wine, however, brings out their inner nature, and critics and humourists soon become enthusiasts. Hardly has an hour gone by, the newspapers fly from the tables, the discussion flowers and becomes livelier, warmer and fiercer. Wit and the desire for freedom know no limits, and the champagne corks rejoice like the Berlin souls which have been freed from convention and police repression…"

In Imperial Berlin, a bastion of Social

Democracy, the revolution did not take place on the streets but in the workers' taverns. The renowned and notorious mechanism of verbal wit helped wash away the political anger at reaction and militarism.

Claire Waldoff, "raisin of the programme" in the Linden cabaret club ("Who's throwing mud around?"), encountered difficulties in the Third Reich because the Berliners openly associated her song "He's called Hermann", composed long before the Nazi seizure of power, with Hitler's paladin, the Prussian Prime minister and later Marshal of the Reich, Hermann Göring. In Berlin he was nicknamed the "Quell-germane" or "swollen German". The Berliners had long since been used to such equivocal texts by their beloved Claire. In one of her most popular chansons in World War I the refrain ran: "(Kaiser) Willem, don't talk so much, I'm sick to death of it."

Hitler, who grew up in Bavarian beer halls, was not a very popular man in Berlin, not least on account of his lack of humour. "I'd rather believe than start wondering", Berliners would say during the Third Reich. Later, when bombs were falling on the German capital, it was with bitter irony they said: "Think practically, donate coffins!" Districts which had been razed to the ground were appropriately renamed: Charlottenburg became "Klamottendorf" ("Rags Village"), Lichterfelde "Trichterfelde" ("Crater Field"), and Steglitz, "Steht nichts" ("Nothing Standing").

East Berliners today are no less critical. A sample joke: Maria Callas sings in the Palace of the Republic. Honecker goes to her dressing room after the concert and says, "Dear lady, you were wonderful! With your art you have given our people a thing of beauty. You may ask of me what you wish!" "Tear down the Wall!" says the opera star. Honecker stops short. "I understand", he replies feeling flattered, "you want to be alone with me."

On both sides of the Wall the Berliners keep their grim humour on alert, as a lifebelt, for they lead a life which is by no means peaceful. It is part of the machinery of this city of millions: fast, unsettled, hectic, sometimes a dance on a volcano.

"In this city people work a lot," wrote Kurt Tucholsky, "here there is drudgery. (Pleasure as well is work here, you roll up your sleeves and expect to get something from it.) The Berliner is not busy, he is always wound up. Unfortunately, he has completely forgotten why we are on this earth. Even in heaven—assuming a Berliner gets to heaven—he would be engaged in something at, for example, 4 o'clock in the morning."

Above, the summer drink: "Berliner Weisse mit Schluss". **Right**, young spectator at the East Berlin May Parade.

THE TURKISH MINORITY

Currently, some 254,000 foreigners live in West Berlin. About 150 nationalities, ranging from Afghans to Zambians, are represented. Of these, the Yugoslavs (12.1 percent), Poles (4.6 percent), Italians (3 percent) and Greeks (2.8 percent) are especially numerous. However, the largest community by far, at nearly 45 percent, are the 114,000 Turks. Berlin has become the city with the most Turkish inhabitants outside of Turkey.

The booming 1960s, when the German Federal Employment Office recruited the first "guest workers" from the slums of Turkish cities and the villages of distant Anatolia, have long since gone. Many of these first immigrant workers, who had originally planned to spend a limited time in Germany, have since arranged for their wives and children to follow them, and have found cheap accommodation in the decaying tenement houses of the traditional working-class districts.

Today, the Turks are a clearly defined minority within Berlin; they have developed their own distinctive community, with their own wholesale and retail businesses, restaurants and banks, their clubs and religious festivals, to say nothing of travel agencies offering regular flights to Ankara and Istanbul. Turkish doctors are treating (not only) their compatriots. Turkish typing agencies help sail past the reefs of German language, while special Turkish schools help to surmount the obstacles of obtaining a driver's licence. There are daily newspapers, radio programmes, video shops and, the newest acquisition, cable TV—all in Turkish.

In the Berlin districts of Moabit, Wedding, Kreuzberg and Neukölln the Turkish immigrants, most of whom adhere to the Islamic faith, characterise the street scenes: women with shawls covering head and most of the face, sometimes even veils, and men with kepi (*takke*) and, of course, a black moustache. Most Turkish Berliners live in Kreuzberg, where a true "Little Istanbul" has burgeoned around Kottbusser Tor and Görlitzer Bahnhof. The subway line 1, heading for the Schlesisches Tor in east Kreuzberg has, not unexpectedly, been nicknamed "Orient-Express" by ever-present Berlin wit. The Maybachufer market merchants offering everything from very colourful piles of fruit and vegetables, to clothing, material and all sorts of household goods, are mainly Turkish.

To the occasional visitor to Berlin, this unfamiliar folklore may appear colourful and exotic.

It has, however, brought a lot of problems in its wake: the differences in language, culture, religion and mentality which form the background to the Turks' distinct lifestyle are, for many native Berliners, incomprehensible. The notion of Turkey as an oriental fairy-tale land of minarets, bazaars and ladies of the harem is one thing. Daily contact with large Turkish families as neighbours, whose customs are felt to be strange, if not disturbing, or a workmate from Anatolia communicating in barely comprehensible "Pidgin" German, is a different thing.

It may well be that kebab stalls have become a welcome contribution to the local cuisine; and that locals appreciate Turkish restaurants as a

change from their daily diet: and the small store at the corner, long abandoned and now revived by Turkish families may be seen as an atmospheric alternative to the supermarket's anonymity; and nobody would want to miss the next-door cobbler or tailor: yet, at the root of it, the "garlic eaters" as fellow citizens, have remained alien to the majority of Berliners. In addition, the high unemployment in recent years and the lack of educational facilities for young people have strengthened the prejudices of many Berliners against Turks who are, for many natives, the epitome of "the foreigner" taking away German jobs.

The Turks increasingly are being thought of as competing for jobs: some even blame them for being responsible for one's own economic misery. No Berliner, however, would be keen to work in the badly paid jobs on the assembly-line, to collect garbage or to do cleaning jobs. Families have joined their bread-winners and in view of the high Turkish birth rate, irrational fears of an oriental immigrant group "swamping" the domestic culture have arisen. Racism and hatred of foreigners, incited by right-wing extremist circles, results on occasions in the cry: "Turks out!" or even physical attacks on Turkish people.

The Turks, who for their part had only a vague idea of what their future homes would be like, they feel insecure and discriminated against. The more difficult it is for them to be friendly with their fellow German citizens, the more inclined they are to withdraw to the familiarity of their own traditions which provide a code of conduct for both everyday life and personal behaviour. In the course of time, some 25 mosques have been consecrated, most of which are located unobtrusively in former factories. This is also where the Koran (the Muslim Holy Book) is taught. The children, strictly divided according to sex, have to learn whole sections of the Holy Book by heart in the Arabic language. They are indoctrinated by the "Imam" with values that are little suited to the reality of their daily lives and which are even more likely to increase the distance between them and Germans of the same age.

At the same time, this has led to identity crises and family conflicts in the Turkish community. The relative liberalism of Berlin school life and the visual stimulation of advertising on the city streets on one hand, and the strictly patriarchal structure of the Turkish family on the other, divides the world of many second- and third-generation Turks into "mornings Germany, evenings Turkey".

Parents who want to keep growing daughters under lock and key and to marry them off as virgins to orthodox Turkish men according to old custom, show little understanding of the young people's desire to wear fashionable mini-skirts or pleated trousers instead of traditional shawls or even the veil. The older folk still have strong emotional links with their homeland and would prefer to return to their Turkish homes rather sooner than later; ideally, of course, with the whole, often numerous family. Their daughters and sons, however, often want to remain in "rich" Germany.

On the other hand, it is not easy for many young Turks to gain access to the free life which Germans of their age lead. They are often denied entry to discotheques on the flimsiest pretences. Experiences of rejection and discrimination of this kind exacerbate the conflict.

In the meantime, programmes and initiatives have been developed to promote mutual understanding and to improve daily living with one another. Besides German-Turkish kindergartens and women's houses, as well as "mixed self-help groups", a variety of joint activities, particularly those of a cultural nature, like German-Turkish theatrical groups, rock festivals and street parties take place throughout the city.

The "Berliner Treffpunkt" functions as a co-ordinating centre for events of every kind to facilitate integration. Turkish artists and writers were involved in the preparations for Berlin's 750th anniversary celebrations. The Senate department concerned with foreigners is campaigning with the slogan "Living together in Berlin" for more tolerance between young Germans and foreigners. The aims of the campaign are to encourage more young second- and third- generation foreigners to adjust to their local environment, to help reduce mutual prejudices, and to promote and develop existing contacts.

Nevertheless, many Turkish Berliners, particularly of the first generation, remain firmly attached to their cultural and religious traditions in order to preserve their Turkish identity. Ultimately, they still want to return home and, with savings and possibly the Senate Repatriation Premium, make a new start without being scorned again—as "Almancilar" ("like the Germans") in Turkey. The majority of young Turks, however, are more interested in assimilation and integration and in the long term will undoubtedly exercise their option of becoming German citizens. In theory, more than half of the Turks living in Berlin have the right to do so. All the same, their complete absorption on an equal basis into German according to Berlin society, will probably take generations, according to some sociologists, as was the case with foreign immigrants in the past. The Huguenots were envied by the local population and were met with rejection. Only when the language barrier was lifted, did integration finally become possible.

Aras Ören, a Turkish writer living in Berlin, expressed the ambivalent feelings of the Turks regarding their national and cultural identity in the following poem:

As regards me,
Whatever life they cut out for me,
I know it is a garment that does not fit.
But how will the descendants
Really judge me?
If not by my truth,
then surely their own.

STREETS AND PLACES

One thing is certain: over the next 750 years Berlin will constantly be changing its face. It also is no coincidence that the Berliners ironically say: "As long as the Spree is still flowing through Berlin...", so often has the city changed its identity. When talking about Berlin today, any one of three things could be referred to: the city as a whole, West Berlin or East Berlin. Therefore, wherever it seemed appropriate, places and sights are clearly distinguished as to whether they are in West or East Berlin. The Wall, saddest monument of the once Imperial capital, is dealt with in a separate chapter.

It is now time for a closer look at this bizarre double faced city. But even 150 years ago Adolf Glassbrenner asked: "Where is Berlin in Berlin? Just because you hear the locals speaking their dialect and you have had a glass of the popular *Weissbier* doesn't mean you know anything about Berlin".

The real Berlin is best found in its districts: they alone make this huge city in any way comprehensible and habitable. A district in itself, even if not shown on the city map, is the new West Berlin city, the downtown area around the Kurfürstendamm and the Gedachtniskirche. The travel section commences here at the focal point of international tourism. Around this core stretches Charlottenburg, Wilmersdorf, Schöneberg and Tiergarten. Each of these districts has its own traditions and sights and each is honoured with a chapter.

Then, beginning with the southeastern districts of Kreuzberg and Neukölln, the remaining eight districts are visited. When we do this we are proceeding clockwise around Berlin and radiating from the centre to the periphery. In this way the reader will come to appreciate in detail the outer green belt which ends in North Berlin's concrete jungle of Wedding.

Two chapters on East Berlin cover a one-day visit to the historical district of Nitte which is between the Brandenburg Tor and Alexanderplatz. A one-day trip to Potsdam with Sanssouci Palace is also included.

Many visitors despair at the sheer size of Berlin. The Tip Boxes (see Travel Tips section) should be of help. All begin with information about the major public transport routes. They also contain general information which should be useful on a visit to a district. West Berlin's museums are dealt with in detail in the feature section: the treasures of East Berlin's Museumsinsel in a special box.

Preceding pages: Tobogganing at Teufelsberg; enjoying summer at *Insulaner*; taking a ride in Grunewald; having a dance.... **Left**, sunbathing in the sea of houses.

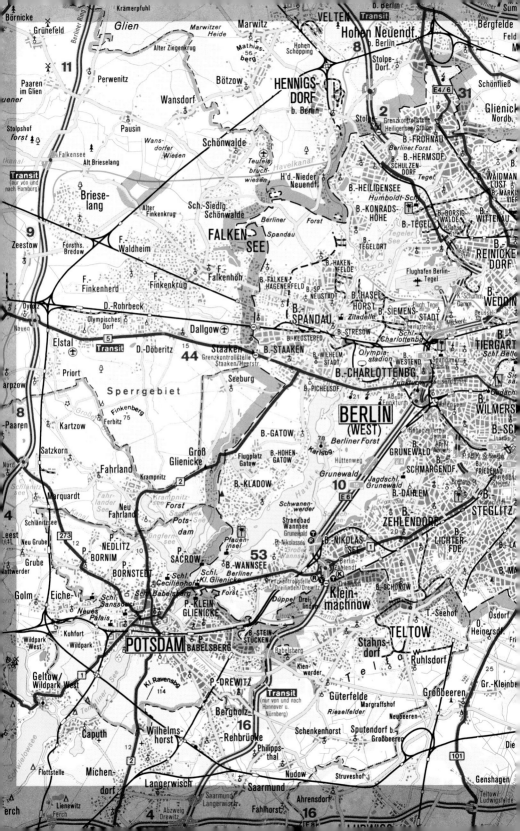

KURFÜRSTENDAMM

"Ohne Ku'damm keen Berlin", ("without Kurfürstendamm no Berlin"). So went the serenade of the Schöneberger Sängerknaben chorus to their "splendid avenue" on its 100th birthday celebrations. The choir-boys were right: the Kurfürstendamm was, and remains, the focal point of western Berlin. It is difficult to imagine the city today without it.

Opinions differ as to the exact birthdate of the Ku'damm. It has existed as a country road since 1542, beginning as a narrow path leading to Elector Joachim II's hunting castle in Grunewald. For centuries, the renowned boulevard passed through sand and swampy land. Then, in 1871, chancellor Bismarck caught sight of the *Champs Elysées* in Paris. From that moment on, the "Iron Chancellor" never gave up his dream of having just such a majestic avenue for the capital of the newly founded German Empire. In 1875 his cabinet prescribed the following measurements: "Length 3.8 km from the zoo to Grunewald; 53 metres total width, space for 7.5 metres front-gardens on either side, four metres of pavements and 10 metres for roadways, in the middle a bridle-path of five metres and a promenade of also five metres width." All this was meant for the "comfortable open-air promenading of the people of Berlin" and "equestrian training for the upper classes".

Construction on the country road proceeded slowly until, in 1882, the "Kurfürstendamm Society", created by the Deutsche Bank, purchased and developed the area. On 5 May 1886, steam-driven streetcars began running between Grunewald and the zoo. This event marked the real beginning of the Kurfürstendamm. But, as with many things on the Ku'damm, the streetcars did not last long. What, however, has lasted since the 1930s, is the Ku'damm

Left, vintage rally on the Ku'damm.

myth, which expresses itself in an undefined longing called "homesickness for the Kurfürstendamm".

No monument: He who strolls along the Kurfürstendamm today must be very observant if he wishes to find traces of its brilliant past: little has survived. However, the Ku'damm should not be approached with too much respect or in search of the good old times—the less brilliant times are far too obvious. Yet, a fresh and lively breeze is blowing in this part of Berlin: this is no place for the dusty and outmoded past. The Kurfürstendamm is as lively as ever, just as pleasure-bent, voluptuous and full of contrasts as it was at the turn of the century.

In any case the Ku'damm is a symbol. It is, without doubt, almost synonymous for downtown West Berlin. In earlier times, this role was played by "Unter den Linden" and Friedrich Strasse and their surroundings. Since the division of the city, however, the old Kurfürstendamm has taken over, for the Western half, a role for which it was not prepared. There are no government or other official buildings and those national shrines which one expects in a traditional city centre are absent.

The decayed tooth: Other than the protest against the razing of the Gedächtniskirche, the Kurfürstendamm did not witness political demonstrations until the mid-1960s. After the war, the Gedächtniskirche stood where it always had, in the middle of the roaring traffic of the erstwhile Viktoria-Luise-Platz, now called **Breitscheidplatz**. It was named after Social Democrat Rudolph Breitscheid who was murdered in Buchenwald concentration camp in 1944. However, eventually the ruin did not fit into the concept of a "car-adapted city." In 1957 the *Tagesspiegel* newspaper circulated a questionnaire in which 90 percent of the city's inhabitants voted to keep the "decayed tooth". In 1961 it was finally integrated into the design of the new **Gedächtniskirche** by professor Egon Eiermann. A brass plate in the tower-ruin states: "The tower of the old church shall remind us of the judgment that God passed on our people in the years of war."

The interior was re-opened to the public in 1987 and is now an exhibition room. It is clear from those mosaics which remain that the Gedächtniskirche once was an extravagant monument honouring the Kaiser and the state. Built with donations from prosperous burghers, this neo-romanesque edifice was consecrated to the memory of Wilhelm I in 1895.

Its location in the heart of the city also resulted in the Gedächtniskirche gracing the political headlines. During the 1960s and 1970s, church services were disturbed when Rudi Dutschke, the leader of the student protest movement, tried to discuss the Vietnam War with church-going Christians. Some priests and parishioners supported the student protests, while others resorted to violence against the intruders.

Young outcasts, punks and tramps always make the headlines when they set up house on the front steps of the church. Once, the altar was destroyed by a drunkard. A few years later, a clergyman was beaten up when he tried to keep someone from scribbling on the walls. The parish spends 80,000 marks a year to repair damages resulting from vandalism. In spite of all this, the church remains true to its mission of reconciliation and peace. It houses a shelter where the homeless can have a shower, a meal and a bed for a few pfennigs. Once a year, Breitscheidplatz is crowded with hundreds of heavy Honda and BMW motorcycles when hundreds of Berlin bikers come together for a memorial service dedicated to friends who have died in accidents.

At the "Wasserklops": The rest of this area is usually taken over by youngsters performing acrobatics with their skateboards, bicycles and roller-skates. Then the square is alive until late at night. People sit on benches, steps and granite seats around the "**Weltkugel-Brun-**

The "Show-case of the West" in the fifties.

nen", nicknamed "Wasserklops" ("Water Meatball"), as Berliners call Joachim Schmettau's fountain of 1983, a massive, angular serrated globe of rust-coloured granite. They listen to street musicians from all over the world, have their portraits drawn by local artists, or read the pamphlets distributed by all sorts of organisations and religious sects. Others lazily study the merchandise of the street-stalls, where the leather belt seems cheaper than in the shops, the jewellery more trendy, and the silk shawl more exotic.

In the Europa-Centre: In 1965 the Europa-Centre sprang up, the first of many such projects following speculation, at a place where in the 1950s some food-stalls and an amusement tent had shared the nights. The **Europa-Centre** today houses some 100 stores, restaurants, bars, cafés; a movie centre with five cinemas, a "Multivisions-Show" offering a 40-minute crash course in Berlin history; the "Vip-Club-Disco"; the "Spielbank Berlin" (a casino whose entrance is on Budapester Strasse); the cabaret "Die Stachelschweine"; a revue theatre; Berlin's largest sauna and, last but not least, a 353-feet (106-metres) high platform with telescopes and a panoramic view.

One could spend an entire day investigating the inner life of this outwardly not very attractive building. The "Uhr der fliessenden Zeit" (Flowing Time Clock), a technical art object by Paris physicist Bernard Gitton, tells the fast passing time. The Berliners have christened this 43-foot (13-metre) water-clock the "fruit juice machine" because of its neon-coloured liquids.

The "Romanisches Café": Until its destruction in 1943, the legendary "Romanisches Café" was also located here. In the same way that the "Café Grössenwahn" (Café Megalomania) had been the spot for bohemians in pre-World War I Berlin, so the "Romanisches" filled the gap in the years of the Weimar Republic. It was the focus for expressionist literature, freely ex-

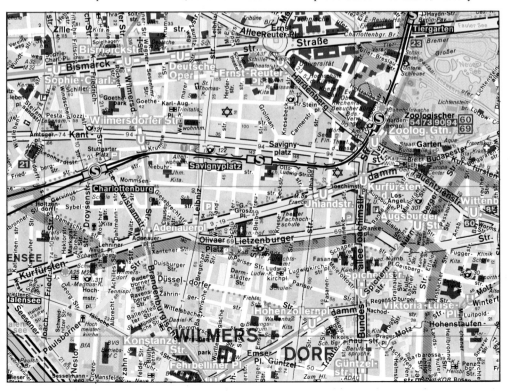

pressed opinions and a meeting-place of the avant-garde and their retinue dressed-up as anarchists. The smoke-filled interior of the café was not especially interesting. Across from the revolving door was a buffet that offered the same mediocre food that is found in the waiting-room of any Prussian railway station. Night after night, the same guests sat with their cliques in either the rectangular "basin for non-swimmers" or in the square "basin for swimmers". Upstairs, the mezzanine was the realm of the chess-players.

Today, this legendary coffee house is a symbol for the cosmopolitan Berlin of the "Roaring Twenties" where hedonism ruled unhindered. The list of the guests who frequented the "Romanisches" and the other artists' cafés around Kurfürstendamm reads like an encyclopedia of the history of modern literature, stage and screen: Else Lasker-Schüler, Kurt Tucholsky, Alfred Kerr, Robert Musil, Joseph Roth, Egon Erwin Kisch, Gottfried Benn, Carl Zuck-mayer, Thomas and Heinrich Mann, Klabund and many more. Another regular, Billy Wilder, became famous as a journalist writing *A Gigolo at the Hotel Eden.* Others, like the directors Robert Siodmak and Ernst Lubitsch, were on the road to fame—until Hitler came.

With the expulsion of the Jewish intellectuals in 1933, the Nazis also succeeded in eradicating the spirit of liberalism from the Kurfürstendamm. "We watched the coffee house and its terrace blow away, disappear along with their ghostly load, dissolve into nothingness as if it had never existed…", wrote Wolfgang Koeppen describing the end of the café. "The guests…were dispersed all over the world, arrested and killed; they committed suicide or sitting bent in the café over mediocre publications, ashamed of the fawning press and great treachery…"

Ten years later, on one November night, British bombers razed this part of the city to the ground. The demolishing and rebuilding craze of the 1950s and

Tourists at Café Kranzler.

1960s did the rest. Today, the boulevard, lacking in orientation, is a hotchpotch of glass and steel architecture dotted with some historical buildings.

An apartment building at Ku'damm **No. 213** at Uhlandeck, which also houses some shops, was built to reflect the original Kufürstendamm architecture. The tasteful exterior matches the stately staircase with carved interior jewels, bronze medallions and paintings on the walls. In keeping with Berlin tradition around the turn of the century, the five-storey buildings also had smaller apartments in the rear. Most of the flats were spacious, with separate entrances for the servants and unusual technical equipment for the time, such as elevators and central heating. The **Iduna-Haus** on the corner of Leibnizstrasse, with three small baroque towers adorning the façade, is another example of patrician architecture and has been declared a national heritage monument.

Unclear transition: Where does the Kurfürstendamm actually begin? With house number 11 on the north side of the boulevard just behind Breitscheidplatz…? It would be pointless to search for the first 10 numbers: they disappeared in 1925. At that time this part of the Kurfürstendamm, which is today occupied by the Hotel Intercontinental, was renamed **Budapester Strasse**.

Other people believe the boulevard begins at **Wittenbergplatz** (except that here it is called Tauentzien Strasse), which is not true either. The transition from one street to the other is unclear, but there is one major difference. **Tauentzienstrasse** is an out and out business street, with no street cafés. However, the **Kaufhaus des Westens** (KaDeWe) stands on the corner of Wittenbergplatz. This famous consumer's palace, with over 51,400 sq yards (43,000 square metres) of space, is the largest departmental store on the continent. About 3,000 employees are waiting to sell to you some 250,000 different articles, from pins to comput-

Pavement artist on Kurfürstendamm.

ers. The **Feinschmecker-Etage** (gourmet section) is worth visiting on any day, but especially on Saturdays, when the upper classes from Grunewald crowd around the oyster and champagne bar. Experts claim that nothing that is edible cannot be found in the food department of the KaDeWe.

Fast-food boulevard: The Ku'damm is no longer as elegant as the KaDeWe. It is a sorry shame, say those who have witnessed small shops with style being driven out by high rents. Two hundred marks per square yard are far beyond what a small retailer can pay. Who cares, say others, the Kurfürstendamm is a commercial street and therefore everybody takes what he can get.

In the 1970s the Kurfürstendamm was subject to harsh criticism. A "pizza, pop and porno promenade", a "fast-food boulevard", they said. The Kurfürstendamm had become the "trash heap of the nation," they complained, and wilfully ignored that tennis shoe tourists and fast-food chains had long since become the fashion even on the Champs Elysées.

Nevertheless, responsible councilmen recognised that the often cited "Show-case of the Free World" had deteriorated as a result of exclusively commercial development planning. This was particularly obvious with write-off structures such as the Ku'damm-Eck on Joachimstaler Strasse, the Ku'damm-Karree (between Uhland- and Knesebeck Strasse), or the Ku'damm-Center (Kurfürstendamm 142-147), "depressing neon-spangled citadels of consumerism", as they were called. When, in addition, sex-cinemas and peep-shows as well as cheap amusement bars and gambling halls appeared, some critics saw that the end had come. As if sexual entertainment was something new! Already in 'the days of the Third Reich guests of the state had been entertained on the premises of the "Salon Kitty" in Giesebrecht Strasse 11. This notorious bordello later featured in many a film and magazine series as a cunning Nazi spy trap with voluptuous agents waiting on unsuspecting customers. And, nowadays, the police estimate that a couple of thousand prostitutes carry on their trade in the downtown area.

A new façade: Doubtless the Ku' damm was fast degenerating and losing its unique character. To stem this descent, the "City Business Society", a group of concerned business people, met with representatives of the three districts of Charlottenburg, Wilmersdorf and Schöneberg and created a "City Commission". Since 1981, this has resulted in a "boulevard oriented" development of the Kurfürstendamm. Owners of amusement halls, peepshows and fast-food restaurants were discouraged from setting up shop in the "heart of the city". Officially, however, there is no planning. What happens, just happens because of "liberality, multi-functionality and pluralism".

The results of these efforts can readily be seen during a stroll down the

In the Gedächtniskirche.

Ku'damm. Between Breitscheidplatz and Joachimstaler Strasse, where stands Berlin's most expensive real estate at 3,000 to 5,000 marks per square yard, the last gaps between the "Marmorhaus" and the "Café Wien" have been filled. The department store Wertheim has replaced its ugly concrete front with a new glass façade. So-called "Hardenberg lamps" create a nostalgic atmosphere after dark. Many kiosks and advertising columns have been redone in "old-fashioned" style, and stucco-façades have been renovated to brighten up the somewhat run-down image of the Ku'damm. Unexpectedly, these manoeuvres have been successful. Slowly, criticism is being silenced, and the Kurfürstendamm is "in" again.

Abundance of culture: In any case, it offers many kinds of amusement. Firstly, there are first-run cinemas which are mainly located between Gedächtniskirche and Uhland Strasse. Then there is the **Schaubühne am Lehniner Platz**, the current shrine of

Elefantentor at the zoo.

modern German theatre. The **Staatliche Kunsthalle**, with its attractive two-storey exhibition hall and cafeteria on Budapester Strasse 46, can be described as the counterpart in the plastic art field. Mainly concerned with contemporary art, it occasionally organizes retrospectives. The info-shop of the **Berliner Festspiele** and the neighbouring gallery (at No. 48) are where all festival activities are being dealt with.

For a gallery stroll, Wölffer (No. 206) which specialises in naive art, Brusberg (No. 213) with major modern artists or, a little further up, the Majakowski-Galerie of the Society for German-Soviet Friendship, which shows contemporary art from Eastern Europe, are recommended.

The **Maison de France** on the corner of Uhland Strasse promotes the culture of Germany's western neighbour with lectures, films and language courses. An excellent bookstore and a small bistro in the same building impart a bit of Parisian atmosphere to the boulevard. The **Mengenlehre-Uhr** (clock) on the central lane of the Ku'damm inspires passers-by to solve problems of set-theory mathematics. The clock tells time if you add up the rows with lights from top to bottom. The blinking light stands for seconds, in the first row one box equals five hours, in the second row one hour, in the third row five minutes, in the fourth row one minute.

The former Chinese embassy during the Reich era at Kurfürstendamm 218 has been replaced by the restaurant Ho Lin Wah. On the second floor is the "Talk-Club" disco, a popular meeting place for Germans and Americans. Next door is the "King's Teagarden" where one can choose from 170 kinds of tea while listening to classical music. The music at the "Café de Music" and the "Musikcafé" (No. 151 and No. 152) is different. In summer, these two hard rock cafés, behind Lehniner Platz, are crowded with "easy riders" from outer districts.

American writer Thomas Wolfe de-

OASIS OF ANIMALS

The unprimed visitor might be astonished to hear parrots shriek and elephants trumpet at the Zoo railway station. The swift development of the city resulted in Berlin zoo being in the centre of West Berlin.

Construction began in 1844 of a menagerie which was based on the ideas of Alexander von Humboldt, the zoologist Martin Lichtenstein, and the landscape architect Peter Lenné. In those days, the zoo was small and located beyond the city limits. But, when all of Berlin succumbed to the fever of the booming economy in the years after the founding of the Second Reich, the Zoo administration also started to issue shares to raise capital.

At that time, the German Empire was looking for a "place in the sun"—the colonies. The emperor's colonial officers had their headquarters not far from the zoo on the Viktoria-Luise-Platz. They provided the zoo with animals that no other zoo in Europe owned at that time. The first "colonial elephant" came from Cameroon and proved to be a scientific sensation because his tusks grew inward. In this "colonial" period not only wild animals but also "wild humans" took part in huge theatrical shows with magnificent oriental settings.

The buildings which housed the animals were constructed as pagodas, temples and mosques in order to create a picturesque environment. Since 1891, the majestic Elephant Gate on Budapester Strasse has been the gateway to the exotic animal world. In 1913, an aquarium was added to the zoo. With over 4,000 species, this aquarium is one of the largest in the world.

In the 1930's, zoo director Lutz Heck started replacing the customary cages with

open areas surrounded by wide moats, beginning with the baboons' rock and an open-air pool for seals. Until this day his heritage has withstood criticism.

"Be careful! Monkey will grab your hat and glasses!" a sign warns visitors in the monkey house. Coincidentally, there was always a warden around, who, for a tip, would restore proper ownership. It was not until the 1970s that one of the wardens conceded to having trained the animals.

On 22 Nov 1943 the work of 100 years was destroyed in just 15 minutes by an air-raid. During the final battle for Berlin, the "Eastern Front" ran right through the middle of the zoo; one of the last large anti-aircraft bunkers equipped with cannons was located within the zoo. When the last clouds of smoke lifted, only 91 animals were still alive.

The hippopotamus "Knautschke", now 50 years old, became the hero and symbol of the will for survival of the Berliners. The huge animal endured the last days of the war under water. When reconstruction began, Knautschke dozed happily in its pond and let himself be fed. In 1986, all Berlin was glad to hear that "Knautschke" had become a grandfather.

In 1981, the People's Republic of China donated two pandas. A special and regal bungalow was built for the prominent new residents.

Today, the zoo (open from 9 a.m. till dusk, latest 7 p.m.) houses 11,758 species—the most found in any zoo in the world.

On passing through the main gate at Hardenbergplatz, the visitor leaves the busy city behind and enters a different world. To the right majestic elephants welcome him: in front stand the bird cages and the monkey house, followed by the lions' cages, the baboons' rock and the polar bears' compound, not to speak of the magic aquarium and the house of nocturnal animals. Naturally, there is also a special children's zoo.

scribed the Kurfürstendamm as "Europe's biggest coffee house". Each café has its own style. The "Café Kranzler" (No. 18-19) and the "Café Möhring" (No. 213) cultivate the "good old days". In "Café Adlon" on Adenauerplatz, one catches an occasional glimpse of stars, and in the "Kaffeehaus Edinger" (No. 194) hip yuppies turn up in style.

Even the disparaged "consumer paradises" are good for an occasional surprise. "Over 400 of the most interesting people in Europe", according to the signs, await the visitor in the **Wachsfigurenkabinett**, Berlin's Madame Tussaud's in the Ku'damm-Eck at the corner of Joachimstaler Strasse. Tourist attractions abound in the Ku'damm-Karree, including a flea-market and a **Teddybear Museum**. All these invite people to come and to stay, and since the city's closing-down laws are handled fairly loose, the café terraces and pavements remain crowded until morning on warm summer nights. There is no shortage of discos, and street musicians, la-

ser spectacles, juggling festivals and similar happenings attract throngs of curious people to the Ku'damm during the organised Berlin "Midsummernight's dream". Its transformation into a "sculpture boulevard" for the 750th anniversary celebrations created quite a stir with both residents and visitors. Passers-by discussed the works with the artists, art came to life, and for moments it was part of everyday life. On no other street in Berlin would the eight sculptures have received so much attention. The Kurfürstendamm managed to regain some of the flair it had lost in years past.

"Off" Ku'damm: Whoever has seen the Kurfürstendamm has also seen Berlin's claim to fame as an international city but is still far from knowing the town. Straying into side and nearby streets helps to broaden the view. On **Fasanen Strasse** we get a look at how the "chic" off-street became an art gallery strip in recent years. **Villa Griesebach** at No. 25, inaugurated in 1986, helped Fas-

Left, a zoo caretaker. **Below**, at "Foffi", one of the many "in" places.

anen Strasse acquire its current character. After many years of neglect, it was planned to demolish this villa, together with a neighbouring green-house, and build instead a garage. A citizens' initiative successfully fought the plan. Today, the **Galerie Pels-Leusden** uses the villa for stately exhibitions and auctions. The **Käthe-Kollwitz-Museum** moved in next door. The **Wintergarten** has become a new gathering point for Berlin's literary scene. A basement bookstore, a restored café-restaurant and a garden constitute the **Literaturhaus Berlin**.

On to Kant Strasse: On the north side of Fasanenstrasse, diagonally across from the Hotel Bristol-Kempinski, stands the **Jüdisches Gemeindehaus,** the Jewish community centre. Of the original synagogue only the portals remain. The rest of it was burned down on 9 November 1938, during the so-called "Kristallnacht". The portals were harmoniously integrated into a simple building constructed in 1959. The large hall in the upper storey is used for prayer on holidays. A Jewish school conducting courses in Hebrew, a library and a kosher restaurant are all included in the community house.

The large theatre with Latin gable ornamentations on the corner of Kant Strasse has had a colourful past. It went bankrupt many times as a private operetta and comedy theatre. From 1950 to 1961, it was called the **Theater des Westens** and housed the "Städtische Oper Berlin". The première of *Cabaret,* at the end of 1987, with German star Horst Buchholz, launched a new career for the theatre as a stage for musicals. Several successful productions such as *Peter Pan* and *La Cage aux Folles* have consolidated the artistic reputation of the house. On occasions, guest performances from New York bring a genuine Broadway flavour to the lavishly renovated building, which dates from the Kaiser's time (1896).

The clock and the glass hall at the **Bahnhof Zoo**, formerly a disgrace to the area, are now an essential part of the inner city. In co-operation with the East German railways, the train station was superbly rebuilt for 40 million marks just in time for the 1987 celebrations. Before that, many travellers arriving at Berlin's only long-distance train station would have preferred to turn around and go back to where they came from. The hall, filthy and dark, smelling of toilets and disinfectant was a twilight zone of dealers, male and female prostitutes, and boozing tramps of all sorts.

Little St. Germain: Going west, the Kant Strasse widens into the Savignyplatz whose numerous bookstores and bars recall St. Germain in Paris. This section is also a much sought-after residential area, particularly along the **Carmer Strasse**, where the renovated façades are a reminder of how beautiful Berlin once was. "Projekt Weltbaum 2" in the **Savignyplatz** subway station was initiated by environmental artist Ben Wargin. Joseph Beuys and Günter Grass, among others, had a hand in creating the wall paintings. The side streets are quiet compared with Kurfürstendamm. During a stroll through Bleibtreu-, Knesebeck-, Mommsen- or Giesebrecht Strasse, the stroller might discover many things missing on the boulevard: delightful little boutiques, second-hand shops, kitsch and art, the local and the exotic, stand side by side.

This quiet district is a relief from the honky-tonk atmosphere on **Lietzenburger Strasse. In Sperlingsgasse**, south of Ku'damm, numerous pubs claim to be "olde Berlin", but Berliners are rarely found here. On Lietzenburger Strasse itself (so-called "Lietze"), between Uhland- and Knesebeck Strasse, striptease bars and brothels dominate. **Loretta im Garten** is a noteworthy exception, a charmingly lit beer garden with several pavilions where one can sit and socialise under the trees on summer evenings. The amusement stalls can scarcely be compared to the Prater in Vienna, but are a joy nonetheless, especially for children.

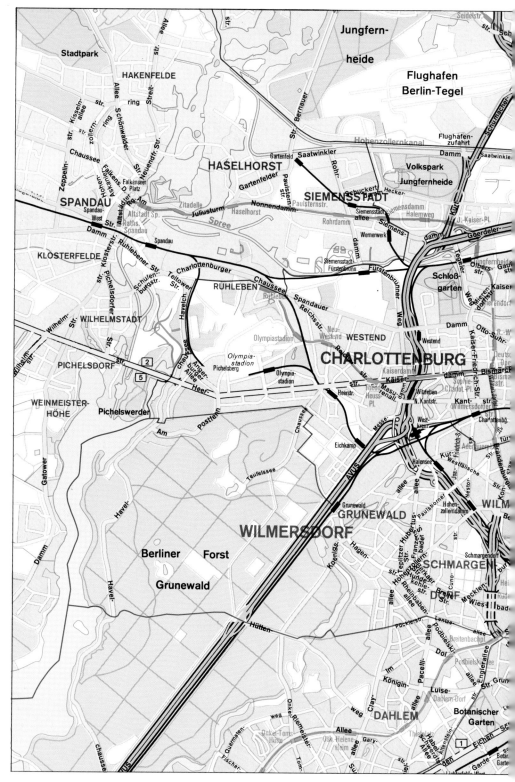

CHARLOTTENBURG

Anyone roaming the Kurfürstendamm and its side streets will see a part of Charlottenburg—but only a part. The entire district has 190,000 inhabitants and its 12 sq miles (30 sq km) cover the whole of the city centre's northwest, an area with many interesting sights. These include the "Funkturm" (Tower Radio) and, further out, the Olympic Park. Above all, however, Charlottenburg, formerly a residential suburb, represents a chip of old Prussia in West Berlin.

The student quarter: Crossing the rails under the Zoo station viaduct, on Hardenberg Strasse we reach the heart of Charlottenburg's student quarter, the **Steinplatz**. On the way one passes the "Bundesverwaltungsgericht" (Federal Court of Appeal in Public Lawsuits) on the corner of Jeben Strasse, the "Industrie- und Handelskammer" (Chamber of Commerce) and the hexagonal pavilion of the "Berliner Börse" (Stock Exchange).

The area grew into a university quarter at the start of this century as more and more professors, artists and wealthy people "moved west" and settled in Uhland Strasse, Fasanen Strasse, Carmer Strasse and Knesebeck Strasse. Now, the district sports a motley mix of bars, galleries, cafés and a good selection of bookshops. The 29,000 students enrolled at Charlottenburg's two universities, 25,000 of them at the Technische Universität, create a distinctly youthful atmosphere.

The whole university quarter grew out of the former Hochschule für Musik (Music Conservatory) at Fasanen Strasse 1. Its multi-purpose concert hall ("Musikbahnhof") seats over 1,340. The lecture hall, built in 1902, was designed by the architect who was responsible for the adjoining neo-Baroque Hochschule der bildenden Künste (Fine Arts Academy). These two, and parts of the Pädagogische Hoch-schule (Teachers' College), were combined to form an arts academy, the **Hochschule der Künste** (HdK), in 1975. The **Technische Universität** (TU), started as an academy for construction and industry on Werderscher Markt, and has been in Charlottenburg since 1884. It currently has 22 departments and virtually forms a city within a city. Its institutional and administrative buildings occupy the remaining east side of Hardenberg Strasse as far as Ernst-Reuter-Platz.

Three of Charlottenburg's thoroughfares, the Bismarck Strasse, the Otto-Suhr-Allee and the Strasse des 17. Juni, originate at the Brandenburger Tor and converge on the **Ernst-Reuter-Platz** (formerly "Knie") which, like the Grosser Stern in Tiergarten, is one of the busiest traffic intersections in Berlin. The eastern edge of the TU campus is delimited by the Charlottenburg bridge over the Landwehrkanal and the **Charlottenburger Tor** with its statues of Frederick I and his spouse Sophie-Charlotte, the eponym of the district.

Charlottenburg, at one time the richest town in Prussia, erected the gate on the border to Berlin on the occasion of its bicentenary in 1905 as an expression of civic pride. It was intended as a counterpart to the Brandenburger Tor, but the monumental effect was lost when the structure had to be split in two due to the enlargement of the old Charlottenburger Chaussee.

A popular and folksy **Trödelmarkt** (bric-a-brac market), similar to the "Krempelmarkt" on the Reichpietschufer in Kreuzberg, is held on weekends in front of the Ernst-Reuter-Haus. Connoisseurs of rococo porcelain from Frederich the Great should visit the **Staatliche Porzellanmanufaktur** (Porcelain factory) at Wegely Strasse 1 next to the Tiergarten S-Bahn station.

From Sophie-Charlotte-Platz onwards Bismarck Strasse and the Kaiserdamm lead to Charlottenburg's western centre of gravity, Theodor-Heuss-Platz. On the Bismarck Strasse two

**Left,
Charlottenburg
Castle.**

theatres deserve attention because of their architecture. The **Schiller-Theater** (1951) and the **Deutsche Oper** (1961) at the subway station of that name. Both are considered pleasant examples of contemporary theatre architecture.

To the Rathaus: "The wide Berliner Strasse that cuts through Charlottenburg passes by a number of cafés and ale houses, all looking to make as much as they can from the pockets of the convivial Berliners. Between them peer the summer villas of Berlin's senior citizens and bankers...." That was how Robert Springer described the **Otto-Suhr-Allee** in 1850 (later named after the town councillor and mayor in 1955-1957). The tranquillity and elegance have all but vanished. Sterile apartment blocks present a shabby façade to motorists driving to Tegel airport, Siemensstadt or Spandau.

The **Rathaus** in Charlottenburg's (Richard-Wagner-Platz subway station) is unmistakable because of its 293-foot (88-metre) high clock tower, which was inaugurated on 20 May 1905 on the occasion of Charlottenburg's bicentennial. This public building, with a rather subdued Art deco style, is quite enormous as many have discovered to their chagrin when getting lost in its halls trying to pursue some piece of official business.

Behind the Rathaus, the Alt-Lietzow street recalls the district's modest birth as a village named Lützow or Lietzow. In this street, the former **Villa Kogge** which was built in 1864—now the registry office—is worth a visit. On Guericke Strasse, the 1815 **Luisenfriedhof** is the final resting place of several famous Charlottenburg families. In the traditional "Charlottenburger Kiez" around **Gierkeplatz** on Schusterruh Strasse one of the last yeoman residences suggests how Charlottenburg looked in 1705 when King Frederich conferred the city privilege.

The **Luisenkirche**, the district church built in 1216 and later extended

ICC with Funkturm.

by K. F. Schinkel, and Charlottenburg's first school (1786), which today houses the local branch of the regional office for addiction problems, also help maintain the atmosphere of old Prussia.

Prussian baroque: After the castle was built Charlottenburg was symmetrically planned and furnished in the manner of a residential town. The castle is considered to be West Berlin's most important historical building. Court officials and the military lived opposite, at the north end of the **Schloss Strasse.** The officers' barracks of the **Gardes du Corps** (1859), built by Schinkel's pupil August Stühler, house the Ägyptisches Museum (Egyptian Museum) and the Antiken Museum (Antique Museum) of the **Stiftung Preussischer Kulturbesitz** (Prussian Cultural Heritage Foundation).

This last Hohenzollern castle on the Spree river was severely damaged in the Second World War. Now, since its reconstruction, it once again stands as one of the finest examples of Prussian baro-

que. Its imposing front, 610-yards (550-metres) long, took almost 100 years to build and remodel. It was originally a small castle for the princess and later Queen Sophie-Charlotte (1688-1705), and was built in 1675 five miles (eight km) from the gates of Berlin by the master-builder Arnold Nering. It was enlarged in the 18th century to a residence, with an "Ehrenhof" (nobles' courtyard) and a French garden. The court architect, Eosander von Göthe, added on the west side the 159-yard (143-metres) long **Orangerie** with a typically domed mid-section where, at a height of 160 feet (48 metres), the temperamental goddess Fortuna turns in the wind. Under Frederick II, the court architect von Knobelsdorff added the "Neuer Flügel" (New Wing) on the east side. C.G. Langhans' designs for a small orangery and the **Theaterbau** of 1790 (today the museum of Pre- and Early History) completed the complex.

The **Reiterdenkmal des Grossen Kurfürsten** (Equestrian Statue of the Great Elector, 1698) arrived in the Ehrenhof because of wartime confusion. Andreas Schlüter's bronze statue originally graced the bridge in front of the town castle on the Spree river. During the war it was transported to Potsdam for storage. When the baroque statue was being returned to Borsighafen on Tegel lake in Berlin in 1946, the overloaded lighter sank under the considerable weight. Several years later the statue was raised to the surface and restored. It was finally placed in front of Charlottenburg Castle in 1965.

Restoring the rooms to their original appearance took decades of painstaking artistic work. Today, in their beautifully-renovated condition they serve as a museum. The **Goldene Galerie**, from Frederick's rococo period, is especially attractive. It is on the top floor of the Knobelsdorff wing, where the collection of paintings and the private library of Frederich the Great are displayed in his former personal rooms. At the end of 1986 the **Galerie der Romantik** moved

Flight-simulator in the Technische Universität.

into the first floor.

"A view such as that from the bridge over the lake to the castle cannot even be found in the best parks", wrote Robert Springer in 1850 about Charlottenburg's **Schlossgarten**, the castle garden. The original park, which was planned and laid out by Simon Godeau in 1697, was the first garden in Germany in the style of the French under Louis XIV. At the beginning of the 19th century Joseph Peter Lenné gave the purely baroque park a face-lift along English lines.

Three buildings from the 18th and 19th centuries can be found in the park. The **Belvedere**, near the Spree, was built in 1788 by Langhans as a tea house. Frederick William II, nephew and successor to Frederick the Great, often came here with his lover Wilhelmina Encke. The **Mausoleum** (1812) was designed by Heinrich Gentz and K. F. Schinkel as the last resting place for Queen Luise. The marble sarcophagus, a notable example of neo-classical sculpture, was created by Christian Daniel Rauch. Finally, the **Schinkel Pavillon** of 1825, in the southwest of the park, was used by Frederick William III and Princess Liegnitz, his second wife, as a summer house.

Funkturm and ICC: West Charlottenburg is dominated by the **Funkturm** (Radio Tower). The antenna included, it stands 500-feet (150-metres) high and, as a kind of younger brother to the Eiffel Tower of Paris, is a Berlin landmark. The steel lattice construction originated at the same time as wireless broadcasting: on 23 October 1923, the "Voxhaus" at Potsdamer Strasse 14 transmitted Germany's first radio broadcast. Then, in 1926, on the occasion of the 3. Deutsche Funkausstellung (Wireless exhibition), the tower was inaugurated, and six years later transmitted the world's first TV programme. Today, the antenna equipment is only used by the police and fire department. An elevator takes people to the viewing-platform 416-feet (125- metres) up; the

Festive entry into the Olympic Stadium in August 1936.

Funkturmrestaurant at 182 feet (55 metres) is decorated in "olde" style Berlin city. The remarkable **Deutsches Rundfunkmuseum** is tucked away at the foot of the tower.

Over 24 buildings on the **Messegelände** provide 22 acres (nine hectares) of covered space all around the tower. About 25 major trade fairs and exhibitions are held here annually. The nearby **Haus des Rundfunks** in the Masurenallee is still one of the most modern broadcasting centres in Europe and has been planned so that all its studios face the interior courtyard. Hans Poelzig designed the blue-and-black-lined clinker brick building in 1931.

A covered bridge leads from the fair grounds on Hammarskjöldplatz over the city highway to the **International Congress Center (ICC)**, the futuristic construction which, with its silver-grey aluminium panels, is reminiscent of a spaceship. Built between 1973 and 1979 for a billion marks, the main building is 355 yards (320 metres) long and 89 yards (80 metres) wide, and provides about 200 acres (81 hectares) of usable space. If unfolded, it would be even larger than the entire area of the Kurfürstendamm.

The ICC is not so much a building as a multi-functional "happenings" hall whose post-modern architecture must be experienced in order to be believed. The foyer on Neue Kant Strasse, occupies the entire first floor and brings to mind an airport. Each of the great halls can accommodate 8,000 people. The entire building, including halls and conference rooms, has a capacity of 23,800, and the seating can be flexibly divided. The ICC is the scene of many national and international meetings from workers' congresses to shareholders' meetings to political conventions. The silver colossus (which Berlin wits have nicknamed "Charlottenburg's pocket battleship") is an indispensable part of Berlin's cultural scene.

The highway junction to Hannover and Nuremburg leads to the AVUS, for-

Berlin Police motorcycle formation on the Avus.

mer site of Formula One motor races, where Bernd Rosemeyer and Rudolf Caracciola made sporting history. Until recently, Berlin drivers used to arrange private races here, as there used to be no speed limit for the six-mile (10-km) stretch up to Checkpoint Dreilinden. Now a speed limit of 100 km/h has been imposed.

Olympic and other memories: Car traffic going through western Charlottenburg must cross the **Theodor-Heuss-Platz**. The fountain at the square's centre has a commemorative receptacle in which burns a flame lit by Theodor Heuss, the first Federal president after World War II. It is said that it will burn until Germany's reunification.

The Heer Strasse and the Reichs Strasse lead through western Charlottenburg to the Olympic Stadium. At Sensburger Allee 25, a street leading off the Heer Strasse, the **Georg-Kolbe-Museum** offers a short diversion. The former house of the celebrated sculptor and graphic artist (1877-1947) and the

garden exhibit most of his works.

From the **Olympischer Platz** the visitor looks over the former Third Reich's sports campus, which was commissioned by Hitler for the 1936 summer Olympics and designed by Werner March. Its extensive grounds still make it one of Europe's largest sports' complexes. Its centrepiece is the oval **Olympic Stadium**, a concrete structure seating 90,000 spectators.

The adjoining **Waldbühne** is a popular venue for rock concerts, and occasionally an arena for classical musicians with the right mystic atmosphere. When the Rolling Stones appeared here in 1965 in front of 21,000 fans, the open-air theatre was smashed to pieces by disgruntled rockers and for years after no one would rent the place. The British military government has established its headquarters in the north-eastern section of the site.

Very near the Olympic Stadium, at the Heilsberger Dreieck, looms Europe's largest apartment block. The **Corbusier-Haus,** built in 1957 for the INTERBAU (architecture exhibition) by the Swiss architect Le Corbusier, is patterned after his "Shining City" in Marseilles. More than 1,500 residents live in 527 apartments on 17 floors. The duplex maisonettes, when built, were thought to be unique. The apartment complex, which can be seen from Heer Strasse, has its own power station, post office and several shops, but its once visionary power as a model for human living surrounded by greenery has faded. Today, many look on it as a frightening concrete silo.

On the **Hüttigpfad**, where the feeling of still being in Charlottenburg is lost, stands a memorial to the victims of the Third Reich. Here, in the former **Zuchthaus Plötzensee**, 1,574 resistance fighters were executed. Berlin's Catholics dedicated the church **Maria-Regina-Martyrium** on Heckerdamm to the "Martyrs for the Freedom of Belief and Conscience 1933-45" in commemoration of the Nazi terror.

Left, Jewish service in Pesta-lozziStrasse. **Right**, street artists in the city.

105

WILMERSDORF

A bird's-eye view of **Wilmersdorf** reveals it to be a topographical hybrid sitting between the city and the woods of Grunewald. It extends from the Bundesallee into the centre of West Berlin and then westward to the banks of the river Havel. Almost half of the area of 13 sq miles (34 sq km) is covered with a pine forest. The city on one side, the forest on the other: that is the mixture which gives this district its particular charm.

The people of Wilmersdorf (about 160,000) are well aware of this. They belong, for the most part, to the educated middle class, with an above average proportion of higher educated professionals and well-to-do widows. This conservative, solidly bourgeois district contributes substantially to West Berlin's elderly population: over one-fifth of its inhabitants are 65 years or over. Among the local social services, there are no less than 49 homes and extensive apartment houses, mostly privately run, for the aged.

Along the Bundesallee: The **Bundesallee** runs from the Zoo quarter southward to **Bundesplatz**. During "the second destruction of Berlin", traffic planners sacrificed what the bombs had left of the former tree-lined boulevard and converted it to an eight-lane thoroughfare. The representative of the Federal government resides at Bundesallee 216-218 in a dark red-brick complex dating from imperial times. Various Federal ministries also maintain representatives in the **Bundeshaus Berlin**.

The former **Joachimstalsche Gymnasium** on the opposite side of the street is architecturally interesting. This neo-classical brick building (1880) with its 145-yard (150-metre) long arcade was inspired by Schinkel's architecture. The building is currently being used by the Hochschule der Künste as well as some other institutions primarily for musical activities.

Hidden behind old trees at Schaperstrasse 24 is the **Theater der Freien Volksbühne**. Like the **Schaubühne** in the Mendelssohn building which is also in Wilmersdorf, this theatre mainly stages works of contemporary authors. In May, the Volksbühne is the venue for the "Theatertreffen Berlin" whose reputation extends far beyond the city limits. Fritz Bornemann's cubic theatre building (1962) with its stucco façades and post-modern wrapping fits harmoniously into the **Fasanenplatz**.

Literary workshop: In the "Golden Twenties" many a creative and restless mind was attracted to this residential quarter near the city. Heinrich Mann lived in the Uhland Strasse. Bert Brecht, then assistant of dramaturgy at the Deutsches Theater, lived in Spiechern Strasse 16 where he wrote *The Threepenny Opera* in 1927. Erich Maria Remarque who was, at this time working on his anti-war novel *All Quiet on the Western Front*, stayed at Wittelsbacher Strasse 5. For Erich Kästner, who had come to Berlin from Saxony, the city was "the only place where something was going on." His novel *Fabian* is a stinging satire on Berlin's pre-war decadence which he experienced at close hand when living in a furnished room at Prager Platz.

Next door to some 300 artists, critical authors and philosophers, such as Ernst Bloch, Alfred Kantorowicz, Manés Sperber, Arthur Koestler, Erich Mühsam, Walter Hasenclever and Johannes R. Becher, were living in a public housing estate on today's Ludwig-Barnay-Strasse. The **Künstlerkolonie** (Artists' Colony) gained notoriety as the so-called "red block". When elections were held, it stood like "a solitary, challenging island in the midst of a foaming sea of swastikas and black-white-red" (the nationalist colours), contemporary author Axel Eggebrecht reported. In the evenings the SA troops waylaid the "cultural bolsheviks" on their way home. The colony in turn organised its own protection ostracising whomever sympathised with the Nazis. When Hitler seized power the brown-shirted police terror against the hated "communist nest" on the south-eastern edge of Wilmersdorf could unfold uninhibited. Many residents were imprisoned, abused, deported to concentration camps or banned from their professions. Others fled into exile. The postwar tenants knew nothing of the fate of their predecessors and the anti-fascist past of the Künstlerkolonie was soon forgotten. Recently this chapter of Berlin's history has again roused some interest among the media.

Religious diversity: The onion-shaped towers of the **Christi-Geburts-Kathedrale** (Christ's Birth Cathedral) recall an entirely different aspect of Berlin's history. More than 100,000 Russians came to the Spree after the revolution of October 1917. They established five Russian theatres, about 50 publishing houses and many restaurants. The immigrant colony's cultural centre in Wilmersdorf included, of course, a cathedral. The present Russian-orthodox church at the junction of the Hohenzollerndamm and Konstanzer Strasse, however, was not consecrated until 1938 by which time most of the Russians had moved on to Paris, London or New York. The cathedral, whose parish numbers about 2,000, is the bishop's see for Berlin.

Adjacent, in the **Islamisches Zentrum** (Islamic Centre), Imam Butt summons the faithful to prayer. The mosque at Brienner Strasse 7, a domed structure in the Indian Moghul style, was erected in 1928 with the support of the Muslim Ahmadiyya Society whose headquarters are in Lahore, Pakistan.

Wilmersdorf prides itself on being a haven of religious tolerance, with 32 places of worship for most of the different creeds who reside here. Especially striking among the modern protestant churches is the **Kirche am Hohenzollernplatz**, a 1930 creation of the

Bauhaus architect Fritz Hager, balancing between expressionism and "New Objectivity". The clinker building has been dubbed "God's Power Station". The 1929 **Kreuzkirche**, further south at the junction of Hohenzollerndamm and Forkenbeck Strasse features a strangely shaped massive tower of red-blue stone.

Berlin's biggest office: The **Hohenzollerndamm** connects the inner city with Grunewald and Dahlem. At **Fehrbelliner Platz**, the muncipal centre of the district, it passes through an administrative precinct where 30,000 civil servants are employed. The oval nucleus is made up of official buildings in the characteristic monumental style of the Nazi period. They were meant to be a "Forum of the Third Reich" around Fehrbelliner Platz. The former headquarters of the Nazi "workfront" now houses the **Rathaus Wilmersdorf**, while next door the **Kommunale Galerie** (Municipal Gallery) exhibits contemporary art and local history.

Various Senate departments have headquarters in the government buildings. The Senator of the Interior, employer of 28,000 public officials and servants, including 12,000 uniformed police officers, has his office at Fehrbelliner Platz 2. The Senate department for construction and housing, located in an 18-storey "public silo", spends 2.6 billion marks annually, making it the city's biggest contractor.

The pension funds of 16.5 million people are administered by the Federal Employees' Insurance Agency with headquarters at Fehrbelliner Platz. A high-rise building on Hohenzollerndamm houses a further 1,600 employees. At the Steglitz exit of the **Stadtautobahnring**, the city highway ring, another municipal landmark catches the eye—the **Autobahnüberbauung Schlangenbader Strasse,** a 15-storey concrete mountain of 1,000 terraced council flats towering above a highway tunnel which is nearly 700 yards (600 metres) long.

Costumed party at iceskating stadium Wilmersdorf.

Alt-Wilmersdorf: For most of its 700-year history, Wilmersdorf was a simple peasant's settlement in the March. The inscription on a granite stone at the historical centre of **Wilhelmsaue** so aptly states that the "farms surrounded by fields lent Alt-Wilmersdorf its character in the old times." The last vestige of these rural times is the cosy **Schoeler-Schlösschen**, a farmer's house of 1754 vintage at the former village-green, which was later converted into a mansion.

West of the Stadtautobahn, the district of Wilmersdorf merges into the suburban idyll of Schmargendorf, where at Berkaer Platz one can admire the 1902 **Rathaus Schmargendorf** which is a particularly imaginative example of neo-gothic Marchland brick architecture. Because it houses the registry office, its romantic towers and pinnacles have been immortalised on innumerable wedding photos.

Millionaires' haunt: "Am Roseneck", Schmargendorf borders on the Grunewald quarter, Berlin's most expensive residential area. At Wallot Strasse 19, the **Wissenschaftskolleg zu Berlin**, a German version of America's Princeton University, opened its doors in 1981 to top international scientists of every discipline. As so-called *Fellows*, free of the usual obligations which university posts entail, they have the opportunity to delve deep into their research.

Berlin's upper classes meet at the most posh Berlin tennis club, "Rot-Weiss", at Hundekehlensee, which acquired its reputation during the founding years of the **Villenkolonie Grunewald**. Conceived in 1890 as the crowning touch of the recently extended Kurfürstendamm, this exclusive residential district at the time was the perfect dwelling place for patricians who wished to save on taxes. Until its incorporation in 1920, Grunewald was not administered by the Berlin tax department, but by that of Teltow district which taxed its residents more leniently. The forest department had to

sacrifice 593 acres (240 hectares) of woods, and the upper crust of the growing industrial metropolis unfolded its new-found wealth on the avenues between Bismarckplatz and the Hundekehle. The magnificent burgher mansions of the *Belle Epoque* are characteristic of posh "Berlin 33" to this day. A particularly grandiose example in the style of the Italian Renaissance is the former Palais Pannwitz at Brahms Strasse 4-10, today the **Schlosshotel Gehrhus**.

The Grunewald: A web of paths through the northern part of the Grunewald, along a couple of scenic lakes and nature reserves leads to the legendary **Halbinsel Schildhorn**. Swimming along this peninsula, the last of the Slavonic Wend princes, Jasco, is said to have saved himself from the persecution of Albrecht "the Bear". Grateful to have escaped he vowed to adopt the Christian faith. Nowadays, a strange memorial with a shield and cross recalls this legend. Another destination, the **Grunewaldturm**, 183-feet (55-metres) high, stands on a hill by the Havelchaussee. Teltow district commissioned Franz Schwechten to erect this neo-gothic structure in memory of Kaiser William I. What looks from afar like the domes of a religious building—comparisons range from Sacré Coeur to Russian churches—are actually the gleaming parts of a radar station on **Teufelsberg**. Berlin's highest (383-foot or 115-metres) point was created after the war from 33 million cubic yards (25 million cubic metres) of rubble. Warning signs on the edge of a prohibited zone indicate the presence of the British and Americans. From the summit they survey the radio-communications of the "Eastern Block".

Somewhat lower, at **Teufelssee-chausee**, a hill acts as a substitute for the Alps for West Berlin's sporting women and men. Hang-gliders and hikers practise their skills on the slopes of this mountain of debris, which offers pleasant panoramic views to the walker.

111

SCHÖNEBERG

Many people may know Schöneberg from TV news broadcasts. The town hall with its rectangular clock tower and the flag with a bear on it are both well known. Famous visitors from all over the world have signed their names in the city's golden book. On the square out front 400,000 Berliners cheered U.S. President Kennedy when he addressed them on 26 June 1963, from the balcony with those unforgettable words: "*Ich bin ein Berliner!*" As a memorial to the assassinated president the square is now called **John F. Kennedy-Platz.** Everyday at noon a copy of Philadelphia's *Liberty Bell*, a gift of the Americans, rings from the tower of the town hall, which can be climbed as far as the observation platform.

In May, 1911, when the mayor of the independent district laid the foundation stone of the **Rathaus Schöneberg**, nobody had any idea that, 40 years later, the imposing official building would be the administrative and political centre of the western half of the city. It is now the official seat of the district's mayor and the mayor of West Berlin. After a thorough cleaning for the 750th celebration the Silesian sandstone façades are now a brilliant white.

The **Rudolph-Wilde-Park** begins immediately behind the Rathaus, and is Schöneberg's finest park. This is where the "Goldener Hirsch" (Golden Stag) statue stands. The golden stag is the coat-of-arms' animal of Schöneberg and serves as a reminder of the original inhabitants of this formerly heavily forested area. At Kufsteiner Strasse the park turns into the Wilmersdorf recreational area.

Since 1946 the **RIAS Building** has been the home of "Radio in the American Sector" which, after the SFB, (Station of Free Berlin), is the second largest radio station in West Berlin. Its powerful transmitters reach large audiences in East Berlin and GDR.

Millionaire farmers: The Dominicusstrasse runs from the Rathaus directly into Schöneberg's historic centre. The oldest building by far is the **Dorfkirche** of Frederick the Great, a church built on a rise beside the **Hauptstrasse** in 1766. Between Kaiser-Wilhelm-Platz and Dominicusstrasse, the Hauptstrasse still is a verdant promenade, a reminder of its past as a village pasture.

Schöneberg was mentioned in documents as early as 1264 when the Askanian prince Otto III of Brandenburg donated "five hides of land in the *villa sconenberch* " to the Benedictine nuns of Spandau. When the village came into the possession of Elector Joachim I in 1506, thus becoming regal domain, it gained in importance. Lying on the Berlin-Potsdam route, a major communications artery, proved to be very advantageous, except during the Seven Years War when the whole village was burnt down by Russian troops.

One of the most important aspects of the reconstruction was the paving of the carriage track to Potsdam. Now that Schöneberg was located on Prussia's first major carriageway, the time needed to travel to Berlin was considerably reduced. Travellers stopped here for a rest. Innkeepers, handicraftsmen and market gardeners set up shops. Nevertheless, Schöneberg retained its village atmosphere, and became an attractive place for day visitors from Berlin, a tradition which continued into the start of the 20th century. The operetta melody *Das war in Schöneberg, im Monat Mai* (Once in Schöneberg, in the Month of May) referred to this and Schöneberg citizens adopted the song as their "national anthem".

When the Berlin-Potsdam railway was opened in 1838, many farmers had taken the opportunity to sell their land profitably to the rail company. They became known as "Schöneberg millionaire farmers" long before the building boom during the founding years of

**Left,
Rathaus
Schöneberg
after
restoration.**

the Second Reich. This wealth is illustrated by many exclusive villas on the Haupt Strasse and by the richly decorated mausoleums and chapels in the old cemetery behind the village church.

Imperial times: Between 1875 and 1898 the district's population rose from 7,500 to 75,000. Schöneberg was granted city rights, and as the population grew at explosive speeds more and more housing areas had to be created. One of these was **Friedenau** at the south-western tip of the district. It was founded in 1871 as a settlement of elegant villas for wealthy government officials and retirees. The French-Prussian war had just ended, and this is how Friedenau ("Peaceful Meadow") got its name. Friedenau has indeed maintained an especially peaceful character with tree-lined streets, gardens, green squares and stuccoed mansions. The inhabitants were not particularly pleased to be made part of Schöneberg in Berlin's great administrative reform of 1920—they had thought elegant

Steglitz much more suitable.

Around **Friedrich-Wilhelm-Platz,** on the seamless border between Wilmersdorf and Friedenau, the curving streets reveal the geometry of the former building plan. The "Burg" stands on the corner of Schmargendorfer Strasse and is considered an excellent example of Friedenau villa architecture. In the north of the district in **Perelsplatz** there is a noteworthy Art deco fountain—the "Sintflut-Brunnen" ("Deluge Fountain"). Like Schöneberg, Friedenau also underlined its communal independence by building an imposing Rathaus (townhall), which stands prominently in **Breslauer Platz**, where the Haupt Strasse runs south and changes its name to **Rhein Strasse**.

Rusting rails: A huge gasometer in Torgauer Strasse near the Schöneberg S-Bahn station symbolises the proletarian Schöneberg of old. A network of rails and rail bridges criss-cross the area west of the highway intersection. Near **Priesterweg** in the direction of Tempel-

Berlin senate in plenary session.

hof, Berliners tend small garden plots in allotment colonies with romantic names such as "Glück im Winkel" ("Happiness in a Corner").

A decision as to whether the allotments, the only green at Schöneberg's borders, will remain, is pending. The planned construction of a central goods station for Berlin on the **Südgelände** has become superfluous, but the contract with the GDR railways is still valid. However, not only would the allotments be endangered, but construction on them would also destroy an ecological oasis where a number of rare plants have, over the years, developed into a small jungle that has grown between the rusty roads.

An artificial mound heaped up with the rubble of the "Bayerisches Viertel" after the war rises 100-foot (30-metre) high at Munsterdamm, and has been turned into a park by the city's gardeners. On the summit of the **Insulaner**, at 250 foot (75 metre), the dome of the **Wilhelm-Foerster-Sternwarte**, the largest observatory open to the public in West Germany, is a regular meeting place for amateur astronomers. At the foot of the mound, the **Zeiss-Planetarium** simulates the course of the stars under its 67-foot (20-metre) high aluminium dome.

Working-class "Kiez": The Insulaner hill with its parks, swimming pool and toboggan-run is the most important recreational area for the **Schöneberg Insel**, a densely populated tenement area between Schöneberg's goods station and the Yorck Strasse S-Bahn station, which is only accessible over a series of rail bridges. At the beginning of the century these proletarian housing estates became a stronghold of the workers' movement. Nowadays, the "red island" could scarcely be called elegant. With its apartment blocks, workshops and corner bars, it typifies the petty-bourgeois Berlin "Kiez". Incidentally, in such surroundings, in today's **Leber Strasse** (the former Sedan Strasse) two world-famous Hol-

West-east banner decoration at the Allied Control Commission building.

lywood film stars—Marlene Dietrich and Hildegard Knef were born.

Lovers of cemetery romanticism and old gravestone paintings should stop by the **St.-Matthäus-Kirchhof** on Monumenten Strasse (entrance on Grossgörschen Strasse 12-14). The brothers Grimm, Rudolf Virchow and Senator Bolle ("Bimmelbolle"), founder of the dairy company with the same name, are all buried here. Immediately after the unsuccessful assassination attempt on Hitler on 20 July 1944, the bodies of Colonel von Stauffenberg and his fellow plotters were buried here, but were then exhumed by the Nazis and burnt. An engraved stone marks their short-lived resting places.

Kleistpark: From the "Insel" you can reach **Kleistpark** on Potsdamer Strasse in a few minutes. This historically important area was the royal vegetable garden from 1679 onwards, and then the location of Berlin's first botanical gardens. Adalbert von Chamisso, the much-travelled poet and naturalist who wrote *Peter Schlemihl*, was the custodian from 1819 to 1839. In 1897 the botanical gardens were transferred to Dahlem, and the area was turned into a park named after the poet Heinrich von Kleist. The **Königskolonnaden** (1780) at the main entrance were designed by Carl von Gontard for the Königsbrücke at Alexanderplatz. The colonnades have been standing at their present location since 1910.

The "Rossebändiger", two bronze groups in front of the **Kammergericht** (built in 1913) in the park behind, constitute examples of Russian sculpture from the last century. The sight of this Palace of Justice, in its north-German baroque style, produces uneasy feelings. For a time the infamous "Volksgerichtshof", the supreme "court" of the Nazi regime, held session here and, among many others, sentenced to death, the men of the 20 July conspiracy. Between the capitulation in 1945 and 1948, Germany was governed by an Allied Control Commission. Now, in

Market woman in Friedenau.

116

the former **Kontrollratsgebäude**, about 500 of the 540 rooms are empty; only the first floor is used by the Allied Air-traffic Control Centre.

Einstein was here: The Berlin public transport company has its offices at Kleistpark subway station and so there is no need to be surprised at the large number of blue-uniformed employees making their way to the offices on the Potsdamer Strasse 188. The **Haus am Kleistpark** accommodates the district's arts council, music school and local history museum; in an annex the **Hochschule der Künste** (Academy of Fine Arts) trains future art teachers. A few blocks away on **Grunewald Strasse—Akazien Strasse** stands the district's most distinctive private house, a magnificent building erected in 1892 in neo-renaissance style.

The **Bayerisches Viertel** begins west of Martin-Luther Strasse. This elegant residential area was known before 1933 as "Jewish Switzerland" because a number of Jewish scientists lived in these apartments. The most famous was professor Albert Einstein, who in 1921, at Haberland Strasse 5, (today Nördlinger Strasse 8) learned that he had won the Nobel Prize. The district was heavily bombed during the war, but the **Viktoria-Luise-Platz** on its northern edge has regained its former harmony after being restored. It is no coincidence if you see a number of pretty girls sitting at the fountain or in the café "Montevideo"—most of them come from the **Lette-Haus**. In 1866, founder Wilhelm Adolf Lette had started an "Association to Promote Professional Education of the Female Sex", at that time a far-sighted pioneering initiative. The association's college in Viktoria-Luise-Platz has an excellent reputation and offers courses in commercial art, photography, fashion, domestic economy and various technical and scientific professions.

Around Nollendorfplatz: At Wittenbergplatz (note the expensively restored 1913 subway station) Sch-

öneberg borders the downtown area. Mainly uninspiring postwar architecture is seen on the journey eastward through Schöneberg's northern section. Still, there are many other attractions in store. On **Kleist Strasse** we pass the glass building of the culture association "Urania". At the rear is the Berlin **Post- und Fernmeldemuseum** (Post and Telephones museum). The **Landesarchiv Berlin** (Regional Archives), diagonally opposite on the corner of Kalckreuth Strasse, has occasional exhibitions of city and architectural history. It also houses a unique collection of ancient government papers and social history documents.

Treasures of another kind can be discovered in Schöneberg's **antiques' quarter**. The "best addresses", with matching prices, line **Keith Strasse**. In and around Eisenacher Strasse and Motz Strasse collectors of Meissen porcelain, Russian icons, military paraphernalia and similar rarities may find what they are looking for. High up,

supported by the iron stilts of a disused station, the **Flohmarkt** (flea market) overlooks Nollendorfplatz, where the small **Zille Museum** displays original drawings of the Berlin "Milljöh" ("social atmosphere").

The "Milljöh" around the **Nollendorfplatz** is one of busy night life with neon-lit cafés, pubs, gay bars and the "Metropol", Berlin's biggest disco. On the way to **Winterfeldplatz** and **Goltz Strasse**, you can find second-hand bookshops, junkstores and boutiques with inventive new and second-hand fashion. From the stilted "Hochbahnhof" on Nollendorfplatz a nostalgic ride on Berlin's last street car takes the visitor to the **Türkischer Basar** at Bülow Strasse station, where trade in levantine videos flourishes.

On the "Potse": The **Potsdamer Strasse**, once part of the former "Reichs Strasse 1" from Königsberg to Aachen runs beneath the stilted station. Berlin used to celebrate its legendary six-day-cycling races in the "Sportpalast" on **Pallas Strasse**. This is where Goebbels called for "total war" after the Stalingrad disaster. After its demolition in 1973 a "social palace" zoomed up in its place, a depressingly gloomy prefabricated concrete tenement.

The "Potse", as Potsdamer Strasse is affectionately known to Berliners, became a cul-de-sac when the Wall was built and with it a problem area developed. However, prostitution and drug dealing have been forced into the side streets, while the local brothel owners have converted their shabby lodgings into more profitable homes for political refugees. The senate is trying to find solutions for this area which has a high percentage of immigrants and where banks and supermarkets are found alongside game parlours, sex shops, pawn shops and small Turkish-run variety shops. The Kurfürsten Strasse is the border-line between Schöneberg and Tiergarten, the latter being the only northern inner-city district to adjoin, in the north, the Wall.

Left, café at Nollendorfplatz. **Right**, art in the backyard.

TIERGARTEN

Already in 1764, the English travel writer, James Boswell, was enthusiastic about the "magnificent park at the city's edge, with carriage roads and riding paths." He noted also that provision had been made for those "desiring to exercise themselves." The **Grosser Tiergarten**, two miles (three km) long and half-a-mile (one km) wide, stretches on both sides of the Strasse des 17. Juni, between the Tiergarten S-Bahn station and Brandenburger Tor. For the walled-in Berliners, this recreational facility, with its 19 miles (30 km) of paths and 500 park benches, is a true blessing. Not altogether to the pleasure of the city gardeners, thousands throng the picnic lawns on summer weekends including Turkish families who feel at home with their barbecues.

Enjoying the sunshine in the rosegarden, it is hard to imagine to what extent the Tiergarten was involved in the fighting during the last days of the war in April 1945. The "Reichstag", Nazi Germany's last bastion, fell on 30 April, and the Tiergarten district resembled an apocalyptic moon landscape. Those trees which still stood were cut for fuel in the following cold winter and later the bare terrain was parcelled out into plots in which vegetables were grown.

Reforestation of the Tiergarten started during the Berlin blockade. On 17 March 1949, the first lime tree was planted on the Hofjägerallee by mayor Reuter. Generous gifts of trees and cash have allowed the Grosser Tiergarten to reclaim its former glory. About 40 different bird species—from nightingale to owl—breed here. Specially selected grasslands offer habitats for rare plants and insects.

Between city and Wall: Today, the 524-acres (212-hectare) park once again is the centre of the district carrying the same name. The sharp contrasts between glory and decline and the continuously changing reality of the former imperial capital, are reflected in the district's cramped five sq miles (13 sq km). At its centre is the Grosser Tiergarten, with its mute, witnesses of former German national greatness, such as the Reichstag, Brandenburger Tor and Siegessäule ("Victory Column"). To the south, the "Tiergartenviertel" the former patrician quarters and, to the north, the industrial and workers' area of Moabit lying like an island between canals, reflect the contrasting character of the area. The majority of its 93,000 inhabitants dwell in tenement buildings erected during the last decades of the 19th century.

The Tiergartenviertel: Present-day southern Tiergarten came into being when wealthy Berlin families built expensive country homes on the south side of the park around 1840. Tiergarten rose to become the fashionable west side of Berlin, a residential and artistic quarter. Today, there remain only a few princely relics of this "privileged residence of various aristocracies", as Jules Huret described the area on both sides of the Landwehrkanal in 1906 in the Paris newspaper Le Figaro. There is, for example, the **Villa von der Heydt** next to where the Herkulesbrücke crosses the Landwehrkanal, now seat of the directorate of the Stiftung Preussischer Kulturbesitz. Formerly, this neoclassic Greek-style building adjacent to the Bauhaus Archives, housed the Chinese embassy.

Before and after World War I a number of embassies took up residence in the Tiergartenviertel and the area north of the Landwehrkanal became known as the "diplomats' quarter". Japan and Italy, expressing their alliance with Nazi Germany, built heavy, imposing mansions for their embassies on **Tiergarten Strasse**. After WW II this area lay fallow for a long time, but is now gaining new life. The destroyed Japanese embassy has been faithfully restored and now houses a Japanese-German centre. The ruins of the Italian embassy are being reconstructed to house the **Akademie der Wissenschaften** (Academy of Science).

Immediately to the south of the embassies, in the remaining buildings of the Wehrmacht headquarters at Stauffenberg Strasse 14 is the **Gedenkstätte Deutscher Widerstand** (Memorial to German Resistance). On 20 July 1944, Colonel von Stauffenberg and fellow conspirators were shot in the courtyard of the former Bendler building. *Der gefesselte Jüngling* ("the fettered youth"), a sculpture by Richard Scheibe, commemorates the attempt on Hitler's life.

Not far away, the **Kulturforum** is a never ending construction site where a third museum district is being added to such traditional complexes as Dahlem and Charlottenburg. The final shape of the Kulturforum has not yet been decided as the original plan by Hans Scharoun is being challenged by a new design of Viennese architect Hans Hollein with backing of the Senate. Until the battle is resolved, the complex appears as a disconnected agglomeration of different-style buildings. The southern edge of the Kulturforum at Potsdamer Brücke is made up of Mies van der Rohe's **Nationalgalerie**, whose simple symmetry and enormous windows contrast in a lively manner with the **Philharmonie** at the northern end of the complex. The chamber music hall next door and the **Staatsbibliothek** (State Library) were also designed by Scharoun. The complex is completed by the Musikinstrumenten-Museum (Musical Instruments) which is connected to the Philharmonie, and by the comparatively simple brickwork structure of the Kunstgewerbemuseum (Handicraft Museum). New buildings for a copper-plate engravings museum and an arts library are being constructed.

At the centre of the grounds stands the **St.-Matthäus-Kirche**. The church,

Rock in the Tiergarten.

built by Stüler in 1846, gives the area a special charm, which is mainly due to the contrast with the Nationalgalerie.

Passing the Staatsbibliothek and under the monorail, the Wall at **Potsdamer Platz** is reached. Next to the ruins of the Grand Hotel Esplanade in Bellevue Strasse is the building of an old grammar school which is yet another site where the infamous Nazi court "Volksgerichtshof", presided over by "bloody" Roland Freisler, passed its inhuman sentences. Opposite is a section of the "old" Potsdamer Strasse. The Staatsbibliothek was erected on the axis of the avenue. As the many souvenir shops suggest, the Wall at Potsdamer Platz is an attraction for those tourists who make use of the new border crossing point in the old city centre.

From Zoo to Tiergarten: Thanks to its many entrances, the Grosser Tiergarten cannot be missed. If you wish to explore the full extent of the park, follow the footpath immediately beyond the main entrance to the zoo at Hardenbergplatz. It crosses the **Landwehrkanal** at the Tiergarten floodgate and leads to the victory column along the banks of the **Neue See**.

The "new lake" on Lichtensteinallee was dug out in 1841 as part of a water supply and a system to drain the marshy southern park and to supply the many fountains with water. It was integrated into J.P. Lenné's re-designing of the baroque gardens as a landscaped park open to all classes of society. One hundred and fifty years had passed since Frederick I had the fences removed from the former royal hunting grounds near the city. "Nothing should be done, I don't want any animals there again", Prussia's first king commanded, and a carriage road was cut through the Tiergarten to Charlottenburg Castle. This was the first step to establishing the park which Frederick II initiated for posterity in 1742.

All roads in Grosser Tiergarten cross the Landwehrkanal as does the **Lichtensteinbrcke** at the extension of the zoological garden. After protracted political controversy, two statues have recently been erected to commemorate the murders of Rosa Luxemburg and Karl Liebknecht by units of the Reichswehr in 1919. The **Berlin-Pavillon** at the Tiergarten S-Bahn station is only a short walk away. En route, stop and visit the **Laternenmuseum** Museum which has a nostalgic collection of gas lamps.

Grosser Stern: At the centre of the Grosser Tiergarten, stretching proudly to a height of 223 feet (67 metres), is the **Siegessäule** of 1873. Called "Gold-Elsie" by the Berliners, this gold-coated victory column was designed by Friedrich Drake to commemorate Prussia's victories over Denmark (1864), Austria (1866), and France (1870-71). For Berlin's 750th celebrations, the last of the four patriotic reliefs at the base, which had been removed in 1945 by the Allies, was brought back from Paris as a gift from France's president Mitterrand.

Flirting under the sun.

The reliefs portray important events of the victorious campaigns.

The Siegessäule formerly stood at the Königsplatz (today's Platz der Republik) and was moved to the Grosser Stern in 1938 to adorn the new parade grounds of Hitler's dream of "world capital Germania". So too was the Bismarck memorial and the statues of the Prussian generals Roon and Moltke.

Along the Spree river, the way leads past **Bellevue Castle** towards Moabit. Built in 1755 for the Hohenzollern prince August Ferdinand as a summer residence, the castle has been restored to its early neo-classic form and, since 1959, has served as the Berlin residence of the West German president. When he is not in residence, the grounds are open to the public. They can also be reached via the **Englischer Garten** which has profited from generous donations of trees from the British royal parks.

Altonaer Strasse leads north-west to the **Hansaviertel** which, in its day, was a pioneering urban development con-cept. For the architecture exhibition INTERBAU 1957, renowned architects from all over the world contributed to the reconstruction of the totally destroyed Hansaviertel. The **Akademie der Künste** on Hanseaten-weg stresses its succession to the Prussian academy of arts of 1696. It has taken on the task to "familiarise the public with contemporary artistic movements."

Brandenburger Tor: A walk in the Tiergarten should definitely include the **Rosengarten**, a delightfully restored enclosure where stands a pergola which is evocative of the Wilhelminian era. Past the Rousseau and Luisen islands, past shady duck ponds, the way continues to **Kemperplatz** which, in pre-war days, was the centre of the "olde West" but which today, is merely the terminus of the magnetic monorail arriving from the Gleisdreieck subway station.

A path leads along the East Berlin border fence past statues of Lessing, Goethe, Wagner, Lortzing, Fontane and many others who were all granted a

Left, **Brandenburger Tor** in winter. **Right,** the tent-like roof of the **Philarmonie.**

MAN, SPACE AND MUSIC

The façade glitters in golden colours, and the tent-like roof arches up in a bold curve: Of all the buildings in the "Kulturforum" next to the Tiergarten, the Philharmonie and its smaller twin sister, the chamber music hall, catch the eye. On the opening night, 15 Oct 1963, the Philharmonie was justly praised as an architectonic and acoustic sensation in the world of great concert halls. The exceptional exterior is reflected by the unconventional interior design by Hans Scharoun. By placing the orchestra in the middle of the concert hall, he created a new relationship between man, space, and music. The audience is distributed around the podium on nine terraces similar to a vineyard. The sound can reach unhindered to every single one of the 2,200 seats.

The concert schedule offers a repertoire that, for the most part, contains symphonies; yet the Philharmonie is also well known as the site of the Berlin jazz days, the festival of world cultures, and even some hot rock nights. Above all, however, it is the home of a world renowned elite orchestra that really exists

selves the "Berliner Philharmoniker".

Its artistic director, Herbert von Karajan, has been at the head of the orchestra since 1954. His three predecessors had to be content with a concert hall at Bernburgerstraße, near the Anhalter Bahnhof. Here, Hans von Bülow, Arthur Nikisch, and Wilhelm Furtwängler wielded their batons until the hall was destroyed in an air-raid on 30 January 1944.

The Berliner Philharmoniker gave their debut performance in this former roller skating rink on 17 Oct 1882. Their first subscription concert followed the week after, a brand new concept at the time. On 1 May 1882, 54 "insurgent" musicians left their director and employer-conductor Benjamin Bilse to establish their own orchestra, a revolutionary feat indeed in the authoritarian Germany of Kaiser Wilhelm.

The aged "music sergeant" Bilse directed one of the three private orchestras in the capital that usually entertained the populace in the shadow of the imperial court orchestra. Now, they intended to set up an orchestra founded on democratic

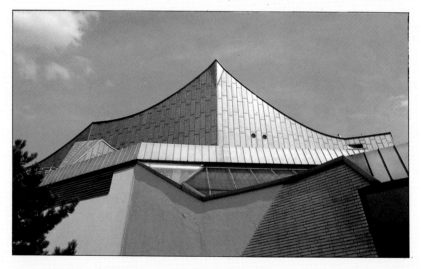

in two versions; on the one hand there is the "Berliner Philharmonisches Orchester" generously financed by the Senate of Berlin, which travels around the world and is basically a cultural ambassador for the city of Berlin. On the other hand, if the same 120 musicians get together for the recording of an album, they call themselves

principles.

Among other things, the agreed statutes required the election by majority of the artistic directors, the board of directors and of any new members. The democratic constitution and a modern pay system characterise the "most famous orchestra in the world" (*Le Figaro*).

place of honour here during the "flood" of statue-building around the turn of the century. And then there rises the **Brandenburger Tor**, 67-feet (20-metres) high and 213-feet (64-metres) wide, the once proud symbol of the imperial capital Berlin. Modelled on the entrance to the Acropolis in Athens, the third of five passages was exclusively for members of the court until the November revolution of 1918. The small customs houses in the wings were remodelled as open halls for pedestrians after the demolition of the "Akzise" ("toll") wall in 1868.

The **Siegeswagen** (Victory Chariot) on the roof, created by sculptor Gottfried Schadow in 1794, is a reconstruction using moulds which survived the war. Until the city was divided, traffic flowed through the gate. Today, as a symbol of Germany's division it stands in isolation in the cordoned-off area at the "national border of the GDR."

Further to the west on the Strasse des 17. Juni, the **Sowjetisches Ehrenmal** (Soviet Memorial) for the approximately 20,000 Red Army soldiers who were killed in the conquest of Berlin, is passed. The memorial with its bronze statue was built from the left-overs of Hitler's chancellery. Significantly, it was placed on the former "victory avenue" that ran through the Tiergarten where Wilhelm II had erected the statues of German princes (Berlin wits calls them "puppets") to honour the glorious house of Hohenzollern.

At the Reichstag: The Reichstag building and the Swiss consulate general are all that remain of the grand buildings of the former Alsenviertel in the Spree bend. The other structures, especially those around the former Königsplatz which filled the empty expanse of today's **Platz der Republik,** were destroyed in the fighting of 1945.

The construction, where the Second Reich parliament, the Reichstag, once stood, was built between 1884-94 for more than 26 million Goldmarks by

Industrial panorama at the western docks.

Paul Wallot in the manner of the Italian renaissance. Its gilded façades and pompous interiors exemplified the taste and desires for representation of Wilhelminian Germany.

In the "Reichstag fire" of 1933, the glass dome and the plenary session hall were destroyed. By the end of 1945 all that was left was an empty shell with black window holes. In 1970, reconstruction was finally completed. Recently, plans have been drawn up to restore the traditional glass dome. The Reichstag building currently has a plenary session hall, conference rooms for the West German parliamentary groups, the Federal senate "Bundesrat" and other bodies, a restaurant and, in the west wing, a highly instructive exhibition on German history **Fragen an die deutsche Geschichte**.

The historical links of Tiergarten with the district of Berlin-Mitte beyond the Wall, become obvious when the visitor walks along the Spree towards the **Moltkebrücke**. People were free to come and go over such Spree bridges until the Wall was built. The bridges are now rusting away in the deserted zones along the river banks.

West of Moltkebrücke, the **Tempodrom** has put up its tents at exactly the correct historical location. This is where the famous "tents", huge recreational and assembly halls of canvas which were later replaced by stone edifices, have stood since the mid-15th century.

The cantilever concrete roof of the **Kongresshalle**, donated by the USA and erected in 1957, simulated the old tradition of canvas tents. After its collapse in 1980, the entire building was rebuilt and inaugurated a second time in 1987 with an exhibition "The Sciences in Berlin". Immediately adjoining is a 140-foot (42-metre) bell tower with a carillon ringing out over the distict, the birthday present of Mercedes-Benz. Tiergarten has always been a favoured place for buildings nobody knew what else to do with.

Left, cleaning the Soviet memorial. Right, Moabit metal workshop.

To Moabit: Crossing Moltkebrücke, the traveller reaches Moabit. Since the Wall was built, this part of the city has lost its attraction. Until 1954 the Lehrter railway station (1869-71), which once connected Berlin with northern Germany, stood at the entrance to Moabit. The station's magnificent forecourt was crowned by Berlin's first exhibition palace. Situated between Alt-Moabit and Invaliden Strasse, it was the site of industrial and art exhibitions. What remains lies under dense shrubbery on both sides of the S-Bahn viaducts.

Invaliden Strasse today is a border crossing point which leads directly to the centre of Berlin. On the other side of the Wall are facilities that once served the entire city, *e.g.* the Charité hospital and Natural History Museum. On the West Berlin side are traces of the past, such as the walls of Moabit's prison on **Lehrter Strasse**, whose name is connected with the tragic destiny of many members of the resistance at the time of the Third Reich.

Hamburger Bahnhof (1847), next to the Sandkrugbrücke over the Spandau shipping canal, is Berlin's oldest long distance railway station. It is almost a miracle that the main building has survived the years. Since 1906, it has housed the Berlin Museum of Transport and Building. This neo-classical brick edifice is once more an exhibition hall having been restored for Berlin's 750th anniversary celebrations.

Many Berliners think of "prison" when the name of Moabit is mentioned. This firstly refers to the **Kriminalgericht** (Criminal Court) and the prison for those awaiting trial in Turm Strasse. Among the many who have been incarcerated in this dingy building, erected in 1903 in ornate Wilhelminian style, are the legendary "Hauptmann von Köpenick", the "Brothers Sass" and, recently, Antes & Co., the main defendants in Berlin's latest corruption scandal.

On the eastern edge of the "Kleiner Tiergarten", a relic of the original Tiergarten which extended beyond the Spree, between Turm Strasse and Alt-Moabit, stands **St.-Johannis-Kirche**, an architectural jewel in this otherwise plain district. The church was inaugurated in 1835 and is one of Schinkel's three suburban churches. His pupil, Friedrich August Stüler, enlarged the church's single nave and gave it a livelier façade by adding a colonnade.

Another vivid architectural monument, easily recognisable by its decorated brick walls, stands behind the district town hall in Turm Strasse. The **Arminiushalle** is the last of the 14 Berlin market halls from the turn of the century to survive in its original form.

North-west Moabit is an industrial area originating from around the end of the 19th century, when Beussel- and Sickingern Strasse were developed. The most notable building here is the 690-foot (207-metre) long front of the **AEG-Turbinenhalle**, which was designed by Peter Behrens in 1909 and is considered a pioneering work in the history of industrial architecture.

HIER STARBEN
FÜR
DEUTSCHLAND
AM 20. JULI 1944

GENERALOBERST LUDWIG BECK
GENERAL DER INFANTERIE FRIEDRICH OLBRICHT
OBERST CLAUS GRAF SCHENK VON STAUFFENBERG
OBERST ALBRECHT RITTER MERTZ VON QUIRNHEIM
OBERLEUTNANT WERNER VON HAEFTEN

Left, 20 July memorial. **Right,** Tiergarten panorama.

KREUZBERG

Kreuzberg is Berlin's smallest (four sq miles/10 sq km) but most famous district. The "Kreuzberg legend" has spread far beyond its boundaries. One hears of the district's special flair, and it especially attracts young people. The reason is the "Kreuzberg mixture," an atmosphere based on the co-existence of Turkish migrants, students, workers, artists and elderly citizens.

Something of the district's mobile nature can be sampled on the way there. Travel from the Zoo station on the subway (line 1) towards Schlesisches Tor and observe that the passengers entering the car are typical of the "Kreuzberg mixture." Looking out of the car—the train travels above the ground after the Gleisdreieck station—it is clear why the district has become home to punks, social rebels, Turks and long-term welfare cases. Dilapidated houses where rents are cheap line the route and there is room for an existence free from the usual social strictures.

Kreuzberg and its innumerable bars harbour an infinite number of eccentrics. Faraway revolutionaries dreaming of an autonomous Kreuzberg, of separating their "Kiez" from the rest of Berlin; singular artists dreaming of their big break; zealous ecologists growing their grains and herbs on balconies and outhouse roofs; old people rhapsodising over the good old days; immigrants from Anatolia (the nickname "Krüzbürg" comes from their pronunciation) propagating a breath of the Arabian Nights. Here life pulsates as nowhere else in Berlin.

Three districts: Kreuzberg is unofficially split into two parts which are joined by a love-hate relationship. One is known as "61", after the zip code; the other "SO 36" (*Süd-Ost*, south-east), according to a pre-war notation. Those living in "61", perhaps in one of the renovated homes on **Mehringdamm**, on **Yorck Strasse** or in **Riehmer's Hofgarten**, are liable to be considered as *yuppies* by those from "SO 36". Such people are not very popular, as the graffiti sprayed on many a carefully renovated façade shows.

Anybody from working-class "Kiez" around the **Kottbusser Tor**—"Kotti"—might easily be suspected of being an anarchist. A satirical cabaret in Kreuzberg put it succinctly: "Somebody from 61 drives a Mercedes, and somebody from 36 breaks the star emblem off the automobile."

This mixture of people, carrying with it the potential for social conflict, has a tradition in Kreuzberg which, as a district, is not very old. The newly created district IV on the southern edge of the city centre received its name in 1920 after Berlin's great administrative reform, when the historic Berlin districts "Südliche Friedrichstadt", "Luisenstadt" and "Tempelhof Vorstadt" were amalgamated into a single administrative district. Initially, some local officials wanted to call the new district "Hallesches Tor", since this important traffic cross roads on the Landwehrkanal was known to every Berliner. However, the name always caused arguments, so it was agreed that the most conspicuous area in the district, the Kreuzberg, should be used as the name of the district.

In the early 1920s, Kreuzberg was mainly a residential area, but structural changes had already been taking place in the "Südliche Friedrichstadt" along Friedrich Strasse and Koch Strasse since the turn of the century. More and more apartment blocks were turned into industrial and commercial real estate and the district's population fell although its social stratification remained mainly intact. Farther to the east in "Luisenstadt", the present-day "SO 36", manual workers and their families mainly lived in dingy one- or two-room apartments without a bath, and with a common toilet in the hall. "Tempelhof Vorstadt" in the south-west, the home of white-collar workers and government employees, formed a self-contained small enclave of villas in Kreuzberg and acted as a middle-class counterweight to the working-class quarter.

"Southern Friedrichstadt", in its heyday a lively part of Berlin's centre, disassociated itself from the suburban character of its southern offshoot. The offices of the press, the Friedrich Strasse with its high social life and the fashionable Wilhelm Strasse (now with its northern tip beyond the Wall), used to house the government, the presidential palace, and the foreign ministry. Then there were two long distance railway stations. Prussia's first private rail company built a station (**Askanischer Platz**) here to link Berlin with Potsdam. The railway began operations on 29 October 1838.

The turn of the century saw millions streaming daily through the huge portals of the Potsdamer and Anhalter stations. An old water tower on the open-air site of the Museum für Verkehr und Technik (Transport and Technology Museum) at Gleisdreieck subway station dates from this period.

Around Anhalter station: Where crowds used to hurry and to scurry, where film and insurance companies did a thriving business, where hotels like the "Excelsior" and "Stuttgarter Hof" once stood, and cafés, restaurants and bars were full all night, there is now nothing but a stretch of urban wasteland. All that is left of **Anhalter Bahnhof**, Berlin's largest long distance station until the end of the war, is a lonely towering portal. **Friedrich Strasse**, once a lively boulevard and inner-city north-south axis from Oranienburg to the Hallesches Tor, is now cut by the Wall. On the corner of the **Zimmer Strasse**, foreigners cross into East Berlin via Checkpoint Charlie. All that remains of the former thriving newspaper district around Kochstrasse are the offices of the Axel Springer Publishing Corporation and the Ullstein

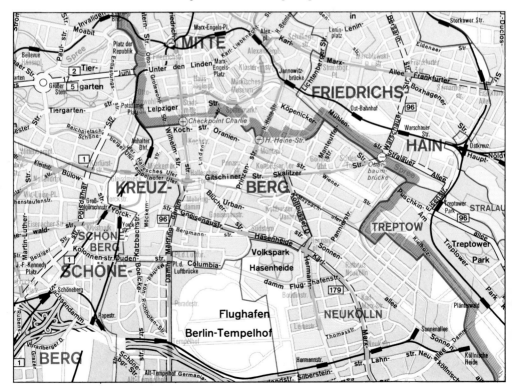

Publishing House.

The wounds left by war, the Wall and radical renovation are best examined from the "Berliner Fenster", a bar on the 17th floor of a housing complex in the Anhalterstrasse. A quick reconnaissance reveals a conspicuous stretch of barren land extending from behind the **Martin-Gropius-Bau** to the Wall. Since its renovation, the former **Berliner Kunstgewerbemuseum** (Handicraft Museum) serves as the focal point for important exhibitions and as the home of the **Berlinische Galerie** as well as of the **Jewish department** of the **Berlin Museum**. The new exhibition centre has contributed greatly to the rejuvenation of the district. In its early days it was of great importance to Berlin's musical life: The "Konzerthaus," where the Berlin Philharmonic celebrated their first triumphs, once stood on **Bernburger Strasse.**

Among the gutted and half-gutted houses levelled after 1945 was Germany's most infamous building of the Nazi period, the former Prinz-Albrecht-Palais at Wilhelm Strasse 102. In this and in neighbouring buildings on Prinz-Albrecht-Strasse were the headquarters of the Third Reich's persecution and extermination apparatus. The SS security service and the dreaded Gestapo were housed here and here were the desks of Himmler, Heydrich, Eichmann and their henchmen.

The view from above shows clearly how ruthlessly the Wall has cut through the traditional street patterns and building groups. The cubic Gropius-Bau (1881) is located in the West and its main portal which points north has lost its function because of the Wall. On the other side of the Wall stands the former Prussian Diet and at the corner of Leipziger Strasse the former Reich's Air Traffic Ministry. East Berlin's striking construction workers demonstrated here on 17 June 1953. The windows are covered by gratings on the side facing west; the building complex, a typical example of Nazi architecture

The remains of Anhalter station.

now houses East Germany's Ministries' House.

New Kreuzberg: Architectural failures of recent years are also obvious from the lofty heights. East and West bristle with unimaginative apartment blocks built in the 1960s. However, the **Mehringplatz** is a rather pleasant exception—a new, architecturally interesting complex of buildings at the **Hallesches Tor** subway station.

Although from a distance, the buildings resemble a collection of highrise apartment blocks, the visitor enters a circularly arranged complex of new buildings in which a pedestrian precinct is bordered by vegetation and shopping arcades. The central court is surrounded by several rings of apartments of differing heights, ranging from three-storied buildings in the innermost ring, to highrise blocks with 17 floors in the outermost. A peace column stands in the middle of the yard.

Mehringplatz was formerly Belle-Alliance-Platz and, leading past it, is Linden Strasse, where the **Berlin Museum** is located. It was formerly the "Kammergericht" (court), where the writer E.T.A. Hoffmann acted as an attorney. Now, the building not only offers informative exhibitions on Berlin's history, but also culinary delights. The museum houses the **Alt-Berliner Weissbierstube**, a traditional Berlin wheat beer saloon, which is famed for its delicious buffets.

However, Kreuzberg derives its real fame from the fact that it is Berlin's number one talent pool. Artists and intellectuals who, in the 1920s, had already made the quarter famous, have remained faithful to it. However, before examining Kreuzberg's legends and flair, here is a practical tip about how best to get to know the district.

Up the hill: The visitor should take the no. 19 bus or subway (station: Mehringdamm), to **Viktoriapark**, and climb the **Kreuzberg** hill which was formerly known as *Goetzescher* or *Runder Weinberg* (round vineyard).

Vines still grow here. The quality of the wine was described by the writer Adolf Glassbrenner as: "Just one-eighth poured on the banner will make the whole regiment shudder." The name of the 219-foot (66-metre) hill was changed after the erection of a memorial conceived by the sculptor and architect Schinkel to commemorate the 1813-15 Wars of Liberation. The 66-foot (20-metre) high Gothic pillar with a mighty cast iron cross on top was put in position in 1878 on a 27-foot (eight-metre) high rock base. The metal sculptures set into the recesses in the memorial portray victorious generals and battles of the Wars of Liberation against Napoleon.

A surprising sight for the uninitiated is the sight of a waterfall joyously gushing down the **Grossbeeren Strasse**. It is an imitation of the **Zackelfall** in the Riesengebirge and is especially enjoyed by tiny tots and pets in summer. The higher up the hill you climb, the better becomes the view of Berlin's

Turkish market.

136

urban development. The concrete jungle to the north-east with old street patterns and hulking modern constructions is Kreuzberg. No foliage is found in this area, just a few green splashes that turn out to be cemeteries. People are packed close together in Kreuzberg: more than 420,000 people were clustered in here in 1910; today Kreuzberg has about 150,000 inhabitants and is still the most densely populated district in Berlin.

It is nevertheless possible to live pleasantly in Kreuzberg. **Riehmer's Hofgarten**, a historic residential area very near to the waterfall, is the best proof of this. The preserved group of buildings can be reached via three entrances: from Yorck, Grossbeeren and Hagelberger Strasse. The complex surrounding a courtyard garden, was named after its founder, master builder Wilhelm Riehmer, who became rich in the years after the Franco-Prussian War (1870-71). It is a splendid example of how quiet, uncrowded living sur-

Krempel-market.

rounded by a lot of greenery is still possible in the big city.

The imposing portal on **Yorck Strasse** leads into a residential park with 24 buildings that demonstrates how sensibly architects planned compact inner-city buildings just before the turn of the century. The apartments are roomy and have private sanitary facilities. The large verdant courtyard with its many quiet nooks and crannies smothers the 24-hour traffic noise from busy Yorck Strasse. Visiting Riehmer's Hofgarten is worthwhile just for the carefully restored stucco façades in the style of the renaissance master builder Palladio. Entertainment is provided by smart cafés, cinemas and a disco. The **Berlin Kinomuseum** at Grossbeerenstrasse 57 fits well into the scenery. It is a kind of flea-market theatre, showing black and white features from the heyday of film.

Discreet charm: Another of Berlin's five "preserved residential areas" is close by: **Chamissoplatz**, lies in an area

largely unaffected by the war and the tear-it-down spirit of Germany's post-war prosperity. The area (formerly "Tempelhof Vorstadt") draws its charm from being an almost perfectly preserved example of the characteristic workers' and petty bourgeois quarter which arose in the second half of the 19th century.

Today, Chamissoplatz once again exudes its old charm. After some years of modernisation—there is even an old Berlin *Pissoir* (gentlemen only) in the middle of it. The rectangular "square" is surrounded by four and five-storied buildings with stuccoed façades and harmoniously partitioned window fronts. Many of old trees, cobblestones, wrought iron balconies, oriels and renovated façades with attention to tradition and colour lend atmosphere, as does an alternative arts gallery which is famous throughout the city. Restaurants, flea-markets and antique shops add colour to the place. Bergmann- and Zossener Strasse, with the **Marheineke Market**
Hall at their intersection, are well worth visiting for the lively trading.

The south side of **Bergmann Strasse** is marked by the start of a quiet, contemplative zone. Four historically significant cemeteries here are the last resting place of a several famous people.

From Südstern to SO 36: The **Südstern** subway station lies opposite the cemetery entrances. Seven streets intersect here to form a star and the **Garnison-skirche**, which is no longer used for services, stands in the middle of this traffic intersection.

Travel northeast to **Kottbusser Tor** and residential Berlin 61 changes to working-class SO 36. The transition is clear and sudden. Old, new and derelict houses jostle each other. The surroundings immediately provide an illustration of the "Kreuzberg mixture". A chic café stands right next to an old-style booze parlour which has the charm of bygone Kreuzberg days when naive painters and traders of anything dwelled here. Traditional small food stores,

Sculpture at Mehring-platz.

second-hand shops, an "alternative" butcher and an esoteric bookshop line the road to the Landwehrkanal.

Sauntering along the **Landwehrkanal** is a real delight because the richly decorated façades have been restored along the whole length. However, many a decorative front may hide dim yards with tiny dark apartments lacking proper sanitation. Lessons learnt from unsuccessful development planning in the 1960s have been implemented in the renovation of the old tenement blocks. Many of the dark and dingy backyard houses in Kreuzberg were simply removed, leaving a number of very fine courtyards behind.

Other examples of successful inner-city renovation can be seen at the Landwehrkanal. On the other side, at **Fraenkelufer**, is the "Ballerbau", a prestigious project of the Internationale Bauausstellung (Architectuaral Exhibition IBA), which has radically changed Kreuzberg's face in the last few years. Already the outer appearence of the

"Ballerbau" catches the eye. The vaulted roof, generous vitrication and a colonnade leading to the interior courtyard pleasantly distinguish this building from other public housing.

Little remains from the typical workers' milieu. A fast pace of urban development has had its grip on Kreuzberg since the "strategies for Kreuzberg", originating in the 1970s, to prevent it from becoming a slum have been practised by the authorities. The IBA took on a major share of the work, with its concept of city renovation; a mixture of the reconstruction of old property, with judicious care taken that the new buildings harmonise with the old.

In "deepest Kreuzberg": The success of restoration efforts is obvious, especially at **Mariannenplatz**, where renovated old homes with stuccoed façades peacefully coexist with modern houses bearing rectangular oriels and sporting glass exteriors. At the centre of all is Kurt Mühlenhaupt's "fire brigade" fountain. Nearby, **Naunyn Strasse** also

Street portal of Riehmer's Horgarten.

bears the hallmarks of recent changes, although these have not really been favourable. It has seen a flat restoration, with brightly coloured, new and indifferently renovated old buildings. Independent theatre groups have occupied an old ballroom.

Even after its restoration, Kreuzberg is still the number one Turkish community, which is clearly audible and visible in the market hall between Pückler- and Eisenbahn Strasse. The hall is firmly in Turkish hands and the variety of goods reflects the way of life of the immigrants from the Bosphorus.

In the **Künstlerhaus Bethanien** Turks have a lot to say in all matters. This former hospital at Mariannenplatz now houses printing presses, artists' studios, exhibition rooms and theatres, a Turkish public library and the Kreuzberg arts' council. Many Turkish artists regularly mill about here. Intercultural exchange is successfully practised in Kreuzberg at several places resulting in day-to-day life going on

normally despite anti-immigrant feelings expressed in graffitis sprayed on some houses. The **Türkenmarkt** (Turkish Market) held on Fridays at the **Maybachufer** offers all the hustle and bustle which is typical of a bazaar until late in the afternoon. The "Uferpromenade" is crowded with veiled women and bearded men bargaining over prices and pondering over fruit and vegetables. Oriental specialties and household goods from all parts of the world are on the stands. The air is redolent with the smell of kebabs and of the oriental spices which are slowly finding their way into the German cuisine.

In the **Oranien Strasse** one can find the genuine atmosphere of Kreuzberg: Turkish cafés and punk bars, neon-lit saloons and Berlin neighbouring corner pubs. When one of the many galleries has an opening the Turkish residents also drop in. As a matter of course many old-established Kreuzberg families these days buy their vegetables at the Turkish shop on the corner.

Cottage industries still flourish as they did in pre-war days in some of the old houses on the **Oranien Strasse**. Sometimes, for example at **Oranienhof No. 183**, the backyards are large and entirely taken over by small workshops. These houses may not look like much from the street but sometimes conceal delightful surprises such as unexpected idyllic corners and architectural refinements behind the peeling façades.

The **Oberbaumbrücke** (1896), which was destroyed during the war is, on the other hand, an architectural monument which nobody can overlook. It was a double bridge for rail and road traffic, a powerful bulwark more akin to a fortress than to a modern-day bridge. It has been closed to traffic since 1961, thus rupturing the connection with the eastern port on the opposite bank of the Spree. Non-functional, the Oberbaumbrücke serves as a crossing point for those walking into East Berlin, and as a favourite model for painters and photographers.

Left, subway line 1.
Right, easygoing Kreuzberg.

NEUKÖLLN

Neukölln, with about 300,000 inhabitants, has the largest population of all the districts of Berlin. Extending to the south-east of the city centre, it made up part of the concrete ring of suburbs that surrounded the German capital in the 19th century. Berlin grew rapidly as hundreds of thousands from the eastern provinces were attracted by the industrial boom. Building speculators hastily erected the notorious tenement houses which led graphic artist Heinrich Zille to state that it was just as possible to "slay a human being with an apartment as with an ax."

Neukölln became the "bedroom of Berlin's workers" and a stronghold of the socialist workers' movement. In 1929, author Franz Hessel wrote about the district, "For its own sake, you would never advise anyone to visit Neukölln." The few prestigious shop-ping centres could not hide the misery and poverty in the side-streets beyond the thoroughfares.

Today, most tourist routes avoid this traditional working-class neighbourhood, although it has more historical sights to offer than Kreuzberg. There is the **Britzer Dorfmühle** in Buga-Park, Berlin's first **Muslim cemetery** on Columbiadamm, and **Böhmisch-Rixdorf** that Egon Erwin Kisch once considered worth reporting on. Unlike Kreuzberg, whose boundary runs along the line Südstern, Hermannplatz and Kottbusser Damm, one has no high expectations about Neukölln, so it is free to unfold its own austere charm with ease. Thus, a bit of unaffected Berlin greets the visitor climbing out of the subway or bus 29 at Hermannplatz, the "Gate to Neukölln."

Like many other places, Hermannplatz was restored for Berlin's 750th anniversary celebrations. In its centre glows a bronze sculpture, the "Tanzendes Paar" (Dancing Couple) by sculptor Joachim Schmettau, who also designed the square "World Globe" in the inner city. The sculpture is surrounded by old Berlin business and apartment buildings with renovated façades.

Rixdorf tradition: Hermannplatz serves as a suitable starting point for a first visit to the district, since the three most important streets in Neukölln—Sonnenallee, Karl-Marx Strasse and Hermann Strasse—start here. In addition, the Neue Welt and the Hasenheide, two famous traditional Neukölln outing places are in the immediate vicinity.

Built in 1865, the **Neue Welt** was formerly the spot for an enjoyable evening of dancing, a "Bockbier" festival or a political gathering. The popular song, *In Rixdorf ist Musike,* was performed here in 1895 by a burlesque dancer. The Rixdorf polka gained world fame through the wooden sculpture of Neukölln sculptor Erwin Schrada. The original now stands in the Heimatmuseum in Ganghofer Strasse. The Schmettausculpture on Her-

Left, the "dancing couple" at Hermannplatz.

mannplatz also alludes to the *Rixdorfer Tanzpärchen*. The Neue Welt was restored as a shopping centre and houses a roller-skating-rink.

The **Hasenheide**, a park with lovely old trees, meadows and an open-air stage is next door to the Neue Welt. In this former rabbit preserve—hence the name "Hasen"-heide—Friedrich Ludwig Jahn built the first German gymnasium in 1811. The bearded "first gymnast of the nation" is remembered here with the Jahn memorial. Gymnastic clubs from all over the world contributed inscriptions and memorial plaques which are now part of the base.

Those who wander further through the park reach the **Rixdorfer Höhe**, the second highest spot in Neukölln. Here stands the "**Trümmerfrau**", a work of the sculptor Katharina Singer. A bench nearby, donated by the "Club der Berliner Trümmerfrauen", is an appropriate place to ponder on the hardworking "wreckage women" who made streets passable again and cleared away the ruins after World War II. The debris and stones that could not be used again were brought to the Hasenheide, and that is how the Rixdorfer Höhe originated.

Around Richardplatz: With its 216-foot (65-metre) high tower, the Neukölln Rathaus, the district townhall, dominates Karl-Marx Strasse, Neukölln's major thoroughfare. **Richardplatz** is where the historic origin of the later Neukölln town is to be found. Originally called "Richardsdorp" and later Rixdorf, the settlement was first mentioned in documents in 1360. Richardsdorp lay on the road between Cölln and Köpenick, and farmers built their houses around this oval square. The Bohemian-Lutheran **Bethlehemskirche** dating back to the 17th century and Berlin's oldest **village smithy** are a remnant of those times. **Kutschen Schöne**, a carriage business founded in 1894, has also survived. Twelve of its 53 carriages are white wedding coaches which couples still hire to take them to the church or to the registrar's office.

Card game contest at Hasenheide.

About 400 Protestant refugees fleeing from religious persecution in their home village in Bohemia found a new homeland in Rixdorf in 1737. So began the **Böhmisches Dorf** (Bohemian village) on Richard Strasse and around the Kirchgasse.

With its own church, humble farmhouses, and impeccably kept graveyard the "village" remained only a few steps away from the big-city bustle of Neukölln. It was described as an "almost displaced idyll", by Egon Erwin Kisch, the giant of German journalism and the author of social investigations in the Weimar Republic.

"The grateful descendants of the Bohemians who have been welcomed here," reads the dedication to the Prussian king Frederick William I on a bronze memorial from 1912 which stands on the village square. One of the three emblems in the district's coat-of-arms is the Hussite chalice of the Bohemian brothers. They named their settlement "Böhmisch-Rixdorf" rather than

Richardsdorf. The two communities were unified in 1874. In 1899 Rixdorf was granted town rights. In 1912, the city council decided to revive the old name of Berlin's original twin town and to rename the community Neukölln.

In the administrational reform of 1920, Neukölln, along with the villages of Britz, Buckow and Rudow which lie further south, became the 14th district of Berlin. All three areas have maintained their rural character till this day. In Rudow, the southernmost part of Neukölln, the ice-age sloughs and fallow-fields give the visitor an impression of what the original Berlin landscape looked like. Here, on the **Waltersdorfer Chaussee**, is one of two Neukölln places in Neukölln where the border can be crossed. Travellers take this route to the East Berlin airport in Schönefeld.

The histories of Buckow, Britz and Rudow supposedly began in the 13th century. Buckow's ("Buckow" being a Slavonic expression for beech) landmark is its church, built of granite blocks and field-stones. It is the most beautiful village church in Berlin and, with a small graveyard and pond, constitutes a true rural oasis.

"Blub and Buga": Just a few hundred yards away are the "Buga" grounds. The official Federal gardening show 1985 (BUGA) in Berlin presented forest-poor Neukölln with a beautiful recreation area. The 247-acre (100-hectare) terrain, with forest and meadows, streams, flower beds, and a large man-made lake is very popular, attracting visitors from all over the city. The park was specially designed to provide living space for endangered animal and plant species. Wetlands and areas of natural vegetation have been created in which frogs, rare water birds and many types of dragon-flies thrive.

None of the bridges over the lakes and brooklets resembles the other. Each one was built to fit its own environment and fulfill its own function. The other buildings are also unique, each an integral

part of a work of landscape design, architecture and art. The pleasant **Café am See** is a good example. The hallmark of BUGA '85 was the **Britzer Mühle** with its mill house: both were restored for the garden show.

At the same time as BUGA '85, the "Berliner Luft- und Badeparadies" or "Blub" for short, opened its doors on Buschkrugallee. With a beautiful wave pool and waterfall, a sauna garden, bathing grottos, and opulent gastronomic catering, it is thought to be the most attractive "water park" in Europe. Nearby, on Ganghofer Strasse is yet another water attraction, Berlin's city pool. It opened in May, 1914, and was built in the style of an ancient bath house. High columns support the domed ceiling whose splendid mosaic makes swimming here an event.

Two experiments: In the past, depressed living conditions in Neukölln created explosive situations. A large settlement of 2,500 apartments was built between 1925 and 1931 on the former Britz estate to help alleviate the situation. Part of it is the **Hufeisensiedlung** (horseshoe settlement), a public housing project designed by architects Martin Wagner and Bruno Taut, which happily combines two important elements: a good social environment and modern building techniques. This "Reformsiedlung" (Reform Settlement) from the Weimar years is still regarded as exemplary, in contrast to the **Gropiusstadt**, the second largest housing experiment in the Neukölln area.

The foundation stone of this satellite town was laid in 1962. Walter Gropius, founder of the Bauhaus, designed the basic plans for the complex where more than 60,000 people now live. Also of Walter Gropius design, and the distinctive mark of the settlement, is a 31-storey building, the highest apartment building in Berlin. It is surrounded by buildings that vary in height from one to 16 storeys, creating a semi-circle opening to the south.

Already in the planning phase, the architects paid careful attention to the installing of playgrounds and verdant terrains. Of particular importance in this context is a sickle-shaped park in the centre with four subway stations nearby. In spite of all these good intentions, the "Gropiusstadt" has provided much work for psychologists and sociologists, because the inhabitants of this large settlement often find themselves dissatisfied with what has been sold to them as "modern urban living".

Adventuring through the "Kiez": Neuköllners can be happy, even proud, of the cultural offerings in their part of town. The reputation of the **Neuköllner Oper**, an independent music theatre group, has for some time extended beyond the district. Neukölln artists no longer need desperately cry, "Die Wüste lebt!" (The Desert Lives!) to attract attention. Today, they have the **Galerie im Körnerpark**, where their works are exhibited and appreciated.

In the centre of Neukölln, between Hermann Strasse and Karl-Marx Strasse, the Körnerpark with its flowerbeds, fountains and suspended stairways is a gardener's dream. This hideaway is rather surprising in a densely populated area dominated by industry such as Neukölln. A film factory, a cement factory, the Berliner Kindl brewery, the Trumpf chocolate factory and Philip Morris corporation are all within the district boundaries, but cultural activities and business are not mutually exclusive. Philip Morris offers prizes and scholarships to encourage artists, and thus helps Neukölln's artistic endeavour both directly and indirectly.

Past and present, local and tourist, big city pace and village serenity intermingle in Neukölln. Here, one experiences the unaffected "Berlin Kiez" off the beaten tourist paths. The observant visitor who strolls these side-streets or enters one of the countless small corner pubs will come to know the most interesting part of the city: the Berliners.

At the Bohemian cemetery.

TEMPELHOF

The name Tempelhof is automatically associated with "airport" and because of its airfield the district is known all over the world.

The birth of civil aviation, the pioneering days of "Aunt Ju 52", the rapid expansion of air-traffic after the Airlift, the present day jet age— all this has been witnessed by the Tempelhof residents at close hand. Now, fenced off on all sides, the airport covers over 1,110 acres (450 hectares) between Columbia-Damm in the north and the disused peripheric railway tracks.

The community of Tempelhof is much older. It was founded in the 13th century by the Knights of Templar order, as were the parts to the south, Mariendorf, Marienfelde and Lichtenrade. All three once were, like Tempelhof, plain farming villages in the March. In 1772, Frederick William I converted the farming and grazing lands into a military training and parade ground. The "Tempelhofer Feld", as it was called, was the venue of numerous military spectacles outside the gates of Berlin.

The first international airport: In 1883, the Kaiser's new air transportation unit was based on the Tempelhof field, which also had other aeronautical sensations to offer. On Sundays, Tempelhof became a favourite picnic spot as large crowds gathered to watch painter Arnold Böcklin, engineer Dr. Wölfert and Frenchmen Armand Zipfel making astounding attempts to fly away from the airfield. In 1909, Orville Wright, one of the two celebrated American flying brothers, performed audacious show flights over the field. The era of motorized flight had begun.

The "Flughafen Berlin" was officially opened on the eastern part of the former parade ground on 23 October 1923. At first, it consisted of little more than the signboard, some aircraft han-

gars and a check-in hut. Airplanes took off and landed on a grass landing strip. Five years later the huts gave way to a respectable airport with a hotel, restaurants and concrete-paved forefield. Between 1936 and 1939, this terminal became the centre of the huge present-day complex at the Platz der Luftbrücke. The war prevented its final completion and it was not until the 1950s that the new **Zentralflughafen Tempelhof** was entirely devoted to civil aviation.

When the larger commercial airlines moved their regular operations to Tegel in 1975, Tempelhof became less busy. Over a period of 50 years, 60 million passengers had flown to and from the airport without a single air accident. Despite its location on the edge of a heavily built-up urban area—the eastern landing corridor passes right across rows of Neukölln's lined houses— Tempelhof proved to be one of the safest airports.

Airlift memories: Today, Tempelhof

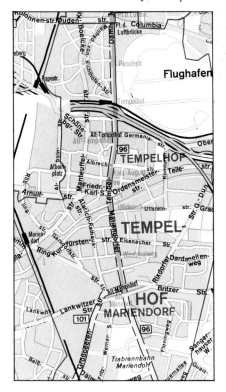

Preceding pages: trotting race in Mariendorf. Left, Platz der Luftbrücke.

stands forlorn and almost forgotten. The formerly busy runway is now usually deserted and used only by regional airlines and air taxi services out. The Berlin airport company has rented parts of the office buildings and maintenance hangars to private companies and departments of the city administration. The reception building, once again with barred windows, is part of a military airfield from where the Americans on Columbia-Damm operate their *Tempelhof Air Base*.

The days of the Berlin airlift are commemorated further east at **Gate 5**, where the Americans keep a "raisin-bomber"—a four-engined DC 54—on display. The 40-year-old veteran is parked near the fence. Every year, at the beginning of May, on "open house day", the oldtimer is towed out onto the runway for the enjoyment of sightseers.

Another memorial to the blockade is the statue in the airport's forecourt. Eduard Ludwig's concrete sculpture represents the arch of a bridge, and the spikes at the top symbolise the three air corridors which kept West Berlin alive at the time of the blockade. The memorial bears a bronze plaque on its base with the names of 70 Allied airmen, 39 British and 31 Americans, as well as four German helpers, who were killed during the airlift.

Soon after, the memorial was unveiled in 1951 Berliners, with their typical black humour, nicknamed it the: "*Hungerkralle*", or "Hunger-Claw", alluding to the meagre blockade rations. Its twin, although smaller in size and with the three spikes aiming north, stands alongside the Frankfurt-Darmstadt Autobahn on the American *Rhein-Main Air Base* at Frankfurt's international airport. It was from there and Wiesbaden that flights took off for Tempelhof during the blockade.

"House of Peace": In 1910 a real estate company acquired the western part of Tempelhof field for 72 million goldmarks. The transaction was hailed by the press as the "world's biggest real

estate deal." Before World War I bourgeois apartment blocks were built on this land, and later, in the 1920s, a garden city, **Neu-Tempelhof**. The area is nick-named "Fliegerviertel" ("Airmen district") because during the Nazi era, many streets were named after highly decorated combat pilots.

Between **Bayernring** and **Duden Strasse,** coming from Schöneberg, stands a five-storey, green apartment block, built in 1912 and typical of the area. A modest plaque at the entrance indicates that in May, 1945, world history was made on the first two floors of this house on Schulenburgring 2. The first floor housed the commander of the 8th Soviet Guards Regiment, General Wassili I. Tschuikov and his combat staff during the Battle of Berlin. One storey up General Katukov and his staff of the 1st Armoured Guards Division directed the operations to conquer the "Reichskanzlei " and the "Reichstag", Hitler's chancellery and the parliament building.

Also on the first floor, on the morning of 2 May 1945, Nazi-General Helmut Weidling, Berlin's last commander, signed his troops' capitulation, and thus ended the war for Berlin's sorely tired population. The oak table on which the historic document was signed now stands in Tempelhof's local history museum. It was not until the former Russian war poet, Jevgeni Dolmakowski, who drew up the protocol at the negotiations, visited the house 30 years later that its inhabitants learned about those events. Three of the tenants have since compiled an anthology of documents titled *Ein Haus, das Weltgeschichte erlebte* ("A House, where History was made").

The former "Reichsstrasse 96" runs in a straight line from **Platz der Luftbrükke** through the district to Zossen. On the border between Schöneberg and Kreuzberg, it is known as **Tempelhofer Damm** after which, when passing through **Mariendorf** and **Lichtenrade**, it bears the name of the

SPRING BOARD OF LUFTHANSA

Tempelhof Airport was once prominent in the world of civilian international air traffic. Berlin-Tempelhof was the first home for *Lufthansa*, Germany's airline, it's stepping stone to the world. In 1920 it developed into the most important and modern airport in Europe. With over 247,000 passengers and 63,000 take-offs, in 1938 it recorded a higher air-traffic intensity than the airports of London, Paris or Amsterdam.

Other airports, in and around Berlin, such as Johannisthal and Staaken, played a prominent role in the early days of aviation: this was where, after World War I Berlin's air traffic began with flimsy biplanes.

However, travelling between the city and Staaken and Johannisthal took quite some time, so city officials and the airlines started to look for a more convenient location outside the city gates. Tempelhof field was chosen. *Junkers Luftverkehr AG* and *Aero Lloyd* were the first airlines to establish themselves in the still primitively

equipped new airport. During the night and in winter there were no flights. On 6 May 1926 the two companies merged into one national airline. *Junkers* contributed the yellow and blue colours and *Aero Lloyd* the crane that were to constitute the logo of the airline. The founding of the *Deutsche Luft Hansa AG* (as it was then written) with a fleet of 162 planes proved to be a milestone in civil aviation.

Under the sign of the crane, Tempelhof developed into the centre of a flight network that rapidly expanded to include major German cities and European capitals. Already in 1932 one could fly from here to London in the Junkers G 38.

More and more foreign airlines scheduled flights to Berlin. With increasing passenger numbers, the buildings and technical sophistication of the airport improved. The area grew to three times its original size.

Today, at the sight of the wide oval shape of the airport, many Berliners remember the dramatic days of the blockade in 1948-49. It was lucky for the "political island" of Berlin that Tempelhof happened to be in the American sector. The blockade resulted in the largest air freight transportation enterprise in the history of aviation.

DEUTSCHE LUFT HANSA

At the height of the *Berlin Airlift* up to 1,300 planes loaded with essential provisions landed within 24 hours: at peak hours, a four-engined *Skymaster* either took off or touched down every 90 seconds.

In 1951, after surmounting the worst effects of the war, civil aviation quickly regained its drive. From then on, the colours of the airlines of the three Allies dominated the landing fields. By the end of the 1960s, annual passenger figures reached a record of five million. Tempelhof was saturated. Since 1 Sept 1975, most of Berlin's regular air traffic has used the new airport of Tegel-Süd. However, Tempelhof, a monument in aviation history, is on alert around the clock so that in case of bad weather or other emergencies it can serve as an alternative to Tegel-Süd.

respective districts. Eight miles (13 km) further south it ends at the walled-up border beyond which is the country district of Königswusterhausen.

In the administrative reform of 1920, Tempelhof was grouped with Mariendorf, Lichtenrade, and Marienfelde into Berlin's 13th district. At that time it housed 61,000 residents; today the number has tripled to 185,000.

Tempelhof is a very popular residential area. At the end of the war there were still large open spaces in its southern section but these are now covered by scattered modern housing settlements, semi-detached homes, and recreational parks and allotment gardens.

Village churches and horse racing: Tempelhof is proud of its four medieval village churches, which are evidence of more than 700 years of history. On the street **Alt-Tempelhof**, to the right and left of Tempelhofer Damm, stands the core of the old settlement with enclosed pasture land and the last farmhouses. The half-timbered tower of a 13th-century fortified church is visible in the park opposite the **Rathaus** which was built in the 1930s. In 1956, the church, which was severely damaged in the war, was restored to its original form.

The **Heimatmuseum und Archiv Tempelhof**, displaying furniture, folk art and old documents, resides in the former school house at the village green of **Alt-Mariendorf**. In **Alt-Lichtenrade**, in the former knightly estate, weeping willows ring the village pond. Around it, the idyll of a village survives with a traditional inn and a fire station. The village church of **Alt-Marienfelde**, a late Romanesque building of granite blocks erected around 1220, is considered to be the oldest building on Berlin's soil.

About 800 horses are stabled in Tempelhof–no longer in farms but in the stalls of the **Mariendorf steeplechase track**. This race track out in the country was opened in 1913 and, with its brand-new grandstand, is now a major attraction on the south side of Berlin. The five-storey building is well-supplied with snack bars and restaurants. Wednesdays and Sundays are the big days for racing. TV monitors allow spectators to follow their chosen favourite from start to finish; the electronic totalizator has been operating since 1982. On average, 50 million marks are bet annually by half a million visitors. The "Adbell-Toddington" race and international "Matadoren" race are the social events attended by prominent people and the chic set.

Welcome to the West: In the district of Marienfelde, farther to the south-west, is an institution which many former East Germans will remember all their lives—the "Notaufnahmelager Marienfelde". About one million refugees passed through this transit camp before the Wall was built. Most were flown to West Germany via Tempelhof after completing the usual formalities. The dreary camp-town with its two-storey flat-roofed buildings, was quickly erected on Mariendorfer Damm 66-80 in the 1950s. It still serves as transit home and first address for all legal emigrants from East Germany crossing the dangerous border to West Berlin and is as overcrowded as ever.

Industry at the water front: Economically, Tempelhof is the second largest industrial district in Berlin after Spandau and cannot be ignored. International companies such as Daimler-Benz, IBM, Standard Electric, Fritz Werner, Stock, Gillette, Schindler Elevators and Sarotti Chocolate provide about 10,000 jobs.

The construction of the Teltow Canal at the beginning of the 20th century promoted the industrialisation of southern Berlin. Part of Tempelhof's industrial belt is located along the canal. The **Stubenrauchbrücke** on Tempelhofer Damm provides an interesting view over Tempelhof's port with its cranes and warehouses.

Tempelhof's most noteworthy industrial feature is the expressionist façades of the **Druckhaus Tempelhof**

at the Ullsteinstrasse subway station. Eugen Schmohl designed the printing house in 1925-26 to be Berlin's first steel-reinforced concrete skycraper. The **Ullsteinhaus,** as it was called previously, housed the printing machines and the administrative offices of the then largest newspaper and publishing house in Europe—the Ullstein Brothers. The *Berliner Illustrierte Zeitung,* with a weekly circulation of 1.7 million and before World War II, Germany's leading magazine, was printed on the premises. The 233-foot (70-metre) high clock tower of the printing house is today one of Tempelhof's landmarks. Since large-scale printing ceased the offices of the publishing house have been rented out to small workshops.

The second life of the UFA: "Three things originated in Tempelhof before moving out into the wide world: films, aircraft and the Knights of Templar," was the district council's proud announcement on the occasion of the 750th anniversary celebrations. UFA,

Racing Sunday in Mariendorf.

Germany's pre-war film production giant which had its second largest production site in Tempelhof was only surpassed by the "film city" in Babelsberg. The first silent film studio was already in operation here in 1909, and many a classic was put on celluloid at the studios at Oberlandstrasse 26. In April 1945, Hertha Feiler and Heinz Rühmann, the super-stars of German cinema, were acting in the Terra film *Sag die Wahrheit* (Tell the Truth). The last commerical success for the Berlin film industry, however, was in the 1950s.

Now, the second German Television Channel (ZDF) maintains its largest production unit outside its Wiesbaden headquarters in these studios, which still belong to the Berlin Union-Film. About 70 per cent of all its mid- and long-term projects such as series and plays are produced in the Tempelhof studios. Live productions such as *Hitparade*, the popular quiz *Der Grosse Preis* and the documentary political magazine *Kennzeichen D* are telecast from here.

In Viktoria Strasse, not far from the printing house, dreams of a "greater Germany" were filmed at the time of the Third Reich as were socially critical films such as *Mutter Krausens Fahrt ins Glück*. In 1976, the film processing firm occupying the former UFA site was declared bankrupt and the production buildings became derelict.

However, in June, 1979, a wild bunch of activists occupied the run-down dream factory with "Juppy", a well known eccentric of the "scene", in the lead. Under the motto: "The Second Life of the UFA," they transformed the empty complex into a multi-functional venue for all kinds of activities. The new **UFA-Fabrik**, with its circus, Tempelhof's only cinema ("Ufer-Palast" or "River-Bank Palace"), a tavern, a small theatre and the café "Olé", has become the liveliest patch of colour in a district otherwise ignored as a "cultural desert".

ZDF hit-parade live from Oberlandstraße.

STEGLITZ

"By the way, life here in Steglitz is peaceful, the children look well-fed, the beggars don't press as hard...," wrote Franz Kafka to a friend in 1923.

Apart from the throngs of shoppers in **Schloss Strasse**, life is still rather peaceful in Steglitz and the district, which has 170,000 inhabitants, has maintained its traditional middle-class character. New suburbs and industrial neighbourhoods have sprung up but those quiet avenues that Kafka admired are still there.

The reason to come to Steglitz is to see the splendid orchids in the **Botanischer Garten**; or to enjoy an evening of classical entertainment presented at the **Schlosspark-Theater**; or, if the worst comes to the worst, to be treated at the hospital of the **Freie Universität.**

Shopping paradise of the south: Above all Steglitz is famous for its Schloss Strasse. Berlin has four streets which bears this name, but when Schloss Strasse is mentioned, people generally mean the Steglitz main shopping street which begins at the Walter-Schreiber-Platz subway station and runs south as an extension of Rhein Strasse. Since the end of the war a major shopping centre for southern Berlin has developed here. It extends from the **Forum Steglitz**, a five-storied "Multi-Center", to the Rathaus.

As long as the **Titania-Palast** had its doors still open to the public, people would throng the Schloss Strasse after dark. Its long and brilliant history as a cultural centre no longer can be told by its exterior. However, it is now preserved as an example of the architecture of the 1920s, and city theatre companies use a part of the premises for rehearsals. Until the 1970s the Titania-Palast provided many kinds of entertainment including a movie cinema, concert hall, ballet stage, operetta theatre and burlesque theatre.

It was here, with the permission of the Russian military commanders, that the Berlin Philharmonic gave its first concert after the war on 26 May 1945. The musicians wrote out the tickets and programme by hand. The post-war years also saw international stars such as Maurice Chevalier, Josephine Baker and Marlene Dietrich performing on the stage of the Titania-Palast.

Since 1976, the Schloss Strasse has boasted a new landmark. The **Turmrestaurant Steglitz**, a red-painted concrete tower, called Bierpinsel ("beer paintbrush") by the Berliners, stands near a city highway overpass on the Schildhorn Strasse. A lift ascends to the three restaurant levels which offer a magnificent view through large windows. When asked by a customer what the special features of the structure were, a Berlin cabby enthusiastically exclaimed: "Where else can you see for 20 kilometres while peeing?"

At the end of Schloss Strasse stands the **Rathaus Steglitz** built in 1896-97 in gothic brick style that is typical of the March. It was in a basement restaurant here, which no longer exists that the founders of the "Wandervogel" movement met in 1901. This youth movement had its origins among students at Steglitz's grammar school by the time of its demise, National Socialism had attracted hundreds of thousands of members.

On the corner of the Albrecht Strasse diagonally across the street, the highest office building in Berlin rises above the city. The 432-foot (130-metre) high **Steglitzer Kreisel** was born in the hectic building boom of the 1960s, like many other "concrete bunkers" found in Berlin at that time. Tax incentives during this period attracted a lot of capital to Berlin. In the 1970s, however, the megalomaniac, scandal-ridden, uncompleted "write-off-ruin" was the object of a bankrupt sale. After being finished by a new corporation, the Steglitzer Kreisel became the home of a hotel, of the Steglitz mayor and parts of

Left, Berlin marathon race passing the "Berlin-Pinsel".

the local administration.

"Papa Wrangel's Schlösschen": The old village of Steglitz was conveniently situated on the road to Potsdam. In 1375 it was mentioned for the first time as the property of one Herr von Torgow zu Zossen. By 1920 it had become Prussia's largest village with 84,000 inhabitants. It then joined with the communities of Lichterfelde, Südende and Lankwitz to form the twelfth district of Greater Berlin.

From the old days of Prussia a small castle still remains on the corner of Wrangel Strasse, once the property of Karl Friedrich von Beyme, a Steglitz landowner. Built in 1804, it now houses an excellent restaurant and wine tavern named **Wrangelschlösschen** after its most popular lodger, Fieldmarshal Graf von Wrangel who was known as "Papa Wrangel". The famous cavalry general, who spoke the pure Berlin dialect, is the subject of many legendary anecdotes.

In 1921, the actor Paul Henckels opened a theatre, which was later converted to a cinema, in a building near the castle. In 1945, although still badly damaged as a result of the air-raids, it became the first functional theatre in the American sector. Boleslaw Barlog was appointed its director. The opening production was *Hocuspocus* by Curt Goetz, and the cast included a new talent, Hildegard Knef. "On the first night it was cold, the audience sat wrapped up in horse blankets and old army overcoats." That is her description of her debut in the miserable place that had once again become a renowned theatre.

The Schlosspark-Theater, a comparatively small house with only 478 seats, mainly presents lighter theatre and comedies. The Steglitz subsidiary of West Berlin's state theatres attracts large, enthusiastic audiences every night with its reputation for presenting top-class plays by famous playwrights, both contemporary and classical such as "timeless" Shakespeare.

Meteorology and medicine: Berlin's often lamentable weather is not pro-

duced in Steglitz, but predicted hourly here. The metereological institute of the Freie Universität has operated since 1983 in the old watertower on the Fichteberg. The technical heart of the weather tower is on the sixth floor. Telexes print endless rows of numbers, a television screen shows what the radar eye has spied on the weather front in a 125-mile (200-km) radius; and on the roof of the 133-foot (40-metre) high tower an antenna receives messages from the weather satellites. The weather tower also has a special studio where annually 4.5 million telephone callers are given weather information.

The Steglitz clinic of the Freie Universität on Klingsor Strasse near the Teltow canal was built between 1961 and 1969 with financial assistance from the American Benjamin Franklin Foundation. It is considered to be Europe's most modern medical teaching and research centre and has 1,400 beds. The Federal agency which deals with the testing of materials, the **Bundesanstalt**

Waiting for the bus in Schlosstrasse.

für Materialprüfung, is located at Unter den Eichen and employs about 1,100 people. It operates both as a research and a licensing facility.

A world of botany: Another scientific place, which is also a favourite destination for outings, is the Botanical Garden. The Steglitz entrance is just at the lower end of Schloss Strasse, which joins the Unter den Eichen highway south of Hermann-Ehlers-Platz. Stroll along a pleasant avenue to the exhibition greenhouses which, with their filigree architecture dominate the 116 acres (42 hectares) grounds. The first building to catch the eye is the 83-foot (25-metre) high **Tropical House**.

The visitor walks on a stone footpath past a waterfall under a thick ceiling of leaves. Misty, damp air fills the house and the light is dim. Particularly in winter it is an unforgettable experience to come from ice and snow into a tropical rainforest. The tour through the exhibition houses covers two acres (8,510 sq metres) and leads through the luxuriant world of tropical and subtropical regions. There are ferns, cacti and, in the Victoria-regia-Haus, many exotic water and swamp plants. The Orchid House, where flowers are always in bloom, boasts 120 different varieties.

All in all, 18,000 tree and plant species can be seen in the Botanical Garden. One wanders through the **Freigelände** (open-air-gardens) on beautifully tended, winding teaching paths to observe the flora of the temperate zones of the earth. To the north, the Botanical Garden ends at Königin-Luise-Platz in Dahlem. At this entrance is Germany's only botanical museum with a library with more than 60,000 books.

The military: The Botanical Garden is situated at the western edge of **Lichterfelde**, which in earlier times, like Steglitz, was a small village far away from the gates of Berlin. In 1865, a businessman from Hamburg, Wilhelm Carsten, who later rose to the nobility, acquired the estates of Lichterfelde and Giesendorf from their owner who was heavily in debt. He built streets across the estate and then divided the land and sold the building lots to the prosperous bourgeoisie, claiming that they would live in "one of the most beautiful villa suburbs in Germany."

On what today is **Finckensteinallee**, Carsten, the "Napoleon of real estate speculation" donated a tract of land to the Prussian military and, in 1878, the central cadet college was built there. In 1934, Hitler's bodyguard, the so-called "SS-Leibstandarte Adolf Hitler", moved in. On 30 June 1934, 40 leaders of the SA, rival organization of the SS in the Nazi hierarchy, which had been involved in the "Röhm" rising against Hitler, were executed in the cellars of the Lichterfelde college. Since the end of World War II, the US Army administration has been using the building complex and has renamed it Andrews Barracks.

Without modern vehicles, Berlin

would never have grown so quickly into a large metropolis. In the Lichterfelde of 1881, the inventor Werner von Siemens established his reputation with the world premiére of the "Elektrische". The world's first street car or tram powered by an electric motor had its trial run on May, 1881, from Lichterfelde cadet college to the railway station Lichterfelde-Ost. It was a converted horse-drawn street car with an electric motor installed under the floorboards.

The Father of Aviation: Lichterfelde also prides itself on being the cradle of German aeronautics. The engineer and factory owner Otto Lilienthal who, it is claimed, was the "first flying human being", lived on Booth Strasse. In 1894, he built a 50-foot (15-metre) hill near his house. Eager to see a sensation, the people of Berlin came out every Sunday to Lichterfelde, where the audacious aviator was testing his home-made flying machines and gliding through the air for as far as 100 yards.

Today, a stairway leads to the top of the grassy mound where a stone globe, surrounded by a circular, airy observatory pavilion, open to the sky, symbolises man's conquest of the air. The park along and around the mound on Schütte-Lanz Strasse has been named Lilienthal-Park to commemorate the aviation pioneer who prematurely crashed to his death on his test flight on 9 August 1886.

Compassion for animals: East of Lichterfelde lies the district of **Lankwitz**. The **Animal Shelter** or Dessauer Strasse is known even beyond Berlin. Erna Graffis, living here among her pets, is a resolute elderly lady and president of the animal protection society. She dedicates her life and fortune to "protecting tormented creature".

In a city which has 100,000 dogs and at least as many cats and an infinite number of other pets, looking after stray animals is a major enterprise. The shelter employs about 50 people. It maintains a veterinary emergency service as well as an animal guest-house.

Several hundred dogs and cats are always waiting longingly for a welcoming home in the two-storeyed buildings. There is also a yard where abandoned horses and donkeys, enjoy their bread of charity.

The **animal cemetery** in front of the main building has found its place in a guide-book about "Berlin's hidden sights". Harro and Waldo, two police dogs killed on duty, rest here as do Bimbo, the circus chimpanzee, and other once well-known four-legged creatures from film and television. Two thousand pets have found such resting places in the park.

Some have heart-rending obituaries carved on expensive, marble tombstones. Others, such as the poodle "Little Princess Sissi", have their portraits etched for eternity on the memorial stones. An elderly couple from north Berlin travels each Sunday to gravestone No. 1934, where they pay their respects to their "unforgettable Puppi."

Below, at the animal cemetery. **Right,** in the Tropical House in the Botanical Garden.

ZEHLENDORF

Zehlendorf, which lies to the west of Steglitz, enjoys the reputation of being Berlin's most exclusive district. With a population of 85,000, it is one of the smallest. Yet, covering 27 sq miles (70 sq km) it is the third largest district after Reinickendorf and Spandau.

Statistics show that the Zehlendorfers live in the largest apartments, enjoy the best medical care and have the highest level of education compared to all Berliners. They are situated in the midst of West Berlin's loveliest nature such as the **Glienicker Volkspark**, the Havel river, Grunewald forest, and a sprinkling of lakes, from Nikolassee to Grunewaldsee.

Cloak and dagger: The **Glienicker Brücke**, in the southern tip of the district, has achieved international fame.The middle of this bridge is the border between East and West Berlin. It

was here in 1986 that journalists from all over the world waited for days in the biting cold for the arrival of the Soviet dissident, Anatoli Sharantsky, a Jewish human rights activist who, after years of imprisonment in the USSR, was released in exchange for Soviet spies. And, it was here in 1962 U-2 pilot Gary Powers, who had been shot down over the USSR, was traded for the Soviet agent Ivanovich Abel.

From the Glienicker Brücke one can see the steeple of the **Nikolaikirche** in Potsdam, a neo-classicist church erected at the beginning of the 19th century according to the plans of Karl Friedrich Schinkel, and the **Potsdam Interhotel**. To the north-east is the abandoned romanesque **Heilandskirche**, caught in the no-man's land between East and West. The last service to be held in this church was on Christmas Eve 1961.

After World War II the Glienicker Brücke was called "bridge of union". However, the idea of unity had long

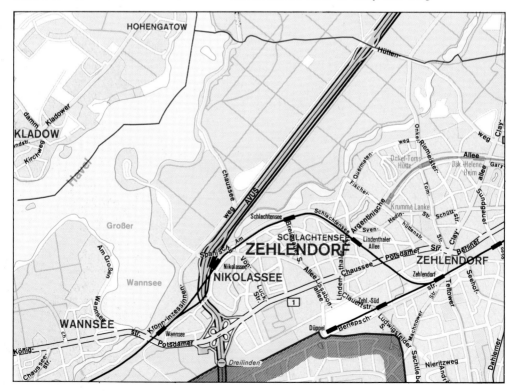

since disappeared when, in 1961, the GDR closed the road to Potsdam. Today, the bridge is open again to normal traffic. Anyone can cross over to the GDR district of Potsdam either on foot, by car or using public transport.

However, 200 years ago, this crossing was especially important to Zehlendorf. The Potsdamer Chaussee, Prussia's first paved road crossed the Havel river on this wooden bridge. On the "stony road" travelling time takes an astonishing six miles (10 km) per hour, reducing the time needed by the coach between Berlin and Potsdam to two hours; and, Zehlendorf was located right in the middle of it. The construction of the Chaussee brought life to sleepy Zehlendorf.

About 50 years after the completion of the Chaussee, the "winds of technical progress" again blew through the venerable village which is rather proud of having been first mentioned in 1241. The Berlin-Potsdam railway was being built; the first train stopped in Zehlendorf in 1838. As villages sprang up all along the railway's route Zehlendorf and neighbouring communities turned into quasi-suburbs of Berlin.

Fun-fair in "Little America": Zehlendorf is no longer the quaint village of yore. The district centre at the intersection of **Potsdamer Strasse, Teltower Damm** and **Clayallee** has a variety of shops and stores, the town hall and other institutions. Only the small baroque village church west of the intersection recalls bygone days. The main entrance to the Zehlendorf cemetery, where Mayor Ernst Reuter (died 1953), Erwin Piscator (died 1966) and other well-known literary figures, are buried is on Potsdamer Chaussee.

On Clauert Strasse, in **Düppel**, a nobleman's estate bordering Kleinmachnow, is now home to a reconstruction of an old Prussian village from around 1200. It is sponsored and run by a volunteer association whose members also demonstrate handicrafts from the Middle-Ages on Sundays.

A second Zehlendorf "downtown" developed after the war further north at the intersection of Clayallee and Hüttenweg in the vicinity of the Oskar-Helene-Heim subway station. The local people refer to it as "**Little America**" because of the many Americans in uniform and in civilian clothes who frequent this area. Since 1945, the US military has made a former Nazi building complex here its headquarters. This is also where the **US Mission** resides. A miniature version of an American town spreads out in every direction around the military installation, replete with movie theatres, schools, stadiums, shopping centres and private residences. However, this does not mean that the Berliners and the Americans do not meet. Once every summer the German-American "Volksfest"is celebrated.

The **Allied High Command** is also located in Zehlendorf. In a quiet manor house at Wasserkäfersteig 1 is the **Berlin Document Center** where the Americans keep an index of the 10.7 million members of the former NSDAP as well as personnel files of other Nazi organisations.

The "Brücke" artists: That part of Zehlendorf which borders the district of Wilmersdorf at Roseneck is called **Dahlem**. This former estate is now a science and research centre. It also houses a treasure trove of art works. The museums of the **Stiftung Preussischer Kulturbesitz** (Prussian Cultural Heritage Foundation) which include the Völkerkundemuseum (Museum of Ethnology), the Gemäldegalerie (Gallery of Paintings) and the Kupferstichkabinett (Collection of Copper Plate Engravings) are located near the Dahlem subway station.

Not far from here, at Bussardsteig 9, at the edge of Grunewald forest, extends a flat building, the **Brücke-Museum.** This new museum construction was conceived in 1964 by the then 80-year old painter, Karl Schmidt-Rottluff, and the then general director of the Berlin municipal museums, Leopold Reidemeister. The museum opened its doors to the public in 1967.

Erich Heckel, Emil Nolde, Max Pechstein, Ernst Ludwig Kirchner and others were members of the "Brücke" artists group which was founded in Dresden in 1905. Heckel and Schmidt-Rottluff, the only surviving members in 1967, enriched the museum's collection with their own works and also donated their personal collections of other "Brücke" artists.

Campus in the park: When it is not semester break, thousands of students flock to Dahlem every day. This is the main location of the **Freie Universität** (FU) and its numerous faculties. The "Free University" was founded in 1948-49 under difficult circumstances. In those years some students and teachers found the political pressures at the venerable Humboldt-Universität, now located in the Soviet occupied eastern sector, to be intolerable. With the support of the military governor Clay, the Freie Universität began classes in December 1948.

Even before World War I, some research institutes of the "Kaiser-Wilhelm-Gesellschaft" had been established in Dahlem. Max Planck, Albert Einstein and other Nobel Prize winners worked here. The "atomic era" was inaugurated in 1938 in the old chemistry institute at **Thielallee 93**, when Otto Hahn and his assistant Fritz Strassmann split the first uranium atom. The tradition lives on at the **Hahn-Meitner-Institut** for atomic research on the Glienicker Strasse in Wannsee.

Parts of the Freie Universität found their first home after the war in some of the old buildings of the Kaiser-Wilhelm-Gesellschaft. In the 1950s the Ford Foundation sponsored the main lecture hall on Gary Strasse and the university library. The "Rostlau-be" ("rusty pavilion")—students here adhere to the Berlin habit of dubbing all and everything—is an extensive flat-roofed construction with an exterior of rust-coloured steel which also stands on

Physics students in the FU.

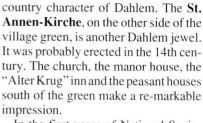

the Dahlem campus. The "Silberlaube" (naturally the "silver pavilion") does not look much different, except for the silver colour. It serves as the university's cafeteria.

At the end of the 1960s the university became heavily involved in the student protest. Under the leadership of the Sozialistischer Deutscher Studentenbund (SDS, the German Socialist Student Association), the so-called "non-parliamentary opposition" movement (APO) held their meetings here. Today, the FU with its 53,000 students is the major university in Berlin.

Martin Niemöller's parish house: The idyllic, country flavour of old Dahlem still persists in the well-preserved, old section called **Dahlem-Dorf**. The history of this village probably stretches back for 750 years. The simple manor house, opposite the thatch-covered subway entrance, which dates back to 1679, is shared by the FU and the "Freunde der Domäne Dahlem", a group committed to preserving the old,

country character of Dahlem. The **St. Annen-Kirche**, on the other side of the village green, is another Dahlem jewel. It was probably erected in the 14th century. The church, the manor house, the "Alter Krug" inn and the peasant houses south of the green make a re-markable impression.

In the first years of National Socialism, the Protestant parish house of Dahlem, under the leadership of Martin Niemöller, was the centre of the **Confessional Church**, which opposed the official Nazi stance of the German Protestant Church. Niemöller courageously preached against the Nazis' policy and was sent to a concentration camp in 1937. The parish house is now known as the "Martin Niemöller Haus" and serves as a research centre for world peace.

Not far away, on Grunewald lake, is a renaissance-style hunting lodge, built for the Elector Joachim II in the mid-16th century. The **Jagdschloss Grunewald** today is a museum exhibiting a collection of hunting weapons and

Left, German-American fun-fair. Right, hunting in Grunewald.

equipment, as well as paintings by German, Dutch and Flemish masters from the Hohenzollern possessions.

Holiday at the Wannsee: In the last third of the 19th century, Berlin began building an ultra-modern commuter train system called the "S-Bahn". Zehlendorf's rapid development into such an exclusive area was in great part due to the construction of this line, called **Wannseebahn** after its terminus station. It passes through the most attractive residential areas of West Berlin and the stations have been designed to blend with their surroundings. Outstanding sights en route to Wannsee are the pure Art Nouveau **Mexikoplatz station** and the **Nikolassee station** which looks like a Gothic fortress. The **Nikolassee** villa colony, situated on the gently flowing landscape of the **Rehwiese** (deer meadow), is especially charming.

A footpath from the Nikolassee station leads to the **Wannsee** swimming area. This is the biggest lakeside resort in the city and, indeed, in all Europe. Swimming in the lakes and rivers of Berlin was officially prohibited until 1907. A public swimming resort was first built here between 1927 and 1930. Berlin's city building councillor, Martin Wagner, and architect Richard Ermisch came up with the idea in order to give Berliners "who live in dark, stuffy tenement blocks and can't afford the luxury of a seaside holiday" a chance for rest and recuperation. Today, the lakeside swimming area of Wannsee brims over with people on warm summer days. Not even the "less-than-pure" water of the Havel can discourage the Berliners.

Literary workshop: Near Wannsee S-Bahn station, at Sandwerder 5, stands a magnificent villa which is no longer used as a private residence. Carl Zuckmayer had the opportunity to work in this little "castle" in the summer of 1925. For the last 20 years, the **Literarisches Colloquium Berlin** has been using the villa as a guest-house and a place where writers and authors from all over the world can come together to communicate. The initiator of the project was the author and professor of literature Walter Höllerer. In 1964, he founded the then avant-garde association to show "literature in relation to science, politics and everyday life". One of the organisation's principle role was to transcribe literary material for other media such as radio, film and television.

The list of scholars and poets who have lived in Zehlendorf, for greater or shorter periods, is impressive. The historian Friedrich Meinecke who was the first director of the Freie Universität, moved here from Freiburg in 1914 and lived at Hirschsprung 13 until his death in 1954.

In the 1920s philosopher and writer Ernst Bloch, the author of *Das Prinzip Hoffnung* (The Principle of Hope) resided on Elfriedenstrasse, which has been renamed Professor-Biesalski Strasse. Many of the beautiful country homes here were planned by some prominent architects. Arnold Zweig lived at Matterhorn Strasse. 67 from 1923 to 1929 where he wrote his most successful pacifist novel, *Der Streit um den Sergeanten Grischa.*

A pilgrimage of sorts is often made to **Kleiner Wannsee** (the "small" Wannsee) by devotees of Heinrich von Kleist, who pay tribute to him by visiting his grave. The path leads through the lot at Bismarck Strasse 3 to that part of the shore where, on 21 November 1811, von Kleist, who was born in 1777, committed suicide with his married lover Henriette Vogel. The red stone marker on von Kleist's grave bears the line of a verse from his work, *Der Prinz von Homburg:* "Now, oh immortality, you are wholly mine."

The Königs Strasse is the thoroughfare which cuts through that part of town called **Wannsee**. The town hall and little houses which stand here and on the side streets are remnants of Wannsee's rural past. **Mutter Fourage** is a gallery set up in an old farmhouse on

Schäfer Strasse, with a pottery and a gardening centre. Lining the shore of **Grossen Wannsee**, (the big Wannsee), are rows of yacht clubs, private spas and clinics, and villas. Just before reaching Heckeshorn hospital, at number 56-58, is a half-hidden villa which once belonged to the SS. It was here on 20 Jan 1942, that the infamous "Wannsee Conference" headed by SA leader Reinhard Heydrich took place.

At this "conference" the Nazi regime decided to come to a "final solution" of the "Jewish question", as Nazi bureaucratic jargon harmlessly described the plan to physically exterminate all Jewish people in Europe. The building later served as a boarding school for the district of Neukölln. As soon as another building is found the **Wannsee Villa** will be transformed into a memorial to the Holocaust.

Exotic enclave: At the last major intersection before the Glienicker Brücke, the Chausseestrasse turns off to run south through the districts of **Stolpe** and **Kohlhasenbrück** to **Steinstücken**, a former enclave. It is under the administrative jurisdiction of Greater Berlin even though it lies squarely in East German territory. This severed section of West Berlin was made accessible again after the 1972 territorial exchange with the GDR. Ever since, the enclave has been "moored" to the "mainland" by a dead straight highway, left and right sides by the Wall. Unfortunately too, that put an end to the peace and quietude of this 80-acre (32-hectare) patch of land.

Steinstücken developed around the turn of the century, as did neighbouring Klein-Glienicke, Babelsberg und Nowawes. In 1920, the residents of Babelsberg successfully protested the incorporation of their village into Berlin, and today they belong to East Germany. Steinstücken, however, agreed to the annexation and became a part of the US sector in July, 1945.

After the completion of the Wall, only residents or those with special ID's

Illusionary "ruin castle" on Pfaueninsel.

were allowed there. The Americans and, on occasion, the mayor of Berlin had to be flown in by helicopter. The rotary blade of an old helicopter now stands prodly on the former landing pad as a reminder.

Castles and gardens: Here in the south of Zehlendorf, one of Berlin's most beautiful parks stretches out along the banks of the Havel. The **Volkspark Klein-Glienicke** was once reserved for noble guests. Prince Karl, brother of Frederick William III, once resided here in a former manor house rebuilt by Karl Friedrich Schinkel and his students. He hired not only the finest master builders in the country but also the most outstanding landscape architects and created a superb masterpiece.

Over by König Strasse rises **Schloss Glienicke**, a castle with a coach house and attendants' quarters. The two round temple-like structures on the roadside are called the "Great and Small Curiosity". They are observation terraces which the prince had built by Schinkel so that he and his guests could watch the traffic on the great road go by. One hundred and fifty years ago, in the age of horse and carriage, such a pastime may still have had a sort of attraction.

The former **Jagdschloss Glienic** stands in a park on the other side of König Strasse. This hunting lodge was rebuilt in the French-baroque style by Ferdinand von Arnim for Prince Karl. It serves today as a centre for conferences and conventions.

Another architectural curiosity, the **Alexandra Loggia**, can be found in the wooded area south of the Chaussee, opposite the road to Nikolskoe. This semi-circular structure on the **Böttcherberg** was erected in 1869. It functioned as a scenic look-out for the lords of Klein-Glienicke. Across from the street "Am Böttcherberg", the **Nikolskoer Weg** branches off and, winding through the trees soon reaches a hill overlooking the Havel on which stands an idyllic inn built in the style of a Russian log house. Next to it is a pretty church with small onion-shaped towers.

King Frederick William III had the **Blockhaus Nikolskoe** (the log house) built as a present for his daughter, Charlotte, whose husband later became Tsar Nicholas I. At that time, the relationship between Prussia and Russia was very much determined by family ties. The graceful church of **St. Peter and Paul** is often chosen by couples as a setting for wedding ceremonies. A midnight service on Christmas Eve in snow-covered Nikolskoe is also a favourite event among Berliners.

An optical illusion: Waiting at the end of Nikolskoer Weg is the ferry to the **Pfaueninsel** (Peacock Island), with its beautiful view of the Havel. The island is cherished by lovers as the most romantic little hideaway in all Berlin. Frederick William II, the very unmilitary successor to Frederick the Great, bought the island in 1793 as a refuge and retreat for himself and his mistress. He ordered the building of a steward's house and a dairy farm. The little "lovers' castle", which looks like the ruins of an old fortress, was intended for his mistress, "Minchen Encke", who later became Countess Lichtenau.

"A splendid little place for fantasy castle", the lively monarch decided in his characteristically scanty language. "Dilapidated castles come to mind, have something gothic built immediately." A half-timbered building was erected between 1793 and 1797, with a façade of oak panels that from the distance looked like white shining stone. Gaping window frames on the third floor give the appearance of romantic ruins. The illusion carries on throughout the entire castle, from the courtyard to the tower chambers.

In 1822, the island was transformed into a landscaped English garden by Countess Lenné. Peacocks were brought over from the Sackrow manor, on the opposite bank of the Havel. Their offspring populated the island and gave it the name which it has kept until this day.

THE AMERICANS IN BERLIN

The Americans occupied Berlin on 4 July 1945. Complying with agreements reached with the Soviet Union, they took over six districts in the south-western part of the city: Zehlendorf, Steglitz, Tempelhof, Neukölln, Kreuzberg and Schöneberg. Since it was Independence Day, they seized the opportunity to hold their first parade in the Lichterfelde Goerzallee. They were only supposed to stay four or five years at the most, but are now in their fifth decade of Fourth of July celebrations on the Spree.

The US-Army has found a home in both Dahlem's Little America and the Lichterfelde Barracks. About half of the 6,600 GI's are married and the American community, including civilian personnel and family members, numbers about 15,000 people. They live the "American way of life" in their housing areas and clubs. Uncle Sam makes sure that they have all the comforts of home, from bingo evenings to bowling and to T-bone steaks all the way from Texas. They do not have to do without home television either. AFN-TV is already on the air at six in the morning; its news bulletins, baseball games, the hit parade, and other novelties are beamed in directly from the USA via satellite. Soldiers serve their two or three years of trouble-free duty in Berlin, without having to cope with German, especially since the Berliners are quite happy to use their brand of English. The British in Spandau and the French in the north also live their lives in the "home" way, but with the Americans everything is just that little bit bigger. They maintain not only the largest force in Berlin, but also the best paid. A *specialist 4*, the most common rank, earns 9,000 to 10,000 dollars depending on marital status, with free accommodation in the barracks or the housing areas. There are also additional overseas benefits, depending on local living costs and currency rates.

The highest ranking officer is a major-general, serving as commander of the American army in Berlin and as the deputy head of the US mission. The core of the army garrison is the Berlin Brigade of three battalions of the *502nd Infantry*. Other troop units, among them a tank company with 22 *M-60s*, engineers, field artillery and radio specialists, are combined into a *Combat Support Battalion*. The Army air force's helicopters are based at Tempelhof which is predominantly ruled by the US Air Force with about 1,000 men, many of whom are employed as radar specialists with electronic eyes and ears pointing to the East. This equipment was installed by the US Air Force under plastic domes at the airport and at Teufelsberg.

A US infantryman on a poster striking a martial pose, tells GI's why they are in Berlin: "To show the Berliners, your Allies and the Communists the best soldiers in our army to fight if necessary like hell for US rights and a free Berlin." The tank grenadiers of the Berlin Brigade practice constantly under realistic combat conditions in *Doughboy City*, a ghost town on Osborner Damm in Lichterfelde, which serves as a training camp for street combat. Tank and artillery crews practice at Grafenwöhr or Wildflekken. On Allied Forces' Day in Tiergarten and in front of McNair Barracks on Independence Day, the best US soldiers parade in impeccable uniforms. The army also spends some time preparing for the "Volksfest" at Hüttenweg which, each summer, is attended by half a million visitors.

SPANDAU

In the centre of Spandau there was, and today probably still is, a saying spray-painted on a railway bridge: "It has always been something special to be a Spandauer!"

There is some truth to that saying, which has also been making the rounds as a bumper-sticker. Spandauers—the inhabitants of the formerly independent town on the Havel—were always conscious of their origins, especially with regard to their relationship with Berlin: "I have 11 districts and one republic–Spandau", Mayor Reuter once joked about the marked local patriotism of the stubborn Spandauer yeomen.

They passionately fought absorption in 1920. Town councillor Emil Müller anticipated the approaching storm before World War I , when a fine town hall was built in Spandau for almost 3.5 million Goldmarks: "May the Kaiser's

hand protect us from Berlin and administrative union", he stormed in 1911 during the laying of the foundation stone. The Kaiser went and Berlin came: Spandau became the focal point of the administrative district of the same name. Its 33 sq miles (86 sq km) make up almost one-sixth of the total area of West Berlin. Spandau shares with Zehlendorf and Wilmersdorf the wet- and woodland areas along the banks of the Havel river, whose meadows Theodor Fontane once compared to those of the river Neckar.

Spandau is the only part of Greater Berlin on the Havel's west bank, and shares a 20-mile (32-km) border with Nauen in the East German district of Potsdam. Those travelling from Hamburg on the highway formerly reached the city at the Heer Strasse checkpoint which now, because of the new access road, has been transferred to Heiligensee. Inter-city trains to and from Hamburg stop at Spandau. Of the historic sights in Berlin, the Zitadelle Spandau with its Juliusturm (tower) is definitely one place not to be missed. After the war, Spandau's name drew worldwide attention because of the war criminals' prison with its infamous payload of high-ranking Nazis. In Kladow, the German Overseas Development Agency (DED) has its headquarters and school that prepares about 250 helpers yearly for future work in the Third World.

Economically, Spandau plays a major role in the life of Berlin. It is the largest industrial district in West Berlin, and is the home of Siemens, the Reuter power station and BMW's streamlined motorbikes. One in five of West Berlin's industrial workers is employed in Spandau's factory. The district's eastern side has many large industrial areas running along the Charlottenburger Chaussee and Am Juliusturm Strasse. These have their own railway networks and port connections. The northern districts of Hakenfelde an der Havel and Klosterfelde which stand in

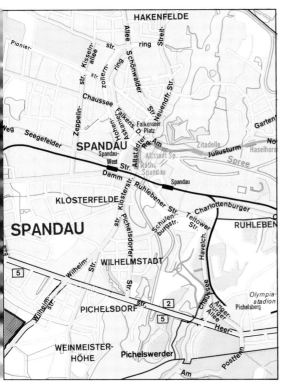

the vicinity of the goods station have been similarly industrialized.

Berlin's big sister: Spandau claims to be the oldest community on West Berlin's soil. Thanks to its suburban location on the Havel's west bank, it has preserved much of its original rural frontier character. The old town was threatened with demolition in the 1960s but it now has protected status. Its narrow rectangular streets and the St. Nicolai church are two reminders of Spandau's royal history. It is proud to be five years older than Berlin and is first officially mentioned in 1232 when a royal letter awarded the *civitas spandowe* market and customs privileges.

Spandau was already able to celebrate its 750th anniversary in 1982. Then West German president, Karl Carstens, travelled "from Berlin" especially for the event—just as genuine Spandauers do not simply go to the Kurfürstendamm, but go "to Berlin". Spandau is alone in offering a local daily newspaper.The *Volksblatt* (circulation 40,000) is now edited and printed in the old publishing house in the Neuendorfer Strasse, where the *Anzeiger für das Havelland* once appeared.

Some believe Spandau's union with Berlin was only properly finalized by the subway link. Since 1 October 1984, the extended line 7 has been transporting people between the city and the heart of Spandau in 25 minutes.

As if to make up to her big sister for the loss of her independence, the Berlin Board of Works took great care with the decoration of the last three subway stations. In the terminus at the **Rathaus** (town hall) "Spandau-at-the-gates-of-Berlin" welcomes its visitors in a post-modern setting: black marble columns, gleaming brass and nostalgic light fixtures. The consecration on the gables of the town hall, which was built between 1910 and 1913, reads: "Under the rule of Kaiser Wilhelm II."

A number of bus routes lead from Rathausplatz on Carl-Schurz Strasse into the suburbs. After the war, 60,000 new homes were built here, mainly concentrated in highrise groups such as those found at Heer Strasse-Nord or at Falkenhagener Feld. Spandau's present population of about 213,000 is almost double that of 1945.

On the citadel: Spandau's importance as a trade and fortress town rested on its choice location near the water. The copper plate engraver Magnus Merian captured this in 1652 in one of the earliest drawings of the city. Directly in front of the old town, at the present-day **Lindenufer**, two navigable rivers meet. The Havel flows from Mecklenburg in the north-east and connects with the Spree on its course to the Elbe. Before continuing on, the medieval trade route from Magdeburg to Poland also passed the town, encouraging the need for a strategic fortified look-out.

Brandenburg noblemen were quick to recognise this need. Documents show that Spandau has had a fortress since 1197. Elector Joachim II ordered it extended in 1557 into an "impregnable modern fortress". The master builder Chiaramella de Gandino composed a mighty moated castle in high renaissance-style with four pointed bastions. Since then the **Zitadelle Spandau**, the Spandau citadel, has often been considered a "masterpiece of modern Italian fortress construction."

No other similar European fortress has been so well preserved. As the mighty brick walls come into view through the trees beyond the **Zitadellenbrücke** (Citadel's Bridge), they glimmer with a reddish hue. The oldest part of the citadel is the 40-foot (12-metre) thick **Juliusturm** (tower) which dates back to the medieval Spandow castle which was the residence of the Brandenburg noblemen and princes. A wooden spiral staircase leads up to a 100-foot (30-metre) high observation platform from where an excellent sweeping view of the dappled Spandau countryside can be enjoyed. The heavily armed citadel was intended to guard the river-crossing on the road to Berlin. When the

Prussian court, including the queen, her sister-in-law and the heir fled to Spandau in the Seven Years War, they took with them the royal finances, silverware and secret documents.

The castle also served as the Prussian state prison where the rulers had officials and political hot-heads locked up. These included, in March, 1848, "Turnvater Jahn" (father of gymnastics) and 1,495 Berlin revolutionaries. After the 1870-71 war, the eight-foot (2.3-metre) thick walls of the tower protected the state war coffers gathered from French reparation payments: 120 million marks in gold coins, packed in 1,200 boxes. In 1919, the gold was returned to the new victor as war compensation. Later the citadel which, from the air, looks like a huge star was used by the military until 1945. In 1817, it already housed a secret rocket laboratory. The top secret military gas research laboratory, where the army experimented with highly toxic substances, which were either simply buried or sunk into wells at the end of World War I was also located here.

Now, life is peaceful on the citadel (open daily except Mondays). In the **Kommandantenhaus** (Commander's House), on the right just after the rail bridge, the **Heimatmuseum Spandau** has occasional exhibitions such as "Spandau and European History". Concerts, art exhibitions and poetry readings are held in the **Palas** (Knight's Hall). In the evenings visitors can dine by candlelight while being serenaded by medieval minstrel music.

Through the old town: The Citadel lies on an island outside the town centre. The bridge **Am Juliusturm** crosses to the right bank of the Havel and the **Old Town**. Just downstream from the bridge Spandau's oldest part, the **Kolk**, stretches to the north. Time seems to stand still when we stroll on the cobblestones past 18th- and 19th-century dwellings. The names of the three streets recall old settlements: **Behnitz** already belonged to Spandau in the 13th

Spandau
Citadel and
tower.

century. A direct passage used to lead from the Kolk to the Citadel, and an army building once stood at Behnitz 3. In the evening the locally billeted artillery troops made merry in the three village inns. The fishing village **Damm** lay on the edge of the Kolk and, to this day, the allotments still possess royal fishing rights.

At the Kolk, or to be more precise, at the intersection of Möllentordamm and the Behnitz, there is a small "balcony" from where one can observe the **Schleuse Spandau** (lock) in operation. Paddle boats, motorboats, yachts, tugs and barges (even the tourist steamer *Moby Dick*) have to pass through this needle's eye linking the upper and lower Havel. The lock will soon be enlarged by a second chamber to allow trans-European ships to reach the industrial area in the upper Havel. Yearly, more than 35,000 boats and ships push their way across the north-south passage. West Berlin has a weekend fleet of about 75,000 yachts and motorboats

and about 100 water-sport clubs have sprouted on Spandau's shores. At the Weinmeisterhorn, downstream from the **Frey-Brücke**, is the start of a 2,000-metre regatta course. The peak season for weekend sailors, of course, is the summer. The lock stays open a full 17 hours a day.

On the other side of the bridge the typically medieval, ovally laid out old town spreads before you. Built in the first half of the 15th century **St. Nicolai**, one of the oldest gothic churches in the March, rises in the middle of the town's historic centre. Rochus, Count of Lynar, the masterbuilder who completed the construction of the Citadel in 1594, was the donator of the renaissance altar. A bronze statue in front of the main door commemorates Elector Joachim II's conversion to Protestantism in 1539. The life of Spandau's towns-people lives on around **Reformationsplatz**.

The remnants of the Middle Ages are in fact lying just under the paving. The walls of a 13th-century Dominican ab-

Changing of the Guards at the now torn down Spandau Allied Prison.

178

bey were discovered during excavation work for a new building. The ruins are carefully preserved in an "archeological basement" which can easily be viewed from the outside through large glass panes.

Two shopping streets, **Carl-Schurz Strasse** and **Breite Strasse**, run through the old town toward the town hall. The **Markt** (market) with its pedestrian zone, the Spandau horse market and the Christmas market is much busier than the reformation quarter. In the surrounding alleys, where craftsmen and yeomen lived, a piece of old Spandau has survived. Although many a half-timbered house fell victim to the post-war craze for new houses, Spandauers have once again learnt to respect the buildings inherited from their ancestors. At Breite Strasse 32 the **Gotisches Haus**, probably Berlin's oldest dwelling, is being restored.

Growing Spandau: Until the beginning of this century, Spandau led the life of an enclosed fortress town. As early as the 14th century, it had already surrounded itself with a defensive wall, some picturesque remnants of which can be seen in **Kinkel Strasse**. Spandau more and more became a military town and Prussia's arsenal ("Waffenschmiede"). Its first factories were set up for military purposes: in the 18th century the Prussian army erected a carbine factory, then came ammunition factories (19th century), artillery works and a canon foundry. Their products are displayed today in the citadel's courtyard. It was only after the removal of expansion restrictions in 1903 that Spandau started to grow beyond its old limits and the **Neustadt** (New Town) grew up along the roads which lead to the north.

Lack of living quarters for the many Spandau armament workers led during and after World War I to the establishment of the **Gartenstadt Staaken** along the lines of an English country town, with 1,200 apartments (bus 31). The sociologist Franz Oppenheimer compared this social settlement of architect Paul Schmitthenner with one of those harmoniously grown Franconian medieval small towns "where the human being was still a citizen and not just a number...." Even today, the colony of semi-detached houses at Heidebergplatz is a coveted piece of real estate.

North of Spandau, in the 3,985 acre (1,577-hectare) **town forest** that stretches from the Havel to the East German border and which is interspersed with idyllic moors lies the **Evangelisches Johannisstift** (Protestant St. John's Home). Father Johann Heinrich Wichern initiated the home as a centre of Christian charity in Moabit in 1858. It moved to Spandau in 1920, and today around 2,500 people including young and old, healthy, handicapped and infirm live and work in this charitable institution. The foundation serves as a meeting place for the synod and other church commitees, and houses a school for church music.

In the south, beyond the disused railway line to Staaken, Spandau merges

Spandau Lock.

with the former Potsdam suburb of **Wilhelmstadt**. The military also dominates here. On the Wilhelmstrasse stand a number of camouflaged vehicles alongside barrack buildings from the Imperial and Nazi eras. Today, the buildings are occupied by most of Britain's Berlin Field Force. The **Gatow military air base** farther out now receives VIP's such as Princess Margaret, Princess Diana and other members of the Royal Family who come to visit their Spandau batallions.

Spandau's former military prison at Wilhelmstrasse 21-24 was surrounded, until recently, by high walls and multi-lingual warning signs . It was erected in 1878-81 and could hold 600 prisoners. In 1947, the four victorious powers used it to intern seven of the main defendants in the Nuremburg trials including Rudolf Hess, Hitler's former deputy, who was sentenced to life imprisonment. After 1966 he was the only remaining prisoner until his suicide in 1987.

Guarded monthly in turn by the British, French, Soviets and Americans, he led an eerie hermit's existence. A pardon would have only been possible by an unanimous decision on the part of the four Allied Powers. However, although Hess was over 90 and half-blind, the Soviets blocked his release even 40 years after the end of the war. After his suicide in 1987 the prison, whose upkeep had cost one million marks annually, was quickly and quietly torn down.

Town among fields: Visiting **Gatow** and **Kladow** reveals the frail charm of the Havelland area. From the Wannsee S-Bahn station, one can take a trip on the regularly operating ferry of the BVG passenger line. Both villages in Spandau's deep south were incorporated in 1920. They still lead a separate life centred on their historic churches, although more and more villas are forcing their way between the last few remaining farm-houses of West Berlin.

In Kladow's former slaughterhouse at **Sakrower Kirchweg**, one can visit Kurt Mühlenhaupt in the studio where

he has lived since 1975. This former barrel organ player and junkman is famous for his paintings of Kreuzberg.

About 40 per cent of Spandau's surface area is either water or greenery. Two fishermen, the last of their trade, cast their nets in the morning mist on the Havel. There are also 69 farms, cultivating a total of 1605 acres (650 hectares) of productive land in the district. Billowing wheat fields in Kladow are no strange sight in summer, and in Gatow a farmer might sell you milk from his cows or fresh eggs. In Gatow, on formerly irrigated fields, rare ferns and birds have reappeared. The **Gatow heath**, a 865-acre (350- hectare) nature reserve, is a beautiful place to enjoy long walks.

Any description of Spandau is incomplete without mention of its industrial antipode, the **Siemensstadt.** In 1899, the rapidly growing electrical firm of Siemens & Halske opened a cable and dynamo factory on the Nonnendamm-allee. Land along the Spree then cost seven pfennigs per square metre, but the workers had to contend with a long walk or commuting by steamer. By 1906, the factory, which stood at the gates of Charlottenburg, already had 10,000 employees, and was absorbed by Spandau and officially christened "Siemens-town".

In the 1920s, it developed into a model example of a factory-town among the fields, with its own housing areas which now spread from Siemensdamm to the Jungfernheide. The skyline of the "electropolis" is shaped by the functional brick architecture of Hans Hertlein. Its most distinctive mark is the 233-foot (70-metre) high **Siemensturm** (tower) at the Werner-Werk für Messwerktechnik.

About 60,000 people were employed in "Siemens town" during the 1930s: today, the number has fallen to only 20,000. However, Siemens, which has moved its headquarters to Munich, remains the largest employer in Berlin's electrical industry.

THE BRITISH IN BERLIN

On 27 May, the Queen's birthday, the *Berlin Infantry Brigade* marches onto the Olympic Stadium's Maifeld. Tanks fire salutes and helicopters with coloured smoke trails buzz past the VIP rostrum. Spectators then witness a spectacle reminiscent of medieval war-fare when the regimental flag served as a regrouping point for soldiers at the height of a battle. Then the Queen's colours are carried past the assembled troops at the *Trooping of the Colour* ceremony. Heir to the throne, Prince Charles, Princess Margaret or another member of the Royal Family fly in from England specially for the occasion.

Military music, colourful tunics, parades: in their sector, which includes the districts of Wilmersdorf, Tiergarten, Charlottenburg and Spandau, the British certainly offer a great deal of tradition and style. On friendship days and district festivals, they send their regimental bands. Scottish pipers in colorful kilts attract great interest wherever they appear. They are a welcome company at private parties or for commercials and can be hired for a fee. The climax of "Britain on Show" is the *Tattoo* in the Deutschlandhalle. Every two years, in the largest military ceremony outside Britain, the army goes through its paces in a two-and-a-half hour show.

Otherwise, the 3,500 or so British soldiers keep a relatively low profile. The Spandau garrison does not expose its activities to public gaze. Fitness training, target practice, weapon instruction, manoeuvres in Grunewald and West Germany fill out the service timetable. Patrols along the East German border, and the monotonous watch at Spandau Allied Prison until the death of Rudolf Hess in 1987 were, some additional

tasks. Surprise practice alarms, day or night, test the defences; even the desk-bound officers in the British headquarters keep their steel helmets and battledress ready near their desks. The commanding officer, a major general, and his aides have their offices in a cordoned-off part of the Olympic Stadium.

The British, like the Americans, maintain a ghost town for practicing street combat. In *Ruhleben Fighting Village* rookie soldiers with blank cartridges and blackened faces act out their combat orders: delaying resistance. If combined with the Americans and the French, the British would be too few to withstand a determined attack from the Warsaw Pact countries. "But, there are still enough of us to prevent us from being taken by surprise," claim Allied military. If it came to the real thing, it would be essential to put up enough resistance to force a period of regrouping and negotiation.

British forces in Berlin consist of an army brigade of three infantry battalions. Each battalion is accompanied by a tank and a pioneer unit with corresponding logistic and administrative sections. The infantry and tank units are rotated every two years. Some, like the 750 Scots of *The King's Own Scottish Borderers* have returned for a third tour of duty. Other troop units, for example the *29th Signals Regiment* or the *Army Air Support* on Gatow RAF air base, are stationed permanently in Berlin. British troops consist mainly of long-service recruits and professional soldiers. About 65 per cent of them are married and bring their wives and children with them.

Including the civilian clerks in the military administration, about 12,500 Britons with Allied status live in Berlin, tucked away mainly in housing areas on the Heerstrasse and in Spandau.

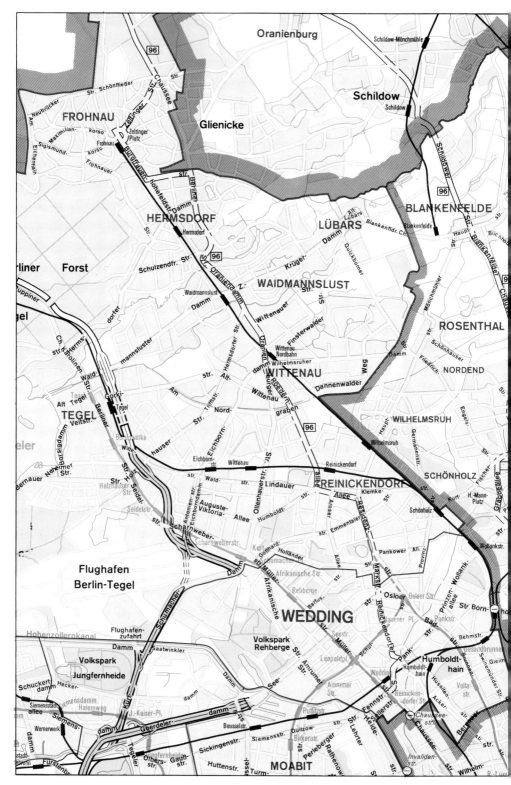

REINICKENDORF

About 4 million travellers annually pass through the hexagonal customs hall of Tegel Airport. Few are aware that they have landed in Reinickendorf, the northernmost of West Berlin's twelve districts. When Berlin's Tempelhof airport could no longer cope with the increasing numbers of arrivals, one of the most modern and large capacity airports in Germany was developed in Tegel. Since 1975, Tegel Airport has been the terminus for all air traffic to and from Berlin.

Tegel has written air travel history. In 1909 Count Zeppelin's airship landed here. In 1931 Werner von Braun and Hermann Oberth fired the first liquid fuel rockets. Tegel was the site of the first landings of the Berlin Airlift in 1948-49, and it was at Tegel that the French introduced the era of jet travel to Berlin with the *Caravelle*.

The "green north": Flying into Tegel Reinickendorf offers a wonderful panorama of woods and lakes that, as with Spandau, make up the greater part of this district. Reinickendorf is called the "green north" and there is a good reason for naming it thus: almost a quarter of its surface area consists of vast forests. However, fields, meadows and former villages such as Lübars, where people still make a living from farming, are also part of the Reinickendorf picture. In addition, there are the luxury villa districts of Frohnau and Hermsdorf, and the contrasting highrises of the Märkisches Viertel, Germany's most notorius large housing project of the 1960s.

The district is the city's largest, covering a total of 34 sq miles (89 sq km). Not only is it a popular area for weekend relaxation, but it also includes an industrial area north of the airport where, among others, the long-standing Borsig company has been operating for more than 90 years.

In the middle of the 19th century the Berlin inventor and engineer August Borsig cornered the market with his locomotives, driving off the British competition. The stature of the firm at the turn of the century is evident by the **Borsig Gate**, an arch ornamented with towers and pinnacles at the factory entrance on Berliner Strasse.

It contrasts sharply with the 12-storey administration building standing behind it, Berlin's first high-rise office complex erected between 1922 and 1924, mainly to overcome the shortage of space on company grounds. Today, the situation is reversed. The manufacture of products takes up less room. Borsig only uses a small part of its premises for production, while the **Borsig Tower**, long considered a landmark, has been rented out to another company. Now, Borsig employs 2,000 Berliners, and a new administrative building is rising on the southern part on company's grounds.

The old village of Tegel, the heart of

BERLIN-TEGEL

AEG-TELEFUNKEN

which lies a short distance to the north, lost its rural character in the wake of industrialisation. On the other hand, it is the only place in Berlin whose shopping area can be reached by steamer. The street Alt-Tegel, a pedestrian precinct since 1976, connects the shopping centre with the **Greenwich Promenade** and the landing stage for the steamers crossing Lake Tegel. The Havel Bay esplanade is the starting-point for many delightful hikes along the shore.

Yet, the picturesque view of the lake is deceptive. Biologists first sounded the alarm 20 years ago when increasing quantities of phosphate threatened to pollute Lake Tegel. A phosphate elimination plant architectonicly shaped like an "environmental steamer" went into operation in 1985, in order to improve the quality of the water. This peculiar construction on the Budde Strasse in Tegel cost about 200 million marks and was part of the International Building Exhibition (IBA).

Castles and guest-houses: Schloss Tegel in the **Tegel forest** is a gem. Built by the Great Elector as a hunting-lodge, it has been in the possession of the von Humboldt family since 1766. Some of the villas in Grunewald seem larger and more prestigious than this small, modest castle in the north of Tegel. However, it was here that the famous brothers Alexander and Wilhelm von Humboldt grew up. Wilhelm, later the owner, laid out the master-plan of the Prussian education system and founded the Berlin University.

Wilhelm had the house extended by Karl Friedrich Schinkel, between 1820 and 1824, in order to provide a suitable setting for his great art collection. The small castle has remained in the possession of a descendant of the Humboldts, who decided to open the park and family crypt to visitors during the summer.

Diagonally across Lake Tegel, on the **Reihenwerder** peninsula, the façade of a castle-like building shimmers through the trees. Ernst Borsig, grandson of the locomotive king and owner of the Tegel works, had this sumptuous villa built in 1911. The **Villa Borsig**, known to most Berliners only from a distance or as the setting for district garden concerts in the summer, has been a conference centre for the **Deutsche Stiftung für Internationale Entwicklung**, (the German Foundation for International Development), since 1959.

Since then, some 30,000 experts and executives from around the world have met here to discuss questions and problems of international development and co-operation.

Not far from the Villa Borsig, at the junction of Karolinen- and Heiligensee Strasse, two restaurants compete for the title of the "oldest inn in Berlin." **Alter Fritz** was still called the "Neuer Krug" when the young crown prince Frederich changed horses and had a mug of beer on his way to Rheinsberg. Other famous guests of the house were the Humboldt brothers and Goethe, who stopped here

Country life in Lübars.

186

in 1778 during his only journey to Berlin. It is said that the innkeeper told him ghost stories, which he later used in Faust II: "The devil's pack, it pays no heed to rules, we are so clever, and yet in Tegel there are ghouls."

Opposite the "Alter Fritz", which currently is closed, stands the **Alte Waldschenke** whose popularity dates to this century. Before that it served as quarters for day labourers. Although there are no exact sources, the simple half-timbered house is said to have been built between 1760 and 1770.

Buddha's Temple: Reinickendorf's country castles reflect its heritage gleaned from the Brandenburg March. Of a more recent period is the **Buddhist Temple** on Edelhofdamm. Approximately 300 members of Berlin's Buddhist community meet not far from the centre of the affluent and exclusive suburb of Frohnau. They are instructed and ministered by four Sri Lankan monks. The temple, which is situated in a park on a hill, was built during the

1920s by the doctor and philologist, Dr. Paul Dahlke. He had converted to Buddhism while journeying in Sri Lanka and, after his death, he was buried in the temple garden.

The Russian orthodox have a small chapel with onion-domed towers and a cemetery on Witte Strasse, overlooking the Tegel Autobahn. In 1894, when the **Russian orthodox chapel** was built in what was formerly Dalldorf, the Berlin congregation numbered just a few members of the court aristocracy and the intelligentsia. So that they might rest in peace after their death far from home, Tsar Alexander III saw to it personally that 40 tons of earth were taken from Russia to Berlin.

The parish grew when, after the 1917 Revolution, thousands of emigrants sought new homes in Berlin. Aristocrats, generals, ministers, artists, and soldiers who died as prisoners-of-war in Berlin, were buried here with their heads pointed east according to Russian-Orthodox custom. Today, the

Into town by bus.

community numbers 200 and is, according to long-standing tradition, ministered by a priest sent from Russia. The language of the church service is Church-Slavonic.

A better life: Around the turn of the century, when Berlin was still expanding, exclusive residential areas appeared in Zehlendorf and Grunewald. The north also became, and remains, a popular place to live for the well-off. The **Gartenstadt Frohnau**, hemmed in on two sides by the Wall, seems as tranquil as a secluded spa-town. In former times, the air here was supposed to have been so good that throat specialists recommended that opera singers lived in Frohnau. Cosy red brick houses line the Zeltinger Platz at the district's centre. The S-Bahn provides nine quick and comfortable connections to the city centre.

The "garden city" was designed between 1908 and 1910 by two university professors, Brix and Grenzmer. One of its special attractions, apart from the good air, is the polo field, the only one in Berlin since 1910. The development society, a novelty, tried to attract affluent Berliners to Frohnau with newspaper ads and even cinema publicity. But it was the beautiful surroundings that moved the poet Oskar Loerke to use his inheritance to purchase a piece of land at Kreuzritter Strasse 8, where he built a house for himself, his wife and an engineer friend. Loerke, who was ostracised by the Nazis, died in 1941 and was buried in the cemetery on Hainbuchen Strasse.

At "Bonnie's Ranch": Reinickendorf, or to be more exact the quarter of Wittenau, is known for an institution which the Berliners cheekily, often discriminately call "Bonnie's Ranch". The nickname is common among junkies. They are referring to the **Karl-Bonhoeffer-Nervenklinik** on Oranienburger Chaussee, West Berlin's biggest psychiatric hospital, which also cares for heroin addicts trying to get off the needle. Between 40 and 50 drug addicts

The historic Borsig Gate.

die each year in Berlin.

In its 100-year history, the clinic has had some prominent patients, such as princess Anastasia, the only surviving daughter of the last Russian Tsar. Following her flight from Russia, she jumped into the Landwehrkanal in despair. She was pulled out of the water by a policeman, and a medical officer had the then unknown would-be suicide admitted to Wittenau. Two years passed before she was recognised by compatriots and released.

The clinic had been founded under the name of "Dalldorf municipal insane asylum." The local farmers felt exceedingly uncomfortable about having a hospital of this nature in their immediate vicinity. The place was therefore renamed Wittenau in 1905, after Peter Witte, the chairman of the local council.

It gained a reputation among experts for its attempts to not only keep the unfortunate lodgers under lock and key, but also to provide therapy for them. However, the clinic's history during the Third Reich was less reputable. Within the walls unscrupulous doctors and nurses comitted euthanasia crimes on the defenceless patients.

The **Rathaus** (city hall) was built by the community of Wittenau in 1911 on what is now Eichborndamm; the building has been the seat of the district administration since 1953.

The Märkisches Viertel: A few kilometres away bristle the 16-storey highrise blocks of a satellite town. This suburb became notorious throughout the Federal Republic as an example of bad town planning. The Märkische Viertel is regarded as a classic example of the impersonal, purely technocratic building style of the 1960s. The nickname of the longest and ugliest of the buildings on Wilhelmsruher Damm speaks for itself: "Langer Jammer" ("Long misery"). It was designed by René Gages and Volker Theissen.

The satellite town, with its 17,000 flats housing 50,000 people, was conceived between 1963 and 1974 in order to offer a new kind of living in "light, air and sun" to families who were forced out of the inner-city by development and high rents. Progress was being "concreted".

In spite of extensive criticism by psychologists and sociologists, there are by now many "Neumärker" who identify themselves with their quarter. By the start of the 1990s, the subway should extend to the Märkisches Viertel. This should alleviate one of the suburb's problems: its the great distance from the city centre.

The **Fontane-Haus** in the shopping precinct provides some cultural diversions for those who do not feel like embarking on the long journey into the city. Sometimes, members of the German Opera give performances here. The Schiller-Theater also offers interesting theatrical productions. At the Senftenberger Ring two attractions are worth seeing: Germany's first **Abenteuerspielplatz**, or adventure playground, created on the initiative of par-

At the northern ring of the "Stadtautobahn", the cityhighway.

ents and children who found the quarter's recreational facilities inadequate; and at Senftenberger Ring 25 there is the **Kinderspielhaus,** the children's playhouse, said to be the first solid and heated edifice built into the ground in so-called "earthern construction style", by the innovative Berlin architect, Engelbert Kremser.

By ferry-boat to Spandau: A favourite goal for the residents of the Märkisches Viertel—and for others—is the village of **Lübars,** its fields stretching right up to the high-rises. Seven farmers still grow corn here on 346 acres (140 hectares) of land. From the Tegeler Fliess nature reserve, which is part of Lübars, one can see the watch-towers of the GDR border posts.

In the west of Reinickendorf, the residential suburbs of **Konradshöhe** and **Tegelort** are squeezed between the Tegel forest and the Havel. This, by the way, is where Berlin's only car ferry runs, taking the traveller from Tegel over the Havel to Spandau's Aaleman-

nufer. The "Hol über" ("haul across") runs in both summer and in winter and rates are reasonable. Everything on wheels is transported, and even a rider on horseback is not an uncommon sight on the ferry which can take loads of up to 65 tons or about 200 people.

Finally, right up in the north is the sleepy fishing village of **Heiligensee,** one of 30 colonies to have appeared on Berlin's periphery during the Middle Ages. The farmsteads around the village green on the Strasse Alt-Heiligensee still suggest the unspoilt character of the place.

Heiligensee's most famous inhabitant lies buried in the churchyard next to the 16th century church: the painter Hanna Höch (1890-1978) who was regarded as the creator of the "collage technique", combining painting and assemblage of other two, sometimes three-dimensional graphic objects. In the early 1920s she was the only woman to join the artists' association "Dada-Berin" through her friend Raoul Hausmann. Ostracised by the Nazis as "degenerate", she retired in 1939 to a kind of summer house at An der Wildbahn 33, and struggled to support herself on her garden produce until the end of the war. She also hid irreplaceable mementoes of the Dada movement in her little residence.

At the edge of the village the Ruppiner Chaussee runs straight towards the border checkpoint Heiligensee. It has been used since 1982 by transit travellers to Scandinavia and for visitors to the German Democratic Republic. In 1988, a controversial feeder road cutting through the Tegel forest to the northern highway that leads to Hamburg, was opened. Since then all long-distance traffic rolls through Reinickendorf. Local residents and conservationists have, for many years, opposed the construction of such roads but without much success. Not only do they cut up the Tegel Fliess reserve, but it also means that numerous trees in the Tegel forest must be sacrificed.

Left, Buddhist Monk in the Frohnau temple garden. Right, "open house" at the Quartier Napoleon garrison.

THE FRENCH IN BERLIN

The striking thing about the 2,700 French soldiers in Berlin is their youthfulness. The explanation is simple: while Britain and the USA have purely professional armies, France conscripts its boys for service on the Spree river.

Almost three-quarters of the contingent are 18- and 19-year-old recruits, many of whom were mustered straight after their apprenticeship or after high school. Every two months, a batch of new recruits arrives at the Tegel garrison station. They come mainly from northern France and Paris, most carrying call-up papers for the 46th Infantry Regiment *La Tour d'Auvergne* or for the 11th Rifle Regiment in their pockets. After two months in boot camp, they join their respective units, where they do intensive combat training in, among other things, street-fighting and anti-tank tactics.

Both regiments make up the nucleus of the Berlin garrison. They also perform tasks specific to Berlin such as patrolling the GDR border or, formerly, doing their guard-duty in Spandau. Supporting them are sapper and telecommunications companies which are stationed in the Reinickendorf *Quartier Napoléon*, as well as transport, staff and medical services. In addition, housed elsewhere, are 300 air force personnel at Tegel airport and a detachment of the *Gendarmerie Nationale*. The city's commanding officer, who holds the rank of major general, functions as Supreme Commander. He has to keep his forces constantly prepared to go on the defensive within two hours. Around the clock, a detachment of motorised infantry and tanks with three *AMX 30's* primed with live ammunition is

available for deployment within five minutes of an alarm. Colonel Jean-Luis Mourrut of the 11th Rifle Regiment who, like all his fellow officers and NOC's on the resident staff, remains in Berlin for three years, is full of praise for his one-year servicemen. "These *garçons* are highly motivated. They see the sense in defending freedom for mankind."

For most, military service in Berlin also means the first lengthy separation from their families. However, this bitter pill is sweetened by a 56-day leave for visits back home. Relatives, fiancées included, are also allowed one visit, with free transportation in a military train. The Berlin district mayors try to help the young Frenchmen to settle in with all sorts of invitations and social functions. Reinickendorf has adopted the Tank Battalion: Wedding the infantrymen.

Once a year the French stage an open house at their military town on the Kurt-Schumacher-Damm, an area of barracks extending over 200 acres (80 hectares) which once belonged to Göring's air force. Then the Berliners, particularly families from the north, come for a visit. Information stands and champagne bars are set up in army tents. For a minor fee one can try all sorts of delicacies such as *crépes* or *merquez*, a hot and spicy speciality from North Africa. The Music Corps of the Marine Infantry is flown in from Paris. Also on Bastille Day, 14 July, the French make a show of their presence in Berlin that is popular among the public. Desire of and curiosity for things French sustain the traditional "Volksfest" on the Kurt-Schumacher-Damm for three weeks, and the *25 kilometres de Berlin* marathon, started some years ago by the garrison, now draws over 10,000 participants with the symbols of Berlin and France.

WEDDING

"Red Wedding greets you comrades, keep your fists ready, close ranks for our day is not far away...!" This proletarian warrior song by Erich Weinert from the 1920s was once typical of the district's reputation. It was already a stronghold of socialist workers' movement during the Kaiser's reign. On 9 November, 1918, AEG and Schwarzkopff workers marched into the government district brandishing the red flag of revolution. Against a background of increasing unemployment, the Communists were winning more and more supporters towards the end of the Weimar Republic. In the Reichstag elections of 1928 they gained more votes than the Social Democrats and, for the first time, became the strongest party.

When the engineering and electrical industries settled in Berlin's northern suburbs at the end of the last century, thousands of workers moved to Gesundbrunnen and Wedding. Both districts had belonged to Berlin since 1861 but now building lots were in short supply. Five-floor tenements with dingy yards sprang up in large numbers. In the 1920s, over 350,000 people lived on a cramped six-sq miles (15-sq km) tract of land: most of them inhabited dank, dark, crowded apartments. Rampant poverty and factory work—those working at all could count themselves lucky—defined day-to-day life in working-class Wedding.

Proletarian existence: "Hallways, rooms, a forest of housing blocks, everything unbearably close together. Everyone smelled each other through the walls, cracks and wooden partitions. Tenants, sub-tenants, lodgers and the curse of this alley—children, not one of whom could sleep in its own bed." This was how Klaus Neukrantz described the poverty in Kösliner Strasse in his banned 1930 novel *Barrikaden am Wedding*, "the street with most poverty-stricken children in the whole of starving Berlin", where tailors and seamstresses had already organised the first strike for higher wages in 1896. After the Social Democratic police president Zörgiebel had disbanded a Communist demonstration, "bloody May", 1929, saw barricades erected and street-fighting in Wedding. Riot police used armoured cars, and 19, mostly innocent bystanders, were killed. A few months later, when the Nazis demonstratively drove a truck with election propaganda through Berlin's "reddest street", they were greeted with stones, bottles and chamber pots thrown from the windows: 98 Weddingers were later to pay with their lives for opposition to the National Socialist regime.

The new Wedding: Present-day Wedding has only 155,000 inhabitants. Slightly more than one square mile (297 hectares), a good one-fifth of the district, has been turned into recreational space, located mainly around Humboldthain, the artificial hill Bunkerberg, the Schillerpark and the Rehberge Volkspark. The last named is well-known for its summer open-air theatre. Promenades with trees and bushes flank the banks of the river **Panke** that flows north from Pankow through Wedding.

Still and yet, the population density of 25,000 people per square mile is about 50 percent higher than Berlin's average. The district is like the neighbouring East Berlin district of Prenzlauer Berg, a place for the common man where, in addition to Turkish, you can hear the real Berlin dialect. A web of train tracks has disfigured the industrial southern section and old Berlin cast iron pissoirs, so-called "eight-cornered cafés" still decorate some street corners. Otherwise one must look closely for signs of the traditional proletarian scene. On Wiesen Strasse 58 the shabby façades of the **Wiesenburg** are hidden behind trees. With 1,282 beds this building was once one of the largest hostels for the homeless in Berlin, and is to be placed on the list of protected monuments.

A glance at the restored **Brunnen-strasse** area indicates how it has changed its appearance since the war. This large area of new buildings was once one of the most poverty-stricken parts, especially south of the **Gresundbrunnen** S-Bahn station. A striking example was "Meyer's Hof" at Acker Strasse 132-33—a run-down tenement with six courtyards. Up to 2,000 people lived in 230 tiny apartments with only outdoor toilets. To once and for all rid itself of its grey stone cubicles and the image of misery, the local government decided in the 1960s to relocate tenants on both sides of Brunnen Strasse and Bad Strasse, which resulted in changes of the local socio-economic structure.

Computers for turbines: Wedding's industrial pattern has also undergone transformation. Nothing symbolises this more than the deserted **AEG gateway** of 1891 in the Brunnen Strasse. One hundred years of Berlin's indus-trial history ended when the electrical concern founded by Emil Rathenau in 1883 had to shut down its production lines in Wedding in 1984. Now the shiny brown façades of an ultra-modern glass palace reflect the former "white collar entrance", a delicate, neo-gothic brick gateway. The computer company **Nixdorf** set up a new company employing 6,000 people on the site (No. 111). The old AEG buildings stretch as far as Ackerstrasse. Among them was a small motor plant on Voltastrasse, and a heavy machine plant on Hussiten Strasse which bore the sobriquet the "cathedral of work".

Today, the area is known as "Silicon Wedding"—the era of micro-electronics has come to the AEG complex. Berlin's "Innovations- und Gründerzentrum" (BIG) is situated at Acker Strasse 76. Technology-oriented small businesses can exchange information here, and have the opportunity to work in close association with the Technische Universität (TU) in order to get off the

Tenement block with cast iron pissoir.

194

ground with newly developed products and services. Other factory buildings are used by the TU as a "Technology and Innovation park". The **Kunstquartier Acker Strasse** has established its exhibition premises in one of the old factory buildings. Environment artist Ben Wargin's highly original work is on display in the courtyard.

On Müller Strasse: The largest employer in Wedding now is **Schering AG**, where about 5,000 people work in an extensive factory complex on **Weddingplatz**. The company, a chemical and pharmaceutical concern, has about 20,000 employees worldwide, a fact it boasts with a 14-floor aluminium-lined construction housing the company's administration. Together with the almost as high research building, it dominates the southwest corner of Wedding. Schering, known for its contraceptive pills and other pharmaceutical specialities, is the only company of world standing to have retained its headquarters in Berlin. It all started at Ernst Schering's

"Grüne Apotheke" ("Green Pharmacy") on **Müller Strasse**, today's main business street and administration centre of the district. The street's southern extension, the Chaussee Strasse, is bisected by the Wall at the corner of Liesen Strasse.

Wedding's **Rathaus** at the Leopoldplatz subway station consists of a 163-foot (49-metre) high administration tower, connected by a glassed-in walkway to the original clinker brick town hall of the 1920s. The Berlin headquarters of the Social Democrats are also on Müllerstrasse (No. 163) in the **Kurt-Schumacher-Haus**. Social Democrats have guided communal politics in the district from the very beginning. The first SPD mayor, Carl Leid, had Wedding's first welfare housing estate built, the **Afrikanisches Viertel** with "cube homes", by Mies van der Rohe. Other architects of the Weimar Republic such as Bruno Taut, Paul Emmerich or Paul Mebes, with their apartment buildings in the **Fried-**

Bernauer Strasse–clearing the death-strip behind the Wall.

rich-Ebert-Siedlung, gave a convincing retort to the degrading tenement blocks of the late 19th century.

Two neo-classical suburban churches based on K.F. Schinkel's designs are amongst the oldest historical buildings in the district. The **Alte Nazarethkirche**, built in 1935 on Leopoldplatz, has round arches which are reminiscent of an early Christian basilica. The **St.-Pauls-Kirche**, on the corner of Bad Strasse and Pank Strasse in the Gesundbrunnen quarter, has pillars and a stuccoed façade giving it the appearance of an antique temple.

Science and research: The district's name is derived from the village and later the estate named "Weddinge" that once stood on the busy, present-day **Nettelbeckplatz**. The **Gesundbrunnen** quarter, named after a beneficial spring near the Panke, developed around what is now Badstrasse. Legend has it that King Frederick I asked for a drink of water while hunting in the area. The water was so refreshing that he had the spring protected by a wooden enclosure and its mineral content analysed. Later in the 18th century, a spa developed around the "Friedrichsgesundbrunnen". The spring was destroyed in 1882 in the course of the canalisation of the Panke. Soon after, the Industrial Revolution came to this area, known as "Plumpe" in the vernacular, and brought with it more radical changes.

During the last decades Wedding has become increasingly renowned as a centre for scientific and medical theory and research. The institutions, many of which are well-known beyond Berlin's borders, are concentrated in the **Institutsviertel** around the Augustenburger Platz and Amrumer Strasse. They consist of the Technische Fachschule (Technical Academy), the Institut für Zuckerindustrie (Sugar Industry Institute) with the adjoining Zuckermuseum, (Sugar Museum) and the Institut für Gärungsgewerbe und Biotechnologie (Institute for Fermentation and Bio-technology), which teaches the noble art of beer brewing.

The **Rudolf-Virchow-Krankenhaus** extends as far as the northern bank of the Berlin-Spandau shipping canal. Virchow, famous doctor and Reichstag member, urged the erection of a hospital in the over-populated north of Berlin. The hospital, opened in 1906, was considered at that time to be a "garden city for the sick", a revolutionary complex with its 57 pavilions. Nature was supposed to help heal the patients. The **Deutsches Herzzentrum**, a private hospital on the grounds which specialised in heart diseases, can carry out up to 2,500 operations a year.

The bacteriologist and Nobel Prize winner Robert Koch (1843-1910), who discovered the cholera agent and tuberculosis bacillus, moved his institute for infectious diseases from the Charité hospital to Wedding's north bank around 1900. Today, the **Robert-Koch-Institut** and its 300 scientists are playing a key role in the fight against AIDS.

The "Hauptmann von Köpenick": Wedding's present-day Sylter Strasse was the scene of a military farce staged by an unemployed shoemaker Wilhelm Voigt. On 10 October 1906, Voigt disguised as a captain of the guards, stopped a troop on guard marching back to the barracks from the nearby **Freibad Plötzensee** (then a military swimming pool). He selected twelve men, "on grounds of high orders", to go with him to Köpenick where he occupied the town hall. In a brusque voice he arrested the mayor and confiscated the city treasury. Berlin's newspapers spread the news of the enterprise in special editions; even the emperor was heard to have laughed uproariously. Voigt, who already had a police record, was given a four year sentence, but only served two of them. For the rest of his life he charged a fee to appear in his uniform which he had rented from a dress shop. Voigt's hilarious exploit is still remembered in the Carl Zuckermayer play based on the above story.

Restoration instead of demolition.

THE WALL

If a newly arrived visitor decides to relax and to watch the news on television, he may well stumble on one of Berlin's peculiarities which may make him sense, even before he sees the Wall, that he is at the interface of two political continents which runs through this unique city.

From 7.30 a.m. to 8.15 p.m., two different men appear on the screen in front of a map of the world. The first gives his report and lays aside his papers. A change of channels reveals a colleague picking up his papers.

One is instantly struck by the close resemblance between these two men. The visitor might assume that they are close relatives, maybe even brothers. However, turn up the volume and the impression changes. Author Peter Schneider writes: "If these two are brothers, they have to be twin brothers who are bitterest enemies. The uppermost goal of each one, evening after evening and point for point, is to maintain the opposite of what the other has just said."

Is the divided city a giant German versus German television soap opera with each half stubbornly feuding with the other? Actually, the Berlin problem goes deeper than this confrontation every evening in front of the television cameras. That's how it was until November 1989. The brutality of the division of an entire city is gradually disappearing from the city itself as well as from the lives of the inhabitants. But even so, while out walking, one is still often confronted with the wall.

It appears suddenly at the end of a street. But its absurdity and ugliness, the neon glimmer, the watch-towers and the notorious no-man's-land are now no longer threatening. But the dramatic events which took place at the wall will never be forgotten. In the first 25 years of the Wall's existence, 74 people, of whom at least 57 were shot, died when trying to reach the west side.

The overall length of the wall around the three western sectors measures 103 miles (165 km), 34 miles or 45 km of it cuts through the city itself.

13 August 1961: Berlin was severed on a warm summer night. It followed a sunny Saturday that saw some Berliners getting out of the dusty city walls, "out to Mother Nature", to the Wannsee or Müggelsee. Others had, as usual, walked or driven to the West sector from the East sector. They had come to see a film, to shop for goods such as western cigarettes, nylons, and coffee, that were not available in East Berlin. Since the partitioning of the city by the victorious powers trade had flourished between the sectors. Stalls and movie cinemas appeared in great numbers along the border and entrepreneurs were quite happy to be paid with East-sector money at the then prevailing exchange rate of about 1:4 to 1:5. Friends and relatives from both sectors visited one another on this warm summer evening. Comrades met in the corner *"Kneipe"* over a beer, went dancing in one of the many ballrooms, or took the beautiful girl who lived a few houses away out on a date to the other side of the border. Jörg Schikowsky, for example, went to visit his 19-year old fiancée Sabine, who had an apartment on Jannowitzbrücke in East Berlin, as he did every weekend.

Almost a normal weekend, but not quite. Once again, on this Saturday, 2,662 refugees from all over the GDR were received at the refugee camp at Marienfelde. Some had crossed the border because they could no longer tolerate the state party invading every area of their lives, while others were attracted by western living standards. Since June of that year, the stream of refugees had swollen to avalanche proportions. After the Vienna Conference with Kennedy, Khrushchev had affirmed his decision to sign a separate peace-treaty with East Germany. A new development in the Berlin situation was

Preceding pages: watch-tower in the death-strip. **Left, remembering** the dead in Bernauer Straße.

in the air. "No one intends to erect a wall", Communist Party chief Ulbricht had said at an international press conference on 15 June. The decision was actually made at the beginning of August when, in Moscow, the party chiefs of all the Warsaw Pact countries conferred. Three possibilities that would meet the requirements of the Communist Party in East Germany for solving the Berlin question were under debate. Two of them—isolating the entire city from the GDR or closing the air-corridor—were rejected. That left the third one, a wall straight across Berlin.

As Jörg Schikowsky cycled home in the wee hours of the morning of 13 August he could scarcely believe what he saw before him. Army trucks were rolling through the eastern sector; tanks rumbled through the sleeping streets. The GDR "Volksarmee" and weapon-wielding members of the worker's militia leapt from troop transports. They took up positions along the East-West boundary, sub-machine-guns poised.

Barbed wire entanglements appeared.

A group of young people in evening attire came from a ball in the Esplanade hotel and watched, bewildered, as uniformed men tore up the asphalt a few feet away on Potsdamer Platz. Jörg Schikowsky was just able to slip into the western sector through a street that had yet to be reached by the soldiers. When his betrothed tried to join him the next morning, the boundary was completely closed. Only a few courageous people succeeded in jumping over the barbed wire during those few hours.

Tragedies at the Wall: During the next few weeks, closely watched columns of construction workers erected the "Anti-Fascist Defence Wall" as it was officially called by the communist regime. It was supposedly needed to ward off an impending attack. In reality, the main objective of the action was to prevent the citizens from running away. Berliners were filled with helpless rage on that Sunday in August and they streamed to the border to vent their protest. **August 1961.**

The Wall cut into the living city of millions of inhabitants like a dissecting knife, sometimes running down the middle of a street. Neighbours who lived across the street from one another were now separated by the Wall and by armed soldiers with orders to shoot. Parishioners were cut off from their churches. So-called "border-crossers" were isolated from their jobs. Even cemeteries were cut in half.

Jörg Schikowsky wrote to his sweetheart, arranging to meet her every weekend at an appointed time and place on the Wall. They waved, cried and shouted their latest news to one another. At the beginning, thousands made daily pilgrimages to the boundary. The Wall became a wailing wall.

Despairing East Berliners tried to escape across the Wall to the west. They dug tunnels, captured excursion boats, waded through sewers (until these, too, were blocked), or fooled the border guards at Checkpoint Charlie with imitations of Russian uniforms. Young men drove through the Wall with heavy trucks or swam under water across the Spree. A circus performer crossed the border hand over hand, hanging from a high-voltage transmission line on an icy winter night. However, as the years passed, fewer and fewer made it over.

About the Wall: With great German thoroughness, the GDR worked to perfect their encirclement of West Berlin with a sensitive alarm system and barriers. The "first generation" Wall was a makeshift, improvised affair. The "fourth-generation" Wall is another matter and is more than 16-feet (five-metres) high. A pipe superstructure with a two-foot (61-cm) diameter discourages all climbers. The seven-inch (18-cm) thick vertical elements of the Wall are joined without any kind of gap. According to a report the actual concrete wall is 77 miles (111 km) long, and five miles (eight km) of the border is sealed off by a metal fence. On the other side is a 56-yard (50-metre) wide prohibited zone, cordoned-off to the east by

Looking across.

an eight-foot (two-metre) high security fence, which consists of copper and barbed wire and is electrically charged. To the west, up to the Wall, stretches a 50-foot (15-metre) wide, sandy and rake strip, the infamous "death-strip". Here, "border-violators" must be shot at without hesitation and on target. Within the prohibited zone are numerous watch-towers, bunkers and run-ways for watch-dogs. Six regiments of the GDR border troops are engaged in watching the Wall, some 13,000 men, 2,200 of whom are always on duty.

From time to time the "modern wall" is whitewashed to beautify it. Western spray-can artists and graffiti painters have taken advantage of the endless expanse of the Wall and the West side is covered with slogans and surrealistic and pop art. That section between Brandenburg Gate and Checkpoint Charlie resembles a colourful open-air gallery. **The estrangement begins:** "It's been more than 25 years now. Incredible how fast you forget these things," says Jörg

Schikowsky, as he looks at faded photographs of the summer of 1961. Meeting at the Wall became progressively more difficult. In the East, the area soon became forbidden territory.

His fiancée? The Wall resulted in their losing track of each other in the truest sense of the word. Each lived his/her own life in his/her own half of the city, married and had children. Until a few years ago he sent a Christmas package every year to her. The children are now grown up and know Berlin only as a divided city. What could they do? Anger cools. One can only cry so long. Feelings do not change, but they fade as the business of living goes on. If you want to survive, you forget. And today, on the official city map of the capital of East Germany, the western half is just a white unprinted spot, faded out like a far-off, unknown continent.

In the meantime, the Wall has lost much of its stark horror for West Berliners. As a result of careful, step-by-step political progress they can now, without **The Wall as a work of art.**

too much red tape, make day-time visits to East Berlin and into surrounding East Germany itself. Harassing investigations at the border crossings are a thing of the past, but the isolated position of the half-city as an "undigested morsel of freedom in the stomach of the GDR" has left tell-tale traces in its consciousness. Especially in summer, when everyone is outside, the hemmed-in feeling occupies the Berliners' minds. Then, the Sunday routine of a trip to the Grunewaldsee or the Krumme Lanke seems to some like courtyard exercises in a prison.

Some people see the aggressive driving behaviour of Berliners in the same light. They vent their need for motion in the inner city which West Germans can "express" on their highways and freeways. The artificial rock-climbing cliff on the Teufelsberg probably owes its existence to the same need. In summer entire climbing parties roped together and outfitted with mountain climbing boots, windbreakers and goggles.

Along the Wall: Sensation-seeking tourism at the Wall has outlived the 1960s. Astonishment at what must be the most perverse construction of the German post-war period has given way to amazement at how quickly the wall has been demolished by officials and knocked down by ordinary people, hammering and chiselling it away. At the Brandenburg Gate in particular, it is actually in danger of collapse. But of course one can still go and see it.

In the district of Wedding, the Wall is a mere 400 yards (360 metres) from the Volta Strasse subway station on Brunnen Strasse. You turn right into **Bernauer Strasse** where the Wall stands on the eastern sidewalk. Along here are numerous crosses, each with a name and a date of death. They are memorials to individuals who tried to get over the Wall, failed and were drowned or shot.

Many heart-breaking scenes were played out here by the wall, where the sidewalk belongs to West Berlin, in the weeks following the building of the

Jogging at Potsdamer Platz.

Wall. Many homeowners and their friends tried to flee by jumping out of a window. The West Berlin fire department was on call constantly, ready to rush to the scene in response to a secret sign and to spread out a life net. Four people missed the net and died. Later, most of the houses in Bernauer Street, which had become a symbol of the inhumanity of the wall, were destroyed.

Another 350 yards (300 metres) away is the cemetery of the Reconciliation Brotherhood, which is divided by the Wall. Not much is left of this cemetery. The gravestones have given way to a fence of metal bars, alarm equipment and guard towers. The Reconciliation Church, which stood within the no-man's-land, was blown up in 1985.

Memorial crosses marking tragedies of known and unknown refugees also stand in the shadow of the Reichstag building at **Seeufer** (Bus 69). A footpath leads along the graffiti-covered Wall to the new border crossing points at the Brandenburg Gate and farther south to what used to be **Potsdamer Platz** (Bus 48). Here is a spot which in the old days pulsated with life. For a long time it had been silent and desolate, without a building left standing. Now with the opening of the crossing points, it is once more filled with traffic and is regaining part of the life which made it world famous right up to the 1920s.

Shortly after the building of the Wall, at the border crossing for non-Germans and diplomats on **Friedrich Strasse**, East German and American tanks met in a head to head confrontation. Several times since the war Berlin has felt the threat of a new war.

At **Checkpoint Charlie** visit the **Mauermuseum** (Museum of the Wall) in what used to be the Café König. Here, the "August 13th Society" has assembled a collection of strange machines used by brave individuals to flee to the West. They range from a home-made submarine to an armoured Opel P4. The collection fills three storeys and is explained in many languages. There are photographs from before and after the Wall, films, literature as well as exhibits called "Artists Interpret the Wall" (Subway station Koch Strasse, Bus 29, open daily from 9 a.m.-10 p.m.).

In the surrounding rural areas, parts of the Wall consist of steel bar fencing. Here we find a deceptively idyllic landscape. In the forests and meadows north of Berlin, where the Wall is set far behind the boundary line, in the underbrush and swamps of no-man's-land at the edge of the little village of **Lübars** and the **Eiskeller** enclave, the Wall has become, over the years, a nature reserve for rare plants, birds and animals.

Garden lovers have settled all over the periphery of Berlin with their little allotments and garden houses which often are directly facing the Wall. The allotments carry such dreamy names as "Harmony", "Peace Garden" and "Satisfaction", and many naively have let their rabbit hutches, compost heaps and radish beds spread right up to the Wall and thereby into the GDR.

Left, demonstrating at Checkpoint Charlie. **Right,** Havel river as well is divided.

THE OTHER SIDE OF THE CITY

Berlin: a name of two different cities or a city with two different names? Whatever the answer may be, East Berlin, for reasons which are manifold, is a story all to itself.

By means of its official name alone, "Capital of the German Democratic Republic", East Berlin dissociates itself from the western part of the city. With all their might those responsible tries to dress up their capital as a socialist metropolis, capable of competing with West Berlin. Simply called "The Capital" East Berlin is everything to Germany's second state: here is the central government of the world's tenth largest industrial country; here are consulates and social institutions; it is the economic and cultural centre, traffic turntable and centre of the media. In addition, East Berlin is rich in historical monuments and is the scene of national events.

Following the trauma of WW II destruction and without an American "Marshall-Plan" and an ensuing "economic miracle" as in West Germany, there came the toil of rebuilding the city. During the early years of the postwar phase a new Germany had to be created at all costs, and it had also to be obvious from the outside. Thus, in 1950, on orders of the SED any restorable remains of the Berlin City Palace on the river Spree were blown up, thus eradicating all symbols of "Prussian Imperialism". Buildings of the late 19th century were condemned because of their "hollow pomp" and the "deceitful show façades covering up inhuman backyards". The 1960's craze of demolition and new buildings also left its mark on East Berlin. Unlike in West Berlin, where the cause was building speculation and profiteering, in East Berlin it had political reasons. Following demolition, wide areas for military parades and political mass-rallies were created, with solitary building blocks on the edges obstructing the horizon, where, as one critic puts it, "the eyes always arrive too quickly and the feet always too late."

Nowadays, however, the architectural heritage is being dealt with in a much more relaxed fashion. No longer is the "certain optical appeal" of the period after 1871 denied. No longer does decoration represent "wasted work effort and squandered material". The restoration of old buildings is progressing on a large scale and entire streets have already been restored and rebuilt in their original form. The Nikolai quarter represents a completely "new" old city in the heart of historical Berlin.

A visit to the Mitte district, whose existence is referred to on signs all over the Western part of the city, is a trip into the history of the whole Berlin. Here, one can still sense something of the splendour of this former capital and royal residence. But, one also experiences something of the reality of a divided nation, and of everyday life in "real, existing socialism"—providing that one faces this Berlin reality without prejudice.

Preceding pages: rally of the East German youth organisation FDJ on Marx-Engels-Platz. **Left**, socialist memorial art as photography background.

UNTER DEN LINDEN

The much-celebrated boulevard, Unter den Linden (Under the Limes), was the historical heart of Berlin until the end of World War II. It is still the central axis of the GDR capital. However, it no longer leads the visitor towards the Tiergarten but rather into the new centre at Alexanderplatz. Gazing westwards from the crossing at Friedrichstrasse, one was confronted by the most famous cul-de-sac in the world. The lime avenue no longer ends as suddenly at the Wall at Brandenburg Gate, but continues through two border crossing points into the Street of 17th July.

In 1647, the Elector, Frederick William, lined his hunting path to the Tiergarten with six rows of trees, each row numbering 1,000 walnut and lime trees. Gradually, rows of simple terraced houses were constructed on both sides of the avenue: to the north, Dorotheenstadt came into being and, to the south, Friedrichstadt. However, the plain residential buildings scarcely suited Frederick the Great's architectural concept and in 1770 he had them torn down and pompous, patrician homes created for the owners. Not all the residents appreciated this gift. For many, the façades were too showy and the heating costs in winter too high. Such problems did not worry the monarch. What mattered was the enlargement of the "Linden" into a suitable mall for the Prussian royal residence.

A fateful woman of fortune: It was his successor Frederick William II, who gave the avenue its final, monumental, touch. In just two years (1788-90), he had the **Brandenburg Gate** built. Of the victory goddess Victoria, her horses and chariot, the master builder Langhans wrote: "The Quadriga on the monument depicts the triumph of peace, the relief beneath signifies protection by the just use of weapons."

What Heinrich Heine may have had in mind when he wrote in his *Letters from Berlin* about Victoria: "The good woman had her turns of fortune...?" was the "robbery" of the Victory Goddess by Napoleon, who took her with him to Paris in 1806. But in 1814 did the Prussian field marshal Blücher brought her back to Berlin again. Heine's words hint at the eventful history which has been taking place at the feet of the charioteer. She saw the display of Prussian pomp and glory and the misery of the empire. She heard Philipp Scheidemann and Karl Liebknecht both proclaim a different republic on the same day in 1918. She experienced the increasing power of the Nazis and finally she felt, as Berlin in 1945 sank into ash and rubble, how the war hit back at the place where it was instigated. The **Quadriga** was also shot to pieces. In 1958 a copy was returned to its original position.

When window-shopping along Unter den Linden today one finds relics of times past beneath virtually every stone, either carefully restored or hidden behind a modern façade. The western side of the street is dominated by new buildings in which the British, French and Italians have their embassies. The Americans reside a little bit away, in the Neustädtische Kirch Strasse. At Pariser Platz, the landmark of divided Berlin, the Quadriga can be observed undisturbed. Before the border was opened, this was the only spot in the GDR where photography of the eastern side and the "Anti-fascist Protective Wall"—as it was officially termed—was not prohibited. The Hotel Adlon, once Berlin's most famous hotel, formerly stood to the left.

Never on Sundays: Leaving the Brandenburger Tor and continuing the sightseeing tour of Unter den Linden, you pass the Ministry for Popular Education on the right. Next door the monumental **Soviet Embassy** testifies to the architectural style of the Stalin era. It was officially opened as the first modern building on the street in 1953. The Bulgarian and French cultural centres,

Left, Frederick the Great in bronze.

the offices of Scandinavian Airlines and of Aeroflot are also on Unter den Linden. Thus, international flair appears to have been retained, but in the evenings and on weekends this quarter is deserted. The East Berliners retreat to their "Datschen", small houses in the countryside. Life on the land is more important to them than a stroll in town past desolate squares and closed shops, even if on Unter den Linden these bear a touch of luxury and the exclusive. On Saturdays, shops—with exception of some big department stores—are closed.

The bleakness and silence of Sundays and public holidays makes one forget that the junction of Friedrich Strasse and Unter den Linden was once the pulsating centre of Berlin. Names like Café Viktoria, Café Bauer and Café Kranzler evoke memories of much-loved meeting places in this district. **Lindencorso**, a café-restaurant with a white-blue glass façade, is scarcely an adequate substitute.

A detour for Schinkel: At this point you should leave the "Linden" for a short detour to Platz der Akademie. The Grand Hotel at the junction of Friedrichstrasse and Behren Strasse punctually opened its doors for the 750th anniversary. Within, the "Café Bauer", re-created to its orignal splendour, is a reminder of old Berlin.

When passing the Behren Strasse, observe the **Komische Oper**, which was first established in 1945. It was here that 30 years ago the famous director Walter Felsenstein (who died in 1975) created the new tradition of a realistic music-theatre, a tradition which is still alive today.

The poet E.T.A. Hoffmann used a quote of Goethe's to describe **Platz der Akademie**, a perfect piece of urban planning, somewhat humorously: "Prophet to the right, prophet to the left, the worldling in the middle." The two prophets to whom he refers are the Deutsche Dom (German Cathedral, 1708) and the Französische Dom

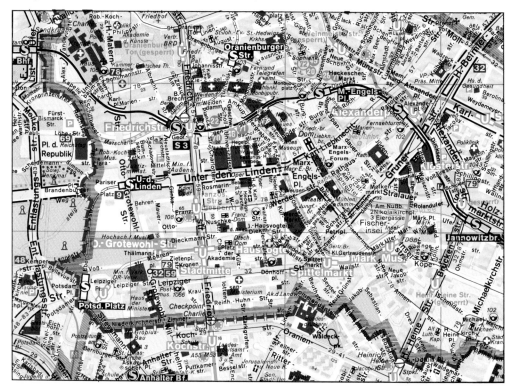

(French Cathedral, 1705), both of whose towers dominate the whole quarter. They were added 80 years later to reflect something of the then late baroque style of building at the square. It was Frederich II's wish to embellish the otherwise rather modest churches, the towers being pure architectural ornaments without function. Today, a winebar has been installed in the dome of the French Cathedral whose nave houses the **Huguenot Museum**, which is small but well worth a visit. After restoration of the German Cathedral, the Academy of Fine Arts moved in with paintings and modern sculptures.

The "worldling in the middle" is the **Schauspielhaus**, one of Schinkel's most beautiful buildings, which was built in 1821. In its time, this neo-classical masterpiece was termed "music becomes form". Since its reopening in 1984 as a concert hall with 1,650 seats it has fully deserved this description. The sounds of music can also be heard by Friedrich Schiller, whose marble statue,

in 1986, was returned to its original position on the Gendarmenmarkt, as the Platz der Akademie was formerly called, as a part of an "exchange of cultural objects" between East and West. In the 1930s the Nazis had exiled the Prince of poets.

Following the Französische Strasse toward the Spree the visitor arrives at the Werderscher Markt. In the building to the right the **Central Committee of the SED** had its seat. Opposite, on the Oberwall Strasse, another modern building houses the **Ministry of Foreign Affairs** of the GDR.

While planning the **Friedrichwerdersche Kirche** (1828), Schinkel abandoned his neo-classical path and built a place of worship in "the character of an English chapel." Thus some aspects of this sacred building in neo-gothic style are reminiscent of London's Westminster Abbey. As a tribute to the man who has left his unmistakable mark in so many places in Berlin, a representative **Schinkel-Museum** was set up in the Friedrichwerdersche church.

On Linderforum: On Oberwall Strasse the visitor returns to the "Linden". The enlargement of the "Linden" into a representative boulevard began in 1695 with the building of the Baroque Old Arsenal. For hundreds of years the building served as an arms magazine and war museum. These days, the **Museum für Deutsche Geschichte** (Museum of German History), on nearly two acres (7,700 sq metres) of exhibition space, displays Germany's past and present from the standpoint of GDR history and geography. The four female allegorical figures at the entrance represent the arts of fireworks, arithmetic, geometry and mechanics. The other sculptures come from Andreas Schlüter's workshop. Particularly impressive are the 22 heads of dying warriors in the inner courtyard, making apparent the horror of war. The entry to the memorial "Lenin in Berlin" is next to the main doorway.

A few steps further on, in front of the

Brandenburger Tor around 1900.

Memorial for the Victims of Fascism and Militarism, a changing of the guards ceremony takes place every 60 minutes, with the soldiers reliving the old Prussian goose-step. Indeed, the Grand Parade of Guards (Wednesday, 2.30 p.m.) is a spectacle which attracts tourists and amateur photographers from all over the world. With all this military pomp the visitor ought not forget that an eternal flame is burning inside the former **Neue Wache** above the graves of the Unknown Soldier and the Unknown Resistance Fighter. They both commemorate the 50 million lives claimed by National Socialism and World War II. The **Neve Wache** (New Guardhouse), built in 1818, was Schinkel's first neo-classical building.

The copse of chestnut trees behind the memorial was, to poet Christian Morgenstern, the "dearest spot" in Berlin. From here he looked onto the aristocratic palais "**Am Festungsgraben**" (today seat of the "Society for Soviet-German Friendship") and onto the **Sin-**gakademie (today, the Maxim-Gorki-Theater) in which Alexander von Humboldt once gave his lectures on the cosmos. Plays by Russian dramatists and young contemporary GDR authors are now staged in this plain 1825 neo-classical building.

The Humboldt brothers: In the **Humboldt Universität**, which stands alongside the Victims of Fascism Memorial, some 13,000 East Berlin students walk about on grounds hallowed by tradition. It was on the iniative of Wilhelm von Humboldt, who is regarded as their "intellectual father", that the university was founded in 1809. Since then, many learned scholars, including 27 Nobel laureates, have established and maintained the international reputation of the Humboldt University. The building was erected according to a plan by Georg Wenzeslaus Knobelsdorff between 1758 and 1766. The east and west wings around the central courtyard are extensions which were added in the early years of this century. In the

Unter den Linden today.

Staatsbibliothek, immediately adjacent to the University, over seven million books are available to the students. The beginnings of this library go back to the year 1661 when the "library of the Elector of Cölln on the Spree" was founded. It was not until 1914 that the building which now houses these books was completed in neo-baroque style.

The former **Gouverneurshaus** (Unter den Linden 11) also belongs to the University as does the **Alte Palais** (Unter den Linden 9). Earlier the Gouverneurshaus stood in the Rathaus Strasse, but during the rebuilding of the city centre it had to make way for modern buildings. In order to preserve its baroque façade it was unceremoniously placed in the space where formerly stood the Netherland Palais.

The **Opernplatz**, opposite the university, scarcely added to its reputation in the early 1930s. Here, on May 10, 1933, at the climax of propaganda minister Goebbels' "campaign against the 'un'-German spirit", some 20,000 books by authors ostracised by the Nazis were burnt. Among them were the works of Heinrich Heine who, long before, had predicted, "Where books are burnt, in the end people also will be burnt." Today, the Opernplatz has been renamed in honour of the socialist workers' leader August Bebel.

Two versions exist of the building standing on the western side of the square: the other is the Vienna Hofburg. This is the **Alte Bibliothek**, which the Berliners call "chest of drawers" because of its ornate façade. Since its restoration in 1969 it has been used as a reading-room by the students of the Humboldt University. The mosaic window, "Lenin in Germany", reminds the students that the Russian revolutionary studied in Berlin in the summer of 1895 when he rented an apartment in the Moabit district.

Friedericus Rex: The neo-classical treasure on the opposite side of Bebelplatz is the **Deutsche Staatsoper**. When Knobelsdorff completed it in

Every Wednesday afternoon: The Grand Guards Parade.

TREASURES OF WORLD CULTURE

Whether one discovers Berlin at leisure or in a hurry, the cultural treasures of the **Museumsinsel** between the two tributaries of the Spree should not be missed. Four of the five museum buildings have been reopened after extensive restoration, the last being the Bode-Museum with Schlüter's equestrian statue of the Great Elector in the domed hall. Work is still in progress on the Neues Museum.

The **Pergamon Museum** contains Berlin's most valuable artistic treasure, the *Altar of Zeus and Athene* (180-160 B.C.), from Pergamon in West Turkey, one of the Seven Wonders of the ancient world. In 1986 the town council of Bergama demanded the altar back. However, it is very unlikely that the GDR will comply with the request. The *Milet Market Gate* is also included in the museum's collection. The Near Eastern section boasts the throne room façade from Nebuchadnezzar II's Babylon. The façade of the desert castle Mschatta (8th century) graces the Islamic Museum. The building complex also houses the East Asian and the Ethnology Museum.

The **Bode-Museum** exhibits artefacts of Egyptian history from the prehistoric to the Greco-Roman period. The approximately 25,000 papyri, parchments, and wax and wooden tablets make this papyrus collection one of the largest in the world. The Early Christian-Byzantine department concentrates on Mediterranean art from the third to the 13th centuries.

While the Sculpture Collection displays South German, Dutch and also Italian works of the late gothic period, the Picture Gallery shows the development of painting in Germany, Italy and the Netherlands from the 15th to the 18th century. The Prehistoric and Early History Museum houses parts of Heinrich Schliemann's collection of Trojan antiquities and finds from virtually every period of early European history. Finally, the Berlin Coin Cabinet, with its 500,000 exhibits, is one of the biggest collections in existence.

The **National-Galerie** exhibits paintings and sculptures from the end of the 18th century to the present day. Contemporary works of art and the Copper-plate Engravings Cabinet are found in the **Altes Museum**. Hours at all four museums are: 9 a.m.-6 p.m. Wednesday-Sunday, 10 a.m.-6 p.m. Friday. On Mondays and Tuesdays only the architecture rooms of the Pergamon Museum are opened.

The **Museum für Naturkunde** at Invaliden Strasse 43 (Hours: 9.30 a.m.-5 p.m. Tuesday-Sunday) houses the zoological, mineral and paleontological collections of the Humboldt University. The focal point of interest is the 40-foot (12-metre) high *Brachosaurus* skeleton, the biggest dinosaur skeleton ever to have been erected within a museum.

The **Kunstgewerbemuseum** (Hours: 9 a.m.-5 p.m. Wednesday-Saturday, 10 a.m.-6 p.m. Sunday) is located in the baroque castle of Köpenick. Emphasis of the collection is on historical furniture, porcelain and leather products from different periods. The treasure-room contains the "Gisela-Jewelry" from around A.D. 1000.

The **Museum für Deutsche Geschichte** (Museum of German History) in the former armoury, the **Märkisches Museum** in the Köllnischer Park, the **Postmuseum** in Leipziger Strasse and the **Hugenottenmuseum** in the Französischer Dom are all worth visiting. These and the **Otto-Nagel-Haus**, **Robert-Koch-Gedenkstätte** and **Brecht-Weigel-Haus** museums are all dealt with in the main text on East Berlin.

1743 it was the first time that a court opera had not been directly integrated into the castle but occupied a detached theatre among the magnificent buildings of Unter den Linden. In the course of its history it was altered again and again—and destroyed twice in World War II. During rebuilding in the 1950s, Knobelsdorff's concept was followed as closely as possible. Only above the main entrance, which in former times was reserved for the aristocracy, did the plain letters "Deutsche Staatsoper" replace the original inscription "Fridericus Rex Apollini et Musis". However, in 1986, after the reconstruction of the foyers and auditoriums was completed, Friedrich's motto appeared once again on the gable-end of the building. To the present day the "Lindenoper" is regarded as one of the most beautiful theatres in Europe.

The domed structure of **St. Hedwig's Kathedrale** was built by Frederick II for the Catholics of Berlin, numbering 10,000 at that time. "Old Fritz" is said to have turned a coffee cup upside down and, according to the anecdote, this gave him the idea for the final form of the house of God which was completed in 1773. It was the dome in particular which created such difficulties for the restorers of the church, which had been destroyed in World War II. The old wooden construction had to be replaced by self-supporting, steel-reinforced concrete segments.

The former **Kronprinzenpalais,** which is now the guest house of the East Berlin magistrate, stands at the eastern end of the "Linden". This is where Heine stood when he admired the great buildings of Lindenforum in 1822, this excerpt of Prussia's splendour and glory, the restoration of which East Berliners are justly proud. There is just one thing Heine did not see: "Old Fritz" himself, high up on his steed, in the middle of the "Forum Fredericianum". This **equestrian statue of Frederick II**, a masterpiece of neo-classical memorial art, was first unveiled in

Left, at the Pergamon Museum. **Below**, the "Operncafé" Unter den Linden.

1851. At the foot of the monument the sculptor Christian Daniel Rauch immortalised all those politicians, military leaders, poets and philosophers whom Frederich II surrounded himself with during his lifetime.

Removed in 1950 and set up at the castle of Sanssouci in 1963, the "return" of the Prussian King to the boulevard 17 years later, in 1980, is another sign that East Germany also wants to include this part of the German past into its national heritage.

Over the Spree: Schinkel also designed the former castle bridge, today's **Marx-Engels-Brücke**, which leads from the "Linden" over the Kupfergraben—a side-arm of the Spree—to the Spree island. Heine still called the wooden drawbridge "dogs' bridge" because it was from here in the days of the electorate that the hunting society, with packs of hounds, set off into the Tiergarten for the joy of the chase. In 1824, the richly-ornamented stone bridge was already completed. The "Gallery of Goddesses", of Nike and Pallas Athene, make up a cycle referring to the anti-Napoleonic Wars of Liberation. During the Second World War the eight statues were stored in the western part of Berlin. In 1981, to commemorate Schinkel's 200th birthday, the Goddess of Victory was returned to her original position.

To the left, walking through the former pleasure garden, is Germany's oldest museum (apart from Munich's Glyptothek). The **Altes Museum**, built by Schinkel in 1830, with its hall of Ionic columns, masks the northern end of the pleasure garden. The great bowl in front of the entrance (cut from an ice-age granite block, 23 feet (seven metres) in diameter and weighing 80 tons was celebrated in 1834 as the "Biedermeier wonder of the world." On looking at the bashed "soup bowl" as it is called by today's citizens, one wonders why.

The Old Museum is a part of the **Museumsinsel** where, in five buildings, treasures of civilisation from all over the globe are on display. The "complete reconstruction" of the Museumsinsel, undertaken in 1976, is almost finished. Only the **Neues Museum** (built between 1843 and 1847) has yet to be reconstructed. The **Nationalgalerie** in the form of a Corinthian temple (opened in 1876), the **Pergamon-Museum** (1930), the first museum in the world devoted to architecture, and the **Bode-Museum** (finished in 1904) house the collections of the State museums of East Berlin.

The **Berliner Dom** on the eastern side of the pleasure garden is a typical edifice from the Williamite period. The reconstruction of the cathedral was begun in 1974 and cost some 40 million marks, financed for the most part by the West German Protestant Church. Since 1980 the baptism and betrothal church has been used again by the Lutheran congregation. The crypt, with the Hohenzollern mausoleum, has been converted into a museum.

Left, outside the state opera. **Right**, Schinkel sculpture before GDR Ministry of Foreign Affairs.

ALEXANDERPLATZ

The Berliner Dom reflects in the bronze-coloured glass façade of the mighty 200-yard (180-metre) long "Palace of the Republic". This mirror image epitomises the diverse character of the East German metropolis: the different architectural and ideological phases, the proximity of old and new.

Built in just under 1,000 days the **Palast der Republik** was officially inaugurated in April 1976. The wing on the pleasure-garden side houses the "Volkskammer", the GDR parliament. On the opposite side, with the former royal stables, the "Grosser Saal" with its mobile floor has room for 500 to 5,000 visitors. Congresses and cultural events are held here. The SED (Sozialistische Einheitspartei Deutschlands) used to hold their party conferences here too. Thirteen restaurants, cafés and bars await guests as do bowling alleys, a discotheque, a youth hall and the Theater im Palast abbreviated "TiP".

Until its demolition in 1950, the huge Berlin city castle complex extended across Marx-Engels-Platz. At the **Staatsratsgebäude**, once the official seat of Erich Honecker, the last remnant of the Hohenzollern residence has been incorporated into the façade as a portal in memory of Karl Liebknecht who, in 1918, proclaimed the socialist republic here.

On the eastern bank of the Spree River, on Karl-Liebknecht Strasse, the **Marx-Engels-Forum** has been adorned with works by GDR sculptors. Towering above all, at the centre of the radial square, are the bronze figures of Karl Marx and Frederick Engels, immediately re-christened "Sakko and Jacketti" by Berliners.

The Gothic **Marienkirche** seems somewhat lost in the modern socialist scenery below the television tower. Enter the 13th century place of worship to escape the roar of traffic on Karl-Liebknecht Strasse and observe such remarkable works of art as the 24-yard (22-metre) long, late gothic fresco *The Dance of Death* (1485) and the marble pulpit by Andreas Schlüter.

The **Neptunbrunnen** stands between Marienkirche and "Rotes Rathaus" and is a fine example of Williamite opulence. The sculptor Reinhold Begas created the bronze fountain in 1891 as a present to the Kaiser from the city of Berlin. The four splashing beauties around the basin symbolise the rivers Rhine, Elbe, Oder and Weichsel.

The new centre: Nothing remains to remind us of the old hay-market which originally stood in front of the city gates: nor of Tsar Alexander I who gave the square his name in 1805 on the occasion of his visit: nor of Adolf Glassbrenner's *Eckensteher Nante*. And very little recalls Alfred Döblin's "quivering heart of a cosmopolitan city", or the "seething human jumble" into which Franz Biberkopf, hero of the novel *Berlin Alexanderplatz*, hurls himself again and again.

Between the 39-storey hotel **Stadt Berlin** and the department store "Zentrum", between the "Haus des Lehrers" and the mural by Walter Womacka (called the "abdominal bandage" by Berliners) and the GDR travel-agency Reisebüro der DDR, tourists and residents hurry or stroll. Walk past the **Weltzeituhr** (world chronometer) and the **Brunnen der Völkerfreundschaft** (Fountain of Friendship), forever feeling in some way lost in the midst of such overpowering architecture. The **Berolina-Haus** and **Alexander-Haus**, are examples of the new objective style at the end of the 1920, which stand at the S-Bahn crossing, somehow fit into the peculiar collection of socialist buildings.

The 1215-foot (365-metre) high **Fernsehturm**, with its weird triangular buildings at the base, is East Berlin's new landmark. "Telespargel" (tele-asparagus) is an all-too-cute nickname for this 26,000 ton colossal television tower. It tapers from a diameter of 140 feet (42 metres) at its base to 80 feet (24 metres) at the level of the gleaming look-out sphere.

Two hundred and twenty yards (200 metres) above the ground, 1.25 million visitors per year look down over a radius of up to 25 miles (40 km) on Berlin and its surroundings. The people seem like ants in a clearing in a forest of concrete when they disappear from "Alex" into the sea of houses. This is true whether one looks to the south down Karl-Marx-Allee, which in the 1950s was still called "Stalin-Allee" and was designed as the "first socialist street in Berlin" in pure Stalinist "wedding-cake style" or, to the east, towards the **Prenzlauer Berg** which to this day remains the most populous and notorious district in East Berlin, with a touch of the bohemian and with the most pubs. Today, the "**Prenzelberg**", which was once a typical workers' quarter, is the East Berlin counterpart of the West's Kreuzberg district.

Proof that the authorities are taking the redevelopment of the city seriously is provided by both the restoration of streets in traditional Berlin style and the newly-designed **Ernst-Thälmann-Park**. This satellite town at the heart of the Prenzlauer Berg provides 4,000 people with flats, shopping precincts, schools, kindergartens and leisure and amusement facilities. Those who are not won over by the 43-foot (19-metre) high Lenin memorial on the square of that name will not be impressed by the monumental sculpture of Thälmann on the edge of the park.

A stroll to the nearby **Volkspark Friedrichshain** is a particular attraction for small visitors. Here they will find the celebrated **Märchenbrunnen** (fairy-tale fountain). The 133-acre (54-hectare) park is just one of the many recreational areas dotted about the city. The zoo in Friedrichsfelde is set in lush countryside as is the park in Treptow— designed in the style of an English landscape garden—in which stands East

World chronometer at "Alex".

Berlin's central commemorative monument. The **Sowjetisches Ehrenmal**, which overlooks the graves of 5,000 Russian soldiers killed in action, is an obligatory destination on all city tours of East Berlin.

Between today and yesterday: The **Rotes Rathaus**, the "red town hall", derives its name less from ideological notions than from the March bricks of which it is built. The fifth town hall in Berlin's history was completed in 1869. The mighty tower which crowns the monumental building testifies to the strength of bourgeois self-confidence at that time, and the growing importance of Berlin as the capital of the Second German Kaiserreich (founded a little later in 1871).

East Berliners took particular care in restoring the **Nikolai-Viertel**. Indeed, much that was restored was not even originally sited here.The result is a historical remake with some deliberate additions. The houses, which snuggle closely around Nikolaikirche, were restored—at least their exterior—down to the last detail with historical exactitude. Included among the "model buildings" is the **Gerichtslaube** from the year 1270, where now drinking, instead of legal, proceedings occur. The old inn "Zum Nussbaum", on "loan" from the Fischerinsel, is renowned mainly because of the drawings of painters such as Heinrich Zille and Otto Nagel.

The **Nikolaikirche** is Berlin's oldest building and was first mentioned in documents in 1264. Following its restoration the church is now administrated by the Märkisches Museum and displays extracts from the history of the city of Berlin. The cobbles, nooks and crannies of the Nikolai quarter tempt one to saunter among the 30 small shops and artisans' workshops. More than 20 restaurants, including the "Am Marstall" complex and the typical Berlin pubs, "Zum Paddenwirt" and "Zur Rippe", provide a pleasant break, particularly in summer, for the visitor.

The **Ephraim-Palais** on Mühlen-

View of the Marienkirche and the "Red Town Hall".

damm Bridge is one of 20 old town houses which are grouped around the Nikolai church. In its time it was regarded as Berlin's most beautiful residence and its magnificent rococo façade caused quite a stir when completed in 1764. Today, it houses temporary exhibitions of Berlin art from the Märkisches Museum. Diagonally opposite on Mollenmarkt (which is the oldest market place in the city), the visitor's attention is caught by the round domed tower of the former **Stadthaus**. Until October 1989 this was the residence of Willi Stoph, former chairman of the Council of Ministers and once head of government of the GDR. Breite Strasse, which is beyond Mühlendamm bridge, is well worth a visit. In former times it was a most respectable address where stood the **Ribbeckhaus**, a Renaissance building from the early 17th century, and the **Alter Marstall**.

To the left of the **Fischerinsel** there is nothing to indicate that this was once the cradle of the double city of Berlin-Cölln. After the war the reconstruction of the old district, which would certainly have been technically possible, was abandoned in favour of demolition and redevelopment on the basis of "new planning free of nostalgia". In practice, this meant demolition between 1967 and 1971, and construction of six 21-storey high-rise apartment buildings. For many visitors, the peculiar charm of the bowl-shaped restaurant "**Ahornblatt**" (maple leaf) is a futile exercise to increase the attraction of the area, however historic the site may be.

The visitor will feel considerably more at home in the **Köllnischer Park**. Here stands the "Wusterhauser Bear", a tower part of a fortification dating from the 17th century. The largest collection of artefacts of regional history in the GDR can be seen in the **Märkisches Museum**. On the way back to Fisherman's Island, the **Ermelerhaus**, a rococo palace on the Märkisches Ufer, welcomes guests to its restaurant, and the **Otto-Nagel-Haus** has a permanent

Revue at Friedrich-stadtpalast.

exhibition of paintings and drawings by Berlin's proletarian artists. From the **Gertraudenbrücke** there is a view of the oldest drawbridge in Berlin, the **Jungfernbrücke**, which was constructed in 1798.

Berlin's old city: In former times, **Leipziger Strasse** was Berlin's main shopping boulevard. The department store, **Wertheim**, had its predecessor here. Seventy-two of the street's 75 houses were destroyed in World War II. Reconstruction has resulted in long rows of concrete fortresses in uniform socialist style. The only embellishment is the **Spittelkolonnade** by Gontard (1776) which seems strangely out of place and is literally overwhelmed by the high-rise buildings.

Those interested in the first telephone exchange on German soil or the first pneumatic dispatch system will enjoy in **Postmuseum** (junction of Mauerstrasse). It was founded in 1898 by postmaster general Heinrich Stephan and preserves the first "Correspondeszkarte" with the 10-pfennig fixed rate stamp on it; the good old postcard in the GDR still costs only 10 pfennigs.

Friedrich Strasse, the 300-year old border-line and north-south axis of Berlin, is still something of a "place of ill repute". It was here that "wild living" rocked the long and hot nights of the 1920s; it was here that the pulse of the big city beat faster than anywhere else; here was high life among the plush velvet and the trash of the cafés, hotels and varietés.

And so, East Berliners reacted with astonishment when, in 1985, the reconstructed one-and-a-half-mile (two-and-a-half km) street in 1985 was named "recreation of the aura of former decades". The new Wintergarten-Varieté, next to the reception building at **Friedrich Strasse station**, contains typical Berlin corner bars, a ballroom, a concert café, a première cinema and a jazz and chanson club. A total of 170 shops, 33 restaurants, and 3,300 flats will be completed by 1990.

But even now there are some outstanding buildings in Friedrich Strasse: the **Hotel Metropol** (junction of Unter den Linden) with its well-stocked Intershop and its expensive luxury rooms (220 Westmarks on average); the **Internationales Handelszentrum**, the trade centre at the junction of Clara-Zetkin-Strasse), which the Japanese put next to the subway lines, though it is both too tall and too massive; the Metropol theatre in the **Admiralspalast** with its comedy attractions is also home of the East Berlin cabaret ensemble "Die Distel"; the **Weidendammer Brücke** whose balustrades date from the nineties of the last century and are decorated with cast-iron candelabra; the theatre of **Berliner Ensemble** on Schiffbauerdamm, Brecht's own stage which is well-known far beyond the borders of the GDR, and—last, but not least—the **Friedrichstadtpalast**, popularly known as the "cave".

What the coloured glass-stones of this former music hall conceal is worthy

Old Berlin pub.

227

of the name "cosmopolitan variety": international pop stars and acrobatics, a famous ballet and perfect staging, plus a mobile stage with all the technical refinements, including a 44,000 gallon (200,000-litre) swimming tank for underwater shows—a bit of Las Vegas made in GDR.

Great names: Director Max Reinhardt had a great formative influence on the **Deutsches Theater** and the **Kammerspiele** which is next door in the Schumannstrasse. For some 40 years he was director of the former and, from 1905 till 1933, of the latter. Both houses continue the tradition of ambitious, critical contemporary theatre.

In the immediate neighbourhood is Berlin's "primordial hospital"—the **Charité**. The "plague house" was built in 1710 as a preventive measure. King Frederich I was afraid that the plague, which had already reached Prenzlau, would spread to Berlin. When the danger was over, the "Königs grosses Lazareth" was retained as a "sick bay" for the

poor under the French name Charité. The red-brick neo-gothic style building covered in ivy was the last extension of 1910 and in 1982, the clinic was enlarged by a 15-storey high-rise edifice. It now can house some 7,000 patients. Names like Ferdinand Sauerbruch, Rudolf Virchow and Robert Koch testify to the fame and importance of this great hospital.

Bertolt Brecht and his wife Helene Weigel lie buried in the **Dorotheenstädtischer Friedhof** in the Chaussee Strasse, near their former flat which is now a memorial. If you are observant when pasing the rows of graves you will notice some illustrious names. The philosophers Johann Gottlieb Fichte and Georg Wilhelm Friedrich Schlegel rest here, as do the writers Arnold Zweig, Heinrich Mann and Johannes R. Becher. Next to them are the artists Daniel Chodowiecki, John Heartfield, and other famous figures of German history and recent GDR past.

Another chapter of German history is found in a few faded inscriptions, memorial tablets and buildings strewn throughout the city: the remains of the extinguished world of Berlin's 160,000 Jews. The area behind the **Oranienburger Tor**, the "barn quarter", was its centre. This poor and rather disreputable quarter, inhabited primarily by the eastern Jewish proletariat, provided the background for many a novel and short story.

Today, only a few hundred of the Jewish community still live in East Berlin . Their former synagogue in the Oranienburger Strasse (which was set on fire during the anti-Jewish program called "Kristallnacht" in 1938 and later even more damaged by bombs in the war) remained a ruin intended to serve "for all time as a place of remembrance and warning". In 1985, however, restoration of the impressive building began, and in 1988, on the 50th memorial day of the "Kristallnacht", it opened its doors again as a museum of Jewish culture.

Lenin memorial Friedrichshain.
Right: celebrating end of school exams.

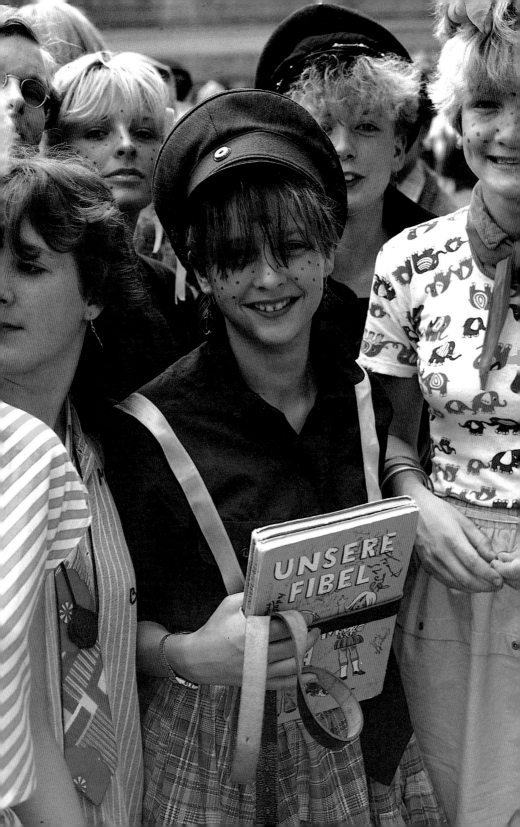

VISITING POTSDAM

Potsdam, with its many castles and gardens, is one of the most important German arts and cultural centres. It is close enough to Berlin to warrant a day's excursion. Since the new travel regulations came into force, West Germans and West Berliners can travel to Potsdam with no further formalities. There is no longer any need for visas.

The first stop on a stroll through the inner city of Potsdam could be the old market. The recently restored **Altes Rathaus**, built by J. Baumann the elder in 1753, today houses the "Hans Marchwitza" cultural centre. Immediately next to it is the **Knobelsdorffbau**, a city palace built in 1750. The old **Marstall**, the former stables, contains East Germany's film museum.

The **Holländisches Viertel** (Dutch Quarter), and the reconstructed **Nikolaikirche** (1830-1839) recreate an at-mosphere typical of a venerable, provincial town. It is hard to believe that cozy Potsdam has a population of 133,000, covers an area of 39 sq miles (100 sq km), is the district capital and is once again a garrison town.

Potsdam became famous because of Sanssouci, the summer residence of the Prussian king Frederick II. It attracted the world's attention in 1945 when J.W. Stalin, Harry S. Truman and Winston Churchill, later replaced by Clement Attlee, gathered here to decide on the future of Germany at **Cecilienhof** castle, picturesquely located in the **Neuer Garten** between two lakes—the Heiligensee and the Jungfernsee. To-day, the castle stands at the Berlin Wall, above Glienicker Brücke.

The Potsdam Agreement was signed on 2 August 1945. It outlined the basic policies for ruling post-war Germany. As with other written arrangements between members of the anti-Hitler coalition, East and West had different interpretations about this agreement. Since

Preceding pages: the Flute Concert of Sanssouci, painting of A. von Menzel. Below, the "Big Three" at the Potsdam Conference.

232

1956, the conference rooms have been open to the public. Guided tours are offered when the significance of the Potsdam Conference is interpreted from the East German point of view. Much of the castle is used by the travel agency of the GDR as a luxury hotel.

The nearby **Marmorpalais** is also a Hohenzollern castle dating back to the 18th century. Today, it houses the **Armeemuseum** which gives an overview of important events in German military history beginning in the 16th century and extending to the present-day GDR. The revolutionary military traditions of the people and the working class are subjects treated with special emphasis.

Castles and gardens of Sanssouci: In Berlin itself, it is difficult to visualise the luxury that the Prussian court once exhibited in Potsdam. This luxury was enjoyed in spite of the fact that Sanssouci Castle has only 12 rooms and was not suited for the demonstration of feudal powers. It was built by architect Knobelsdorff between 1745 and 1747 according to the plans of Frederick II. Because of its rich sculptural ornamentation it is considered to be one of the main works of the German Rococo. The colonnade on the northern side forms a small "honor courtyard" and provides a view over the Ruinenberg. Here is where a large water tank was built in 1748 to supply the fountains of the castle. The artificial ruins are imitations of antique buildings, a tribute to the prevailing Rococo taste. Frederich II never saw the fountains working because the pumps were too weak.

The splendour of the rooms in the castle and the vast gardens underline Frederick II's ambition to spend his time there *sans souci*, "without worry". The name also suggests that the king preferred to speak French while staying at the castle. He wanted to enjoy the arts and music in a secluded country atmosphere whenever possible. His guests included philosopher Voltaire and the musician Carl Philipp Emanuel Bach. Not unexpectedly, the summer re-

Sanssouci Castle terraces.

sidence was also a favoured location for courtly parties and entertainments.

The terraced vineyards of Sanssouci are a particularly attractive sight in summer when the grapevines display opulent green and the chestnut trees blossom. This is how the grounds were carefully planned by Frederick the Great, and this is how they will again be when the long restoration process, which began in 1968, is completed and nature has had a chance to unfold its former glory.

The Neues Palais: Walk down to the large fountain below the terraces, and reach the one-and-a-half-mile long (two-and-a-half km) alley that leads to the **Neues Palais.** On the way, the **Chinesisches Teehaus** shines through the trees, a perfect example of the Chinese tea house fashion so popular at European courts in the 18th century. The "New Palace" was built shortly after the Seven Years War (1763-1796), and initially served as a royal guest castle. The splendour of its architecture

and design was a very costly undertaking yet it assisted in the development of the arts and crafts. The large, richly ornamented banquet halls in the central portion, and the theatre in the south wing with their ornaments, handmade art objects and paintings, richly inlaid furniture and gilded bronze fittings, all demonstrate the impressive skill and quality of the 18th-century craftsmen.

Many architects and builders participated in the construction of this palace. The most famous is probably Carl von Gontard, who also built the **Comuns** in the western part. These were the buildings where employees and lower members of the court lived. The expansive **Kolonnaden** with the **Triumph-bogen**, the triumphal arch, at its centre looks somewhat stately. However, the viewer should consider what the demands of the feudal landlords were in the days of absolutist rule: the impressive scene served to hide the boring swamps from the eyes of the king.

Since 1826, the park and **Charlottenhof** castle in the southern part have been part of the 716-acre (290-hectare) landscaped garden. The castle was built in classical style according to the plans of Schinkel. Behind the castle is the **Dichterhain** (Poets' Grove) and the **Hippodrom**, a clearing in the shape of ancient horse-racing tracks. The **Römische Bäder** (Roman Baths), initially the home of the gardeners, are also proof of a romantic admiration of antiquity. At the end of the park looms the 140-foot (42-metre) tall Roman bell tower of the **Friedenskirche** (1844-54). William IV had this imitation basilica built in the Marlygarten to serve as his court church at Potsdam.

The most monumental edifice, the **Neue Orangerie**, is built in Italian renaissance-style and is located in the northern part of the park. It contains many exotic plants, and is used as a guest house. The "Raffaelsaal", a two storey hall displaying 50 copies of the Italian master and his students is worth visiting.

Left, rococo salon. **Right**, Russian soldiers at the Neues Palais.

234

MUSEUMS FOR EVERY TASTE

It makes no difference whether you are seriously looking for a genuine Rembrandt or a fake, or whether you wish to pay your respects to the beautiful Nefertiti or merely take a copy of her bust home—West Berlin offers more than 30 museums with themes varying from pictorial arts to botany, from ancient history to folk arts to vintage Prussian steam engines.

Whoever believes that there are no fake Rembrandts in Berlin is wrong. The Staatliche Gemäldegalerie in Dahlem recently concluded that the *Man with the Golden Helmet*, one of their most highly valued paintings, is possibly not by Rembrandt, but that it is quite likely the work of one of his students. Experts still believe the masterwork dates to 1650. "We know nothing for quite sure", they say in standard Berlinese. Be it as it may–to look at the *Man with the Golden Helmet* is a fascinating experience. He, however, for his part, seems to gaze quite sceptically at his viewers.

Three centres: The largest art museums in Berlin are concentrated mainly in three areas: in Dahlem, at Schloss Charlottenburg and in the new Kulturforum in Tiergarten, not far from the Philharmonie.

The Dahlem museums once belonged to the state of Prussia. Today they are administered by the Stiftung Preussischer Kulturbesitz (Prussian Cultural Heritage Foundation). The foundation's budget, which covers acquisitions, administration and personnel, building and maintenance, amounts to 160 million marks per year.

A second group of museums, including Charlottenburg Castle, is supervised by the Staatliche Verwaltung der Schlösser und Seen (Public Administration of Castles and Gardens).

Finally, there are the museums of the city of Berlin. These include the Berlin-Mu-

seum, the Berlinische Galerie, the Bröhan-Museum, the Botanische Museum and the recently founded Museum für Verkehr und Technik (Transport and Technology).

There is also a sprinkling of smaller museums, such as a visiting cards and a sugar-manufacturing museum—to name two of the many—and several devoted to individual artists such as Georg Kolbe and Käthe Kollwitz.Then come the museums with special exhibitions; environmental protection, history of the post office, the Berlin Wall, resistance during the Third Reich and the Anti-Kriegsmuseum (anti-war museum). Note that all museums are closed on Mondays, unless specifically stated otherwise.

Prussian heritage: We will turn first to the museum complex of the Stiftung Preussischer Kulturbesitz near the Dahlem-Dorf subway station. The old masters await us here in the Gemäldegalerie. In addition, there is a sculpture gallery, an Indian museum, a collection of engravings, a museum of East Asian art, a museum of Islamic art and—not far away—a museum of ethnology and German folklore.

Those with limited time should at least have a look at the **Gemäldegalerie** (Painting Gallery). Hardly anywhere in Germany are there as many paintings and first-class works of art concentrated in one place. Here hang works from almost every European school until 1800. Italy is represented by Giotto, Mantegna, Botticelli, Raffael and Tizian; the German Renaissance by Dürer, Cranach and Holbein; and the Netherlands by Rogier van der Weyden, Hugo van der Goes, Brueghel, Vermeer, Franz Hals and Rubens. And there are also the masters of the baroque: Antoine Pesne and Georges de la Tour from France and El Greco from Spain.

The Gemäldegalerie opened in 1813. In 1830 it was moved to the Alte Museum, which had been built by Karl Friedrich Schinkel as an art gallery. The original collection consisted of 346 paintings taken from royal castles. Seven hundred paintings from two private collections were later added. During World War II a large part of the collection was stored in mine shafts, safe from the air-raids on Berlin. In 1950 the paintings that had not been destroyed or stolen, and that had found their way back into the western sector of Berlin, were installed in the museum complex at Dahlem that was built in the 1920s.

So here we stand before Rembrandt's mysterious *Man with the Golden Helmet*. There are also 25 other Rembrandts whose authenticity has never been questioned. Along with other Dutch painters we find Peter Brueghel the Elder with *Flemish Proverbs* (1560). Another splendid painting is

represented with, for example, a section of the famous *Männerstädter Altar* by world famous Tilman Riemenschneider.

Next we move to the **Kupferstichkabinett**. The term "cabinet" no longer applies here, as this is one of the world's largest collections of graphics: about 25,000 drawings by old masters, 350,000 engravings and 1,500 illustrated books. All significant artists of the world, from Dürer to Picasso are represented.

The **Museum für Islamische Kunst** (Museum for Islamic Art) was founded in 1904. It presents the development of the Islamic religion from its beginnings in A.D.

the 1476 *Madonna and Child with Six Angels* by Sandro Botticelli.

Next to the Gemäldegalerie is the **Skulpturen-Galerie**. This collection dating originally to the mid-17th century, was also lodged in the Alte Museum in 1830. In 1904, the sculpture collection acquired its own space in the former Kaiser-Friedrich-Museum, which today is the Bode-Museum in East Berlin. During the war the collection was moved to the West. In addition to renaissance, baroque and rococo works, it includes a collection of early Christian and Byzantine art. Sacred art from the Middle Ages is also

600 until the 19th century as reflected in art and decoration. Rugs and textiles, glass, faience, enamels, book paintings, miniatures and other objects tell the story of Islam. A peculiarity of this museum is that it does not present its art following geographical provenance, but rather emphasises the overall importance of Islam for art from Iran, Iraq, Syria, Turkestan, India, Andalusia and other regions whose people are followers of the prophet Mohammed.

Discoveries for young and old: The largest museum in West Berlin is the **Museum für Völkerkunde**, its ethnological sections covering Africa, Early America, East Asia and the South Pacific. Cultural artifacts of distant, and sometimes extinct, people were first gathered here in 1873. The extensive collections from all four corners of the world include paintings, sculptures, religious and household utensils and other objects. A reconstructed men's clubhouse from the South Pacific Island of Palau stands here. Many exotic dolls and masks always thrill children. The Junior Museum offers delightful entertainment and a chance to learn something about the inhabitants of distant continents.

The building also houses the **Ostasiati-**

continent. Here are bronze work, fabric paintings, ivory, glass, objects made of metal and wood, and miniatures from India, Burma, Cambodia and Eastern Turkestan.

Near this large museum complex is the **Museum für Deutsche Volkskunde**, which was founded privately in 1889 but which has been state-run since 1904. Unfortunately, only about 10,000 of the 45,000 catalogued items of this collection of German costumes and folklore survived the war. The orphaned and ravaged collection was kept in various places until its current home was found in 1974.

Here, the focus of attention is the com-

sche Kunstabteilung (Section of East Asian art) which was founded in 1907. Now a museum of its own right, it displays a rich array of porcelain, ceramics, bronzes and lacquer work from China, Japan and Korea.

Last, but not least, is the very new **Museum für Indische Kunst** (Museum of Indian art) which opened in 1963. With over 12,000 objects, it houses one of the most extensive collections of Indian art on the

mon man rather than the beauty and brilliance of lordly houses of the past as in the museums of Charlottenburg Castle. The folklore museum shows vignettes of everyday life from the 16th century to the present, with examples of everyday objects such as textiles, toys, kitchen utensils, regional costumes, tools, furniture and other household equipment. One learns about the religious practices of German-speaking peoples and sees something of the life of a traditional farmer or a 19th-century factory worker, domestic servant or craftsman.

Before leaving Dahlem, a visit to the bota-

<u>Left</u>, puzzled by the *Man with the Golden Helmet*. <u>Above</u>, exotic god at the **Völkerkunde-museum**.

A PLACE FOR ARTISTS

Berlin and art—a sensitive subject, full of contrasts. The barbarism of National Socialism began here in 1933. Its cultural ideology defamed, persecuted, and finally drove away all those painters, graphic artists and sculptors who had made the metropolis of the Weimar Republic an exciting centre of the art world after World War I. For 12 years, Berlin was a dangerous place for art and artists.

However, it has once again become a place where art is nurtured. There is no other city in Germany that has produced or attracted many gifted artists. In the aggressive big-city atmosphere, they find the friction of interaction that artists often require. Since the beginning of the 1980s, the "Jungen Wilden" (Young Savages) with their outburst of colour have made their presence felt. They have made Berlin an international art centre. The city has enough room and atmosphere for many styles, which is clearly reflected in the plethora of galleries.

Two hundred galleries regularly present exhibitions that change every four to six weeks. Most of them are run by private enthusiasts who, like most of their artists, earn a living with non-artistic occupations. Approximately two dozen ambitious commercial galleries operate in this "art jungle". Most of them can be found on both sides of the Kurfürstendamm near Fasanenplatz and Ludwigkirchplatz as well as between Niebuhr Strasse and Savignyplatz. Exclusiveness dictates the order of things: modern painters are high on the list, including Nazi-banned artists such as George Grosz, Max Beckmann and Carl Hofer. There is even an entire museum for the works of Käthe Kollwitz. Together with the Villa Griesebach, probably the most beautiful gallery in West Berlin, it constitutes the beginning of the "mile of art" that stretches the entire length of Fasanenstrasse. On some days one exhibition opening follows another. The public then can enjoy "Kunst konzen-triert", or "Concentrated art", as Berlin art dealers call the chain of events—joint openings and special opening times—which they organise to promote business.

Other galleries do not complain of a lack of visitors. When Ingrid Raab, Carsta Zellermeyer or Silvia Menzel announce an opening, one can be sure that the gallery will be packed to capacity.

The old established Berlin galleries try to counteract this, at times, just fashionable "hunger for pictures" with traditional solidity. The Galerie Nierendorf has had great success with the works of Otto Dix; another pioneer on the new Berlin gallery scene, Rudolf Springer, was already exhibiting internationally recognised painters such as Jörg Immendorf, Markus Lüpertz and A.R. Penck when they were still unknowns. Dieter Brusberg, whose gallery on the Kurfürstendamm receives the most visitors, counts on established artists such as Pablo Picasso, Max Ernst and Ferdinand Léger, though new talents also have a chance here.

But in modern Berlin, art is not found only in the commercial galleries. Works by young artists can be found in a series of autonomous galleries managed by the artists themselves. Of course, in many cases, the names of these galleries are constantly subject to change, along with the management, but many of these "producer-galleries" hold on over the years and create, as in the case of the Kreuzberger Oranien Strasse, a lively counter-weight to the established "mile of art".

The 3,000 or so artists of the city gather in May at the Messehallen am Funkturm when the "Freie Berliner Kunstausstellung" is held and where every Berlin artist is allowed to exhibit one piece of work. The spectrum is composed of established artists and sculptors as well as students and amateur Sunday painters. Many new talents have found their first gallery here. And, maybe, some day they will find their way to the Neuer Berliner Kunstverein, or even the Staatliche Kunsthalle.

nical garden with its **Botanisches Museum** is worthwhile. It was originally in the Kleist-park in Schöneberg but was later relocated in Steglitz. Coming from Dahlem the entrance is at Königin-Luise Strasse 6-8.

A visit to ancient Egypt: The next stop, Charlottenburg Castle, assembles art work from Prussia, as well as from Egypt, ancient Greece and Rome, and of the recent past. It also houses a gallery which is devoted to Romantic painting, featuring prominently Caspar David Friedrich.

The **Ägyptisches Museum** (Egyptian Museum) at Schloss Strasse 70, which is located in an officers' barracks which were

ruled from 1375 to 1358 B.C., is a celebrity the world over. The German archaeologist Ludwig Borchardt discovered the bust in 1912 in the work-room of master sculptor Thutmosis while digging for the lost royal city of Achetaton. It is not known why Thutmosis sculptured Nefertiti as being blind in the left eye, but there are some theories. The figurine arrived in Berlin in the 1920s after a series of trades. East Germany claims the bust to be part of the collection in their Bode-Museum, but authorities in the West have given no sign that they plan to hand over their famous Egyptian lady.

There are other items, in addition to Nefer-

built by architect Friedrich August Stühler, was opened in 1823. It has quite a turbulent past. Its first home was Monbijou Castle (1830) which was destroyed in the first World War. Next, it moved to the Neue Museum on the Museumsinsel in what today is East Berlin where it remained, until evacuated in World War II.

Nefertiti, a 19 inch (48 cm) high limestone bust of the wife of Pharoah Akhnaton, who

Left, sculptor Rainer Kriester with his work. **Above**, St.-Matthäus-Kirche reflecting in the glass-façade of the Nationalgalerie.

titi, to admire. Ancient papyri, whose oldest text is 3,000 years old, utensils, ceramics, toilet articles, and instruments for measuring time, bring the Egypt of the pharaohs to life. The collection comprises objects dating from 5,000 B.C. to the days of Christ. The most spectacular piece of Egyptian architecture is the well-preserved Kalabaschagate.

In the building across the street at Schloss Strasse 1, whose exterior is almost a mirror-image of the Ägyptisches Museum, is the **Antikenmuseum** (Museum of Antiquities) which contains a collection of Greek and Roman works of art including portraits, sculptures and small art objects. Its three sections cover the Roman and Greek and also the Etruscan periods.

Early history and early romanticism: Charlottenburg Castle, built by both baroque and rococo architects, is now a museum. It is the last great Hohenzollern castle in Berlin as a result of the city castle on the Spree and Monbijou Castle being destroyed during the war. The **Belvedere** in the gardens contains a collection of Berlin porcelain while in the simple square **Schinkel-Pavillon**, a collection of small art objects and vases from the Biedermeier period is on display. An exhibition of works from the collection of King

fourth Charlottenburg museum of the Stiftung Preussischer Kulturbesitz is the **Museum für Vor- und Frühgeschichte** (Museum for Pre- and Early History). It was the Great Elector who started this pre-historic and history collection which, in 1830, was moved to Monbijou Castle. It once held the legendary *Treasure of Priam* which was discovered by Heinrich Schliemann in forgotten Troy in 1873 and which was clandestinely brought back to Berlin.

Also worthy of mention is the **Sammlung Bröhan** at Schloss Strasse 1a, near Charlottenburg Castle. Founded in the early 1970s on the initiative of a Berlin businessman, the

Frederick the Great, painted by his favourite artists at court, such as the French painters Watteau and Pesne can be seen on the third floor of the Knobelsdorff wing.

On the first floor, in the **Galerie der Romantik** (Gallery of Romantics), are treasures of early 19th century romantic painting with some of the best known works of Caspar David Friedrich, Schinkel, Spitzweg and others. Architectural motifs from the Biedermeier period by Gärtner and Hummel, as well as fine portrait paintings, also hang here.

In the "Langhansbau" of the castle, the

museum mainly houses 20th century art, particularly *Jugendstil* and *Art deco*. Currently, the founder is in charge of the museum which has been taken over by the city.

Also near Charlottenburg Castle, at Sophie-Charlotte Strasse 17-18, the **Staatliche Gipsformerei** (Plaster Moulding) maintain their workshops. Here, from a stock of 6,000 casts, plaster of Paris copies of Nefertiti and other works of art from all state museums can be purchased. The exhibition and sales rooms are closed on weekends.

At the Funkturm, the radio tower, one finds the **Rundfunkmuseum**, displaying early radios and the first colour television camera. The museum gives a complete overview on the history of German radio, from the first radio show to the start of colour television in Berlin in 1967 (the museum is closed on Tuesdays).

From Menzel to Beuys: At the corner of Landwehrkanal and Potsdamer Strasse 50 is the **Neue Nationalgalerie** (New National Gallery), specialising in 19th-and 20th-century art.

The initial 262 paintings were part of a collection of the Swedish consul and banker Joachim Friedrich Wagener who bequeathed his treasures to King William I in

and Monet, are exhibited.

The collection of the Neue Nationalgalerie, to which new works are added every year, ranks among the most important in Europe. Special shows are held on a regular basis.

A short walk separates the Nationalgalerie from the **Museum für Kunstgewerbe**. Originally, this arts and crafts collection dwelled in the so-called "Gropius-Bau" (named after architect Martin Gropius who planned the building in association with Heino Schmieden) at the Anhalter station. After World War II the collection was kept in Charlottenburg Castle.

1861. Originally the collection was housed on the Museumsinsel in today's East Berlin. After the war it was exhibited in various parts of the city. Finally, in 1968, a new home, built by Bauhaus architect Ludwig Mies van der Rohe, opened its doors . In the low glass building works of Kandinsky, Klee, Malewitsch, Manzel, Grosz, Otto Dix, Joseph Beuys, Newman, Rothko, as well as Realists and Impressionists of the 19th century such as Menzel, Liebermann, Böcklin

Left, Martin-Gropius-Bau at Anhalter station.
Above, Museum für Verkehr und Technik.

Unfortunately, the actual building, which was completed in 1984, is rather disappointing. This could be because the original plan which came from the drawing board of the Stuttgart architect, Rolf Gutbrod, in the 1960s, was frequently altered. The extensive contents are divided into ten areas, each dedicated to a particular epoch, from the Middle Ages to the present century. There are tapestries from Brussels, beautiful silver ware, furniture, chinoiseries, and other exclusively designed and expensive items, such as living-room furniture by Bugatti, and Art deco furniture created for an Indian

Maharaja by Muthesius.

From the harpsichord to the Wurlitzer organ: The **Musikinstrumenten-Museum** (Musical Instrument Museum) occupies a new building near the Philharmonie on the other side of the street. It contains a valuable collection of old musical instruments, including a Wurlitzer organ which is played for visitors. It also changed its habitat more than once since World War II until settling into a finally permanent home in Tiergarten. Each musical instrument is thoroughly explained and children can even try them out. Concerts and readings are given from time to time, and the house also has an excellent café which is open to the general public as well as to museum visitors.

Not far from here, on Landwehrkanal, is Klingelhöfer Strssse 14, where stands the **Bauhaus-Archiv**, a museum in spite of its name. Originally Walter Gropius had intended that the building complex be erected in Darmstadt , but then the city of Berlin offered a beautiful building site in the former diplomatic district.

In the 1920s, the famous school of architecture, applied arts and graphic arts became the hub of progressive teachers and students seeking a coalescence of arts, technology and science. The Bauhaus began in Weimar in 1919 and later moved to Dessau. Then, in 1933, shortly before it disbanded, it transferred to Berlin. Gropius and almost all of his teachers went into exile, and a "New Bauhaus" was founded in Chicago in 1937.

The museum exhibits documents from the curriculum and the work of artists who were trained, or who taught at, the Bauhaus, such as Gropius, Mies van der Rohe, Kandinsky, Klee, Breuer and Itten. (The Bauhaus-Archiv is closed on Tuesdays).

Across the city: The **Brücke-Museum** stands on Bussardsteig in Zehlendorf, not far from Clay-Allee. This gem of a building, by the Berlin architect Werner Düttmann, houses works of important German expressionist painters such as Schmidt-Rottluff, Ernst Ludwig Kirchner and others. The largest part of the museum was paid for by Schmitt-Rottluff.

In Kreuzberg, at the other end of the city, in what was formerly a warehouse at the Gleisdreieck subway station, appropriately housed is the **Museum für Verkehr und Technik** (Museum of Transport and Technology). Opened in 1983, it maintains a 400-year old Berlin tradition which was interrupted only by the war. Berlin has always had several important scientific-technical collections to show. The museum is yet to be finished but how it will eventually look can be seen in a wall-painting in Trebbiner Strasse 9. However, it already contains several exhibits, such as an old *Ju 52* airplane, several steam locomotives and about 100 old cars. Historical and contemporary pieces show technical developments in such areas as street and rail vehicles, shipbuilding, aeronautics, data processing and the art of printing. The "hands-on" area of the museum is exciting for both adults and children, with 50 places where the visitor can try out different technical gadgets and computers.

What would a city be without its own museum of history? Berlin has the interesting **Berlin Museum** at Linden Strasse 14 in Kreuzberg, in the old Prussian court of appeal, a Baroque building from 1735. The collection comprises models and maps, furniture and fashions, signs, graphics, pictures, portraits, busts, porcelain and household utensils which represent a cross section of Berlin's cultural history.

Our last museum will be the **Berlinische Galerie** that has been moved from its old home on Jeben Strasse into the Gropiusbau at the Anhalter station. It was founded in 1969 and is devoted to pictures and historical photographs documenting old Berlin. The Gropiusbau will be enlarged to house a Jewish Museum. Since 1981, various exhibitions have taken place here, for example the Prussian exhibition "Zeitgeist" ("Cultural and Social Trends of the Time"), the "Horses of San Marco" and, in 1987, the Blin Exhibition for the 750th anniversary celebrations. In 1988, a special retrospective of modern times began, and Berlin, under the motto "Locus of the New", was chosen to be "Europe's Cultural Capital"—certainly a welcome encouragement.

Right, porcelain cabinet in Charlottenburg Castle.

MUSIC AND THEATRE

Year-round festival: Berlin became a musical and theatrical centre later than Vienna or Paris. As a provincial court in the Brandenburg March, it lacked all the prerequisites. Berlin first had to become the capital of a respected political entity before it could attract artists and the arts. And, as long as everything depended, in the age of absolutism, on the person of the ruler, time had to wait for the right one to come along.

In 1740, a king ascended the Prussian throne who realised that a people and state would become much more competitive through cultural works rather than through drill books and the militarization of all areas of everyday life which had been the case under the parsimonious "soldier king" Frederick William I. It was Frederick II (to become the Great), the musically gifted son of the "soldier king", who followed these ideas with deeds.

Mecca of opera: Under the patronage of Frederick II (1740-1786), himself a philosopher and musician, Berlin developed some cultural vitality. It still profits today from the heritage of this enlightened Hohenzollern ruler. During the first Silesian war he had the royal opera-house built in Unter den Linden. In 1742, it was inaugurated with a performance of Graun's *Cleopatra and Caesar*. In the following two centuries, Spontini, Meyerbeer, Richard Strauss, Erich Kleiber and Wilhelm Furtwängler produced operatic brillance worthy of a capital. After the war, the Unter den Linden opera-house was one of the first historical buildings in the Eastern sector of the city to be rebuilt. The Deutsche Staatsoper has now re-established itself as one of the leading German opera houses.

It competes ideally with the Deutsche Oper Berlin, its West Berlin counterpart, which was built according to the plans of Fritz Bornemann out of the ruins of the old Charlottenburg opera house. It opened its doors in 1961. Carl Ebert produced *Don Giovanni* with musical direction by Ferenc Fricsay. The Charlottenburg stage quickly gained international renown because of its directors Gustav Rudolf Sellner and Götz Friedrich. Whoever wished to experience a polished *Tosca* under Lorin Maazel, a brilliantly cast *Cosi fan tutte* under Karl Böhm, a sparklingly comic *Figaro* or a daring, forever psychologising *Ring* cycle could feel equally at ease in the functional structure on Bismarck Strasse as in Covent Garden or in the Metropolitan Opera in New York.

In the middle of the 1980s, opera director Götz Friedrich also assumed responsibility for the Theater des Westens. In 1961, on his stage at the Zoo station, where the city opera had been temporarily housed, *My Fair Lady* and the American musical in general began its triumphant run through Germany. Of late, the house has been enjoying the artistic talents of director and choreographer Helmut Baumann who, with an intelligently conceived Kurt Weill revue and a shrewdly cosmopolitan production of *La Cage aux Folles*, has gained wide recognition. Since then the Theater des Westens has made friends with lovers both of traditional operetta and modern musicals.

In 1947, Walter Felsenstein began his revival of realistic music theatre in the Komische Oper, now in East Berlin. His interpretation of the *Opera Comique*, as well as of classical operettas and musicals, is widely admired. The production of Janácek's *Das Schlaue Füchslein* and Verdi's *Othello* were acclaimed as strokes of genius. Today, directors with the innovative fantasy of Harry Kupfer guarantee that the theatre in Behren Strasse will remain what it became in Felsenstein's era: the world centre of contemporary music theatre in the best sense of the word.

World-class orchestras: For Berliners music and singing are "elementary manifestations of life"—as Walther Kiaulehn once put it—but not only the opera. Numerous reputable lay choruses such as the Philharmonische

Chor, the Chor der St. Hedwig Kathedrale, the Berliner Oratorien-Chor and the RIAS Kammerchor, and countless smaller vocal ensembles have many songs, not to mention cantatas and oratorios, to sing.

They are part of the tradition of the " Singakademie" that uttered its first harmonies in 1791 and that in 1829, ushered in the Bach renaissance that persists to this day, by performing the long forgotten *St. Matthew Passion* under the direction of Felix Mendelssohn-Bartholdy.

Berlin's musical potential was not always used optimally. First, the city had to function as a capital. The authorities sometimes meant well but were incompetent. For example, the triumphant premiére in 1821 at the royal "Schauspielhaus" of *Der Freischütz,* in which was a major work in the evolution of Romantic opera, had no positive consequences for its composer Carl Maria von Weber. The king, his heart set on engaging the Italian Spontini, neglected to secure Weber for Berlin. When Mendelssohn applied to the Singakademie to succeed the respected conductor Carl Friedrich Zelter, a more upright but less significant applicant was chosen. "Berlin," remarked Mendelssohn bitterly, "is the sourest apple one can bite."

The aforementioned apple ripened under the sun of bourgeois liberalism. Founded in 1882, the "Berliner Philharmonisches Orchester" played itself into the international limelight under Hans von Bülow, Arthur Nikisch, Wilhelm Furtwängler and Herbert von Karajan. At the end of Karajan's era it was rated, not only by local patriots, but by audiences all over the world, as being among the best orchestras in the world. Karajan's summons to conducting competitions and youth orchestra meetings are followed in Moscow, Tokyo and New York.

The conservative "Berliner Philharmoniker" found serious competition in the younger avant-garde "Radio-Symphonie-Orchester" which was moulded by Fricsay, Maazel and Riccardo Chailly into a first-class orchestra

Progressive restlessness: Critical curiosity which airs itself into daring projects is, as a rule, an expression of the same open spirit that made Berlin an exciting cultural centre in the legendary "Golden Twenties". And, if quality is heard or even suspected in the new and the unfamiliar, then Berliners are the most grateful audience imaginable. In 1974, the 30 instructive concerts of the first, but by no means the last, "Metamusik-Festival" summed up all the new or overlooked works that had been composed from San Francisco to Tibet. To the surprise of the organizers, these concerts were literally stormed by young people.

To be there, to talk about it—that is half the fun for Berlin music fans: it can be a festival première of a work by Mauricio

Kagel or a performance by underground musicians in the Akademie der Kunst or in the Künstlerhaus Bethanien, two venues where artists are free to experiment on the margins of imagination.

This is indeed a characteristic trait of the current music scene in Berlin. Just as an established festival becomes relatively comfortable with its prominence and success, someone else often appears with something, if not better, at least more interesting. For instance the "Berliner Jazztage", the most important festival on the international jazz scene next to Newport, had scarcely settled itself in the Philharmonie when the "Workshop Freie Musik" was formed and took off, more or less, from where the Jazztage stopped. Then the modern cycles of the Philharmoniker and the Radio-Symphonie-Orchester had scarcely found their public when the progressive "Gruppe Neue Musik" emerged to show that, with a smaller group, everything can be performed differently. The friends of music have the benefits: more is offered to them in Berlin than in any other city of the world.

Competition between East and West: Theatre life in Berlin is just as varied. It has doubled through the division of the city and, in some

Because West Berlin's Volksbühne organisation also wanted a place to perform, they built their own Theater der Freien Volksbühne on Schaper Strasse. It opened its doors in 1963. The first director was Erwin Piscator, the creator of the "proletarian theatre" in the 1920s. Shortly before he had distinguished himself as a politically engaged theatre-man at the Theater am Kurfürstendamm with a production of Rolf Hochhuth's *Stellvertreter* with Dieter Borsche playing Pope Pius XII.

In the Theater am Kurfürstendamm, and in the neighbouring Komödie theatre, are examples of theatres typical of London's West

ways, it has profited. Just after the war, each half of the city made it a point of honour to emphasize its own independence and even superiority, in a kind of cultural battle between the two systems.

For example, the "Volksbühne" that made theatre history under the eyes of mistrusting imperial censorship, with productions of plays by Gerhart Hauptmann, Ibsen and Strindberg, lay in the eastern part of the city.

<u>Left</u>, the *Hauptmann von K penick* at the Schiller-Theater. <u>Right</u>, ballet evening in the Deutsche Oper.

End or Broadway type productions, performed by top actors from the world of film and television, are staged. The crowd here is looking for a hearty laugh. The Wolff dynasty, directors in residence for decades at both theatres, has a sixth sense for appropriate comedies, which guarantee laughs and good box office returns.

Berlin's great theatres are found mainly in the old city centre and it is there that most renowned actors such as Werner Krauss, Gustav Gründgens, Paul Wegener, Elizabeth Bergner, Käthe Dorsch and Käthe Gold had their great triumphs. In 1928 the Theater am Schiffbauerdamm housed the première of the Brecht-Weill *Threepenny Opera*. After the war, Brecht returned to East Berlin from his American exile. Thanks to his inspiring authority and generous state support, the Berlin Ensemble in the GDR became an internationally renowned theatre.

After the war, West Berlin countered East Berlin's state theatres with its own organisation of state theatre workshops which operates in the Schiller-Theater and in the Schlosspark-Theater. During the 1950s these became the leading state theatres in Germany under their first director, Boleslaw Barlog who presented, among others, Beckett, Giraudoux, Anouilh, Gombrowicz and Albee, with well-cast ensembles. His directing established Berlin's reputation as *the* German theatre city.

Under his successors, Hans Lietzau and the late Boy Gobert, the three theatres failed to maintain their prominent artistic position. Recently, their direction was turned over to Herbert Sasse, who had earlier brought the light renaissance theatre back to life. Under its new director, Gerhard Klingenberg, this house in Knesebeck Strasse has not left the road to success which lies somewhere between the state theatre and the boulevard.

The Grips-Theater on Hansa-Platz has also attained international fame. The plays for the young given here in stunning productions are subsequently played in other lands and languages. At the première in January 1986 of the subsequently enormously successful musical *Linie 1*, the critics and the public spoke of the birth of the Berlin, or even the German, musical. With *Linie 1*— the title refers to the subway line between Bahnhof Zoologischer Garten and the Schlesische Tor—the German musical emancipated itself from its American prototype: it came of age in a very sprited Berlin manner which is universal and exportable.

Pilgrimage to the Schaubühne: In 1970, in the Hallesches Ufer in Kreuzberg, which at the time was far from an established cultural centre, the Schaubühne unexpectedly caused quite an uproar. Already on the opening night, with Brecht-Gorki's *The Mother* , starring Therese Giese, it set a standard that from then on would only be surpassed by the company itself. They succeeded with Ibsen's *Peer Gynt* and Gorki's *Summer Guests* produced by Peter Stein and, with space—and tradition—defying Shakespeare and classic projects. In 1981, the Schaubühne moved into a ultra-modern new house on Lehniner Platz. Since Peter Stein's success with Chekov's *Three Sisters* and Luc Bondy's success with Marivaux's *Triumph of Love*, theatre enthusiasts make pilgrimages to this house on upper Kurfürstendamm and stand in line for hours in order to get tickets. Here one can experience contemporary theatre at its very, even utopian, best.

It might be said that the Schaubühne is a delayed answer to the Berlin Ensemble and Brecht's epic theatre in to East Berlin. On the other hand, the annual "Ostberliner Festtage" is an obvious answer to the manifold activities of the (West) government subsidised "Berliner Festspiele GmbH". Together with the annual autumn music and theatre festival, they contribute as much to Berlin's attractiveness as the immediately ensuing Jazztage, the international "Filmfest" in winter and the "Theatertreffen" in May. At the last of these the most interesting productions of German-speaking theatres are discussed. In addition, there is the festival of traditional music, the "Horizonte Festival" of world cultures and the "Midsummernights-dreams". They all knit together to create an almost year-round festival.

"Official" and "alternative" cultures fluctuate in Berlin. With about 200 "free groups", the "off" scene has grown very complex indeed, but this complexity creates surprises–it contributes to the liveliness, to the eccentric charm, and (when at its best) to its innovative power. The work, even their mere existence, of all these troupes, should help prevent the "official" music and theatre enterprises from becoming too rigid in their subsidised complacency and stately routines.

It is difficult to tell when night begins in Berlin and even more so when it ends. Night in the city does not simply mean cocktails after sunset on the roof-garden of the "Intercontinental", a steamer-trip on Wannsee under the starry sky of both Germanies, or a furtive taxi journey to the "Madame" club out in the Grunewald where all that flickers on television is the test card. When the barwoman yawns and counts the takings, and the kitchen maid hollers through the swing-doors "no more oxtail soup", for some drinkers at the long empty bars the night is not over by a long shot.

For Uschi, bus-driver with the Berlin transport authority BVG it begins as soon as she steers her "big yellow" into the bus-station on Helmholtz Strasse at 4.30 p.m. She has just enough time to shop the at "Edeka", have a quick look into the letter-box, and give a hasty word of greeting to her daughter who is forever sitting in front of the television consuming videoclips. Mother is going dancing this evening in "Café Keese" on Bismarck Strasse, where the ladies do the talking and the gentlemen, though shy, follow them to the dance-floor in search of adventure.

It is always night in the "Kudorf", which is labyrinth of pubs located in the basement of one of those modern mega-buildings in Joachimstaler Strasse. It is half past five and soon the tourists will roll up. They will be too loud for, in the unusual surroundings, they will want to keep their spirits up with garish jocularity. The women will shriek when men tell their *Playboy* jokes, and the boys will howl when a girl half opens her transparent blouse for fun. Arno and Astrid are students and they know their way about. The pay is shi..., the row caused by the boozed "Wessies" really gets on one's nerves, and when one of them pukes over the draught-tap

Arno just feels like smashing all the glasses on the shelves to pieces. "Come on, don't exaggerate," Astrid always says, "we also once came from West Germany. Here, they can let out their frustration about repressive West German society." Astrid is compassionate and always sees everything in a political context.

"Big Eden", at the junction of Ku'damm and Knesebeck, is also already open. But who wants to shake about in the out-dated

disco-cave when it is 26°C outside and a queue has formed, in front of the ice-cream parlor "Old San Francisco"? Yet, some always do. In the showcases at the disco front door they have seen the owner, one time playboy Rolf Eden, with Elke Sommer, Telly Savalas and other celebrities, whose legends are as faded as the old-fashioned press-photos. And, they have said to themselves, "the night's got to begin somewhere, perhaps things will work out straight away with a tasty chick, then we've got the whole evening in front of us."

Preceding pages: at the revue-theatre "*La vie en rose*". **Left,** Marilyn Monroe parody at "Dreamboy's Lachbühne". **Right,** behaviour is not always as reserved as here.

Between stage and bar: In many bars and

pubs it is time for the "happy hour". Everything is half price until 7.30 p.m. and, once one gets into the swing of things, one could continue till five in the morning. Of course, the 5,000 pubs and bars do not close down then. Berlin is renowned for being "open around the clock": closing time is when the publican has had enough. However, at some time, everyone has to go home to freshen up for the office. At some point the cat needs to be fed, and the flowers on the balcony might be dying of thirst. When these one-timers leave, the taxi drivers on the night-shift drop in for their "lunch break". Otto, the roll-seller, puts

Kneipe" at Wittenbergplatz, diagonally opposite the Kaufhaus des Westens (KaDeWe), encourages senior citizens to take coffee and cake in the afternoon. Any man necking with another man gets thrown out. The lady with the flower hat and strangely wistful smile always sits at her regular seat next to the toilet, a glass of brandy in her hand. Later the window-dressers and buffet people from the KaDeWe delicatessen department turn up. One of them used to do the vegetables at "Bolle's" and is now "Romanova" behind the counter. That's what careers in Berlin are like.

Henriette spent the whole morning at the

down his empty basket after his round of the local bars and orders a round for the locals. Someone buys all the flowers from the shy Tamil boy ("so that he can finally eat his fill"), and in the "Kleine Philharmonie" (in Schaper Strasse on the Bundesallee) Wanja and aging friends reflect on how lovely the bashful gay Tefigalas used to be, while Andreas' tawdry late-autumn "booze" merely attracts purse-proud butchers' wives and parvenue speculators with its phony, commercially-calculated wickedness.

Andreas is the party-king for men who get on incredibly well with men. "Andreas'

visagiste for a television film on cosmetic salons. Powder, cream, paste and colour spread on, simpletons, tassels and brushes on top of it, so that Maestro René can show his skills. And now the stuff has got to come off again. Henriette is an actress and, just before seven, sits in the theatre's dressing-room. "I actually got sunburnt from the bit of sun I saw today," she says to the make-up artist who has to apply the make-up even more thickly than usual. Later, on stage, Henriette is to play a pale young aristocratic lady.

In a cloud of powder, Chou-Chou de Briquette walks her white poodle giving her transparent nail polish a chance to dry. Of course, that is not the real name, but Chou-Chou, or Rainer, loves the gaudy clichés of eccentric transvestites. That is why he has a poodle and the finest collection of Zarah Leander records in town.

The "Sirs/ Madames" who are dancing the "Straps-Can-Can" at "Chez Nous" in Marburger Strasse have honourably grown grey between tulle, tinsel and ostrich feathers. Nobody would suspect that the grumpy elderly gentleman with sparse hair and fat tummy complaining at "Kaisers" that the ham had not been smoked enough lately, would later be swinging his hips at "Chez

"The city is a creative stimulus for the avant-garde, but nobody wears avant-garde."

"Berlin is so terribly rotten and that turns me on", confesses Knut Schaller, who runs the knitting-machines in Lützow Strasse. He once made Berlin rock history with his punk band PVC. The live performances of the sinister ensemble with barbed-wire decor, slide-shows of the blockade and the hooting of air-raid sirens were a clever, well-directed provocation which filled the halls with fans.

In Kleist Strasse another kind of "Domina" (according to a classified advertisement in the *Berliner Zeitung*) lets you ring exactly 13 times before a withered

Nous" like Mae West.

In her living room, a stylishly redesigned former factory floor, Claudia Skoda sits in front of an array of electronic machinery and makes music.*Wir sind die Dominas* was her big hit in the neon-lit alternative dives. Now Claudia is into knitwear fashion goods and has a boutique in the middle of New York's Soho but in Berlin she cannot sell her stuff:

Left, laser disco in the Metropol. **Above**, having one over the eight at the "Zwiebelfisch" on Savignyplatz.

housekeeper opens the door, looking like the late Lotte Lenya on one of her very bad days. Paulette is ready, waiting in her living room on a white skin under artificial palms. She switches off the miniature fountain, because the conversation will be recorded on tape. "So, you are a girl calculating at home what it might pay to walk the streets?" A long, dark red clawed finger presses the stop-button on the recorder. "How dare you, I am an actress!" But the advert said, "Volptuous actress offers all comforts." Well, perhaps she does indeed only give "guest performances" in her theatre-room.

The Schmidts take the S-Bahn home from Lichtenrade. It was a lovely day on the allotment, and it is a lovely journey along the railway line, through so much greenery, over and under bridges, and through stations which appear to be haunted.

Perhaps the Schmidts will "drop by the Turk's place" this evening. His name is Erdal and he is their friend and neighbour. Not all people are deadly enemies in Kreuzberg. The Schmidts eat "Köfte" (Turkish meat-balls) in Erdal's restaurant and again Herr Schmidt will drink far too much raki. And Erdal's wife will explain complicated pieces of embroidery to Frau Schmidt. Live and let live: this is also possible in the neighbourhood "Kiez".

Mascha is bending over the crystal-ball. The black student from Upper Volta wants to know what the future will bring. Mascha has already given tips to many prominent friends. "It runs in our family: we have the power", he explains tersely. All Berliners are superstitious—or why are there so many fortune-tellers, card prophets, diviners and star-gazers here?

Marion also believes in the future. She would really like to make it big. At half-past-nine in the evening she sits in the Hansa Studio in the Tiergarten close to the Wall, for the umpteenth time repeating a simple song into the microphone. The sound-engineers yawn, the technician grins and thinks of the Rolling Stones while Marion gives her best. The song is stupid but the agent has managed to get her an appearance on a short pre-evening show of the second West German channel ZDF, and at the annual lawyer's soirée. That is already something, what else will come will come. Two thousand rock bands, pop groups, hit singers, folk-fuzzies and classical students are hoping for their Big Break in this city.

The Rockabilly rebels sit on the banks of Grunewald lake. They have parked their iron (BMW's, Harley-Davidsons and super-charged Moto-Guzzis) up on the sandpath and lit themselves a camp-fire. Out of their huge portable radios boom Don Gibson, Buddy Holly, Elvis and Carl Perkins. A crate of Radeberger beer stands at the ready; one

of the girls wants to grill curried sausages; and the gang leader's "old lady" has brought along macaroni salad. They will drink, laugh and sing a lot tonight. One will fall into the water dead drunk and nearly drown, while others will want to go "Turk-bashing" but then again give it up, "forget it, they're poor devils themselves."

Living for the moment: "Berlin, it is said, will be the New York of the Eighties," prophesised the British music magazine *Melody Maker* in 1978, and the alternative American urban critic, Nikolaus H. Ritter, stated a little later in *Der Spiegel* : "The long term chances are good that Berlin will become the alternative scene's capital in Western Europe and thus politically active in a new sense." To the dedicated Berlin publisher, Wolf Jobst Siedler, on the other hand, the western half-city looks "strained like a couette who for a last time makes and dresses herself up before it's too late." Too late for what? At any rate, for a life that is worth living in this city. The present moment, not some imaginary future, is important. But rockstar David Bowie was disappointed. On the look-out for stimulating "cabaret-style decadence", the British media-wizard ended up in the arms of the trans-sexual star-imitator Romy Haag. Having exploited the cosmic melancholy of the Schöneberg synthesizer band, *Tangerine Dream* on two LPs, he then denounced author Christopher Isherwood, who once had described the Berlin of the pre-Nazi period between glamour and slapstick so brilliantly in his *Berlin Stories* : "For him Berlin also was one of the most boring cities he had ever been to in his life. But he had to write something, and so he discovered a Berlin which never really existed."

Heike Ruschmeyer sits in her studio in the Kulmer Strasse and thinks. It is half-past-one in the morning and she has just finished painting a picture. She does not want to look at it, because something about it may displease her sponstaneously. She needs distance; a night to sleep over it. Perhaps she will go straight to the jungle, the night-club "Dschungel" in Nürnberger Strasse. Actually they are choosy about who they allow to enter: those who are already inside have the right to feel highly honoured. Here, you can be out of work or in the throes of cold turkey and still glide majestically down a 1950s staircase, as in one of the films of that period. "That period" is the in-thing today—looking like your parents once did has been the latest kick for some time. In the "Dschungel" nobody looks at it, but everybody has seen it: Otto's on Müller-Wipperfürth's mail-order look, crepe shoes, nylon shirts and creamed-up spiky hair—just great. Add to this, pleasant Cool Jazz which, actually is imported from London's black districts.

of the self-exiled rock heroine Nina Hagen, and of us "young wild painters"—as the artistic press pack are fond of writing. You think less of the up-market beauties in pretentious ballrooms, of diamond necklaces, Egyptian cigarettes, less of a touch of precious sin and pricy vice."

Berlin had more a touch of the Balkans, a taste of revolution, meatballs instead of caviar, fizzing beer rather than sparkling champagne. Berlin was never Italian baroque but Jewish expressionism. Berlin was Gallic impudence as well as East European sentimentality. People with hungry eyes, wild imaginations and strong

"A touch of the Balkans": Heike is writing a letter to a friend who fears he will forever rot in West Germany: "Think for a minute of what occurs to you when hearing the name 'Berlin': Max Reinhardt, Marlene Dietrich, Zille and Liebermann, *Nathan the Wise* and the *Threepenny Opera*, the UFA and the 'Cabaret of Comedians'—great names of the old days, historic moments of theatre, legends of the entertainment industry. You think of the Berliner Philharmonic, the Schaubühne at Lehniner Platz, perhaps also

Turkish night-life in Berlin.

hands to help realize these fantasies—those were the typical Berliners who always came from somewhere else and very quickly made themselves at home. The Huguenots, the Jews, the West-Slavian maids, Saxon jacks-of-all-trades, Dutch shopkeepers and Bohemian chauffeurs. In Berlin the ideal of the free citizen became a reality: those who dream of the obvious and realise the impossible. This is as true now as it was in former times. The "Reich's capital" which Hitler so disliked was the centre of the secret opposition to Nazi terror. The youth rebellion of 1968 spread from Berlin to the whole of Europe. Berlin has always been tolerant enough to accept the legitimate wishes of its minorities. Official and sub-culture, mass taste and high-flowing notions, café gossip, pub polemic, and cabaret decadence co-exist in every possible combination. Berlin is likely to make room for its Turkish fellow citizens at the regulars' table. It is here that the rebellious squatter and the crafty granny are likely get together over a "Persiko" and here the exotic blossoms of the long Spree nights can even open their buds in day-time. The example of Berlin proves that once a city has developed a metropolitan mentality and liberality, then these are not so easily lost even when attacked from without and within.

The street-lights are still burning although dawn is breaking over the Tiergarten. Henriette has spent the evening with friends in the "Ax Bax" on Leibniz Strasse. Many theatre people go there, while the art and film crowd tend to prefer the "Paris Bar" in Kant Strasse. Henriette met a " young hero" from Braunschweig but nothing will come of it because she has signed-up for a renowned Bochum theatre. The nice colleague saw her in the "Theater am Kurfürstendamm". "You're good enough for Bochum," he had said and Henriette had been insulted. Playing in Berlin, even on a comedy stage is already something, more than Bochum: she is quite sure of this.

Conspirators of the night: The fast-food stall at the corner of Trautenaustrasse and Bundesallee is open until 5.00 a.m. This is a record in a city which never really sleeps but which has yet very few nocturnal refuges for the hungry stomach. Taxi drivers swear by the fiery shashlik but refrain from the bottle of beer when they see a police-car, whose occupants are going for a round of Thüringer sausages ("with fries, hold the salt") approaching. How many times has the stall-keeper in the white overall dipped his trowel into the same hot fat, how often has he chopped up the burst sausages and poured watery ketchup over them? The ever-green FM station "RIAS 2" blares from the small transistor next to the coffee machine.

Uschi , the bus-driver, allowed herself to be brought to the taxi by a man. But there is no more to it. Once a week, since her divorce three years ago she goes with her friends, Doris and Carmen, to the "Keese" to dance the slow waltz with gentlemen they do not know and, if these are too clumsy, they do not want to get to know. They often end up stirring their straws in their sekt glasses for hours on end, forsaken and waiting for one to come in who could be termed "dashing". The empty dance-floor, the barmen dozing, no tension, no eroticism. Some evenings are a rendezvous with sadness.

"Do you know the worst thing?", some-one asks on bus 19N which runs along the Ku'damm at night to pick up the late-nighters. "The worst thing is eating chocolate cake on Sundays." "Sundays are sad anyway," states a punk-girl with the reflective air of a wise earth mother. "Yes, but then with chocolate cake too..." End of subject: this has to be digested. At the front of the bus, someone has a guitar. "Don't you dare," says the bus driver. But he grins. "Unless it's something Bob Dylan."

Conspirators of the night, allies between midnight and morning. The lonely artist over her writing paper. The clairvoyant woman over her crystal-ball. The aging transvestite in Hollywood costume. The Schmidts in the embrace of Turkish friends. The singing girl filled with yearning at the microphone. The rock rebels at the camp-fire lamenting their lost youth. The divorced woman in the ballroom of false hopes. The lady of easy virtue in the arms of the paying monster. The wedding group; the taxi-driver; the woman from the Salvation Army telling words of purgatory and redemption; the punk; the policeman; the night porter with dreams of might and glory; and the lady high up on the Victory column. There are no nights, there come no mornings. When one gets up yawning, it's time for others to go to sleep. When it is time to say goodbye, others have not even said hello. City round the clock. There are 1.9 million people in this impossible metropolis. And they have 1.9 million tales to tell. Who would know when to stop telling?

Right, rocking through a Berlin night.

"Kann ich
mein Konto
überziehen,
ohne
jedesmal
zu fragen?"

·ENT[A]RTET·

FIGHT B[A]CK

THE THIRD BERLIN: "THE SCENE"

When planning a trip to "Berlin", the prospective visitor first thinks of West Berlin, the Kurfürstendamm, the Wannsee, the KaDeWe and the "Kneipen" that are open till the early hours of the morning. He might also include a visit to the second Berlin, the capital of the GDR, with its museums, the television tower, Alexanderplatz, Sanssouci and Unter den Linden. But, does he know that a third Berlin beyond the tourist office posters, exists beyond a city within a city, where there is living and let live?

This third Berlin cannot be found on any map. No hotel doorman will whisper information about it, and official publicity mentions it as briefly as possible. The third Berlin is the so-called "Szene", the home of the "Spontis" and "Flippies", a gathering-place for drop-outs, protesters and other rebels. The local denizen, which has its secret affiliates also in East Berlin, seem somehow dangerous and attractive at the same time. Dangerous, because the television brought sensationally fictitious reports of squatters in Kreuzberg, of demonstrations in Schöneberg and of Punk riots in Wedding as "crazed alternatives running amuck" into every living-room. Attractive, because the tourist may be tired of the well-trodden sight-seeing trail. Also attractive because he may justly say: "Gedächniskirche, Siegessäule, Brandenburger Tor and Reichstag, that's yesterday. Where are the workshops, the laboratories, the meeting places for the people who are busy creating concepts for the future?"

The first Berlin slogan: While the crowded, cramped city until recently stopped attracting professional people, the legend of an oasis of liberalism, a free city between the worlds, a place where one could dance on the edge of the volcano, began to attract restless types who were eager to flee from the provinces. In the last two decades or so the metropolis on the Spree has become a magnet for individualists, free wheelers and revolutionaries from across Europe.

Berlin's tradition as a meeting place for unruly free-thinkers goes back a long way. Frederick the Great created the slogan "Everyone shall be happy here in his own fashion", a liberal motto considering that it dates back as far as 250 years. Already, in 1685, under his ancestor the Great Elector, the Jews had returned to Berlin because after decades of persecution, they were guaranteed religious and professional freedom. Then, in 1685, under the "Edikt von Potsdam", the Huguenots finally found a new homeland on the Spree.

Prussia, at the time, was a stronghold of liberalism for people fleeing from racial and religious persecution in many other small European states. Initially Berlin profited from this attitude until the beginning of the Nazi era.

When the Allies freed the city in 1945, the former capital of the Reich lay in intellectual and moral ruin. The "pile of debris near Potsdam", as Stalin expressed it, became a vital pawn in the hands of the victors as they each struggled for the upper hand. Berliners saw this all too clearly as the Soviets isolated the city for 10 months beginning on 24 June 1948. A strong feeling of unity that persisted for decades finally developed during the blockade.

In 1945 there was hunger; in 1948 the American "raisin bombers" was running the blockade; in 1961 the Wall—the people in the divided city were fused together by anti-Communist feelings which were not limited to Communists: they concentrated on the Russians, yes, but also focused on West Germans who were suspected of taking up their share of the "burden of freedom" reluctantly. Such defensiveness would not tolerate drop-outs or dissenters who settled in West Berlin to avoid the draft. Anyone criticising the consuming, suppresive philosophy or the hysterical siege mentality was a "nest-soiler" cut off with a curt, "Go join the other side!"

And then Khrushchev came with his cynical prognosis for "the capitalist swamp flower. We don't have to trouble ourselves any longer over it. It will go by itself. One day only the old people, a tired senate and the occupation forces will remain."

Red flags over Kurfürstendamm: However, Khrushchev's prognosis was wrong. A new generation in West Germany, as well as in West Berlin, grew up. A generation who knew nothing of starvation, but was hungry for fresh ideals and felt repelled by the friend-foe clichés of the Cold War.

action, and their battles for social and political change incited the enthusiasm of Berlin's youth. The so-called "extra-parliamentary opposition" (APO) saw its first climax when the student Benno Ohnesorg was shot to death by police on 2 June 1967. He had been taking part in a demonstration protesting against the visit of the Iranian shah. Emotions ran high; the Kurfürstendamm was covered in red flags and the first windowpanes were shattered. Mayor Schütz reacted with helpless cynicism to the half-city's identity crisis.

The Axel Springer press, in its political dream-world and provincialism, angrily

In orderly German living-rooms, among gum trees and kidney-shaped tables, a battle took place between new and old music. The Beatles and protest pop clashed. Parents and politicians were forced to listen to unpleasant questions. Adenauer's ancient slogan, "no experiments", lost its validity.

When the first pictures of war horrors in the jungles of Vietnam appeared on German TV screens, it was as if a dam broke. To young idealists, America no longer was a protector but an oppressor. The revolutionary liberation movements of the Third World became their model, their kind of

mobilised against the refractory students. The result: an incited *Bild-Zeitung* reader shot student leader Rudi Dutschke on the Kurfürstendamm. That night, thousands of vengeful students attempted to storm the Springer publishing house.

"There, look, that's Berlin, a city that can be proud of itself." This complacent anti-communist line from the radio cabaret *Die Insulaner* (*The Islanders*) suddenly had gained a different significance. Students at the Freie Universität not only started airing the dusty robes of those professors who had a Nazi past but, as the "avant-garde of change", they also initiated a reorganisation of West German society as a whole.

The first communes appeared and people began to become accustomed to the existence of alternate life-styles and angry young people sporting long hair, jeans and parkas. The ice of the cold war was broken. In Berlin, it seemed, everyone could again "be happy in his own fashion."

Many activists of the "68 revolution" committed themselves to initiatives more concerned with affairs in their own backyard than to the changes taking place in the Third World. The "march through the institutions" began after idealistic demands for

Tip as well as the left-wing daily *Tageszeitung,* started publishing to provide a media base for the new ideas, and against the still pre-dominant Springer publishing house. And, at the end of the 1970s, the "Alternative Liste" of the Green Party won more than 10 percent of the votes in Berlin elections, and now had elected district councillors and senators.

Toward chaos: At the beginning of the 1980s, what had once been revolutionary and new had become conventional and integrated. Rock music and protest literature from Günther Wallraff and Heinrich Böll, had by now found their way into school

Utopia came to nothing. Feminists predicted the end of the "men only" world and quickly formed women's groups and set up shelters for abused and oppressed women. Money and business had not been abolished but alter-native associations and collectives running pubs and taxi collectives were formed to lay the foundations of a sort of leftist infrastructure.

Magazines such as *Hobo* (later *Zitty*) and

curriculums. The parents of the 1980s' youth—Woodstock still on their minds, long hair and corduroys—discussed their children's education problems in self encounter-groups, and limited their protest to an occasional nostalgic joint. The symbols of protest and drop-out rituals had, in the meantime, become part of the establishment.

The new, younger generation had no interest in their parents' rebellion. Their state of mind was "Null Bock" ("zero, zero"). For them their parents were best locked up at home in their fashionable flats, together with their Rolling Stones records, Bukowski

<u>Left</u>, squatters in lively protest. <u>Right</u>, punk girl facing state authority.

books and politics. The kids had other ways than the "Gruftis" ("Gravies"). They were Punks, Skinheads, Cherokees, Teds, Mods again, and Poppers. Even "super-chic" became a sign of protest. They painted a new way of life—bristled black, platinum blond, or anything else technicolour had on offer; dyed hair, torn T-shirts held together with safety-pins, leather and metal attire, plastic mini-skirts, high-heeled ankle boots you normally would need a weapons license for. This was a new form of protest, this was chaos against normality, against the new order, and against the paradox of the official "bright future" and the unemployment "no

pied and in many cases redecorated in colourful and ingenious ways. To the mostly jobless youths it was more than mere action against speculators. They were also looking for open space to create a new life for themselves. A majority of Berliners, interestingly enough, were sympathetic. The wild, young protesters fought the bureaucrats in a way that frightened their fellow citizens. It also impressed them because the squatters had shown courage against official abuse of power, and had made public the severe shortage of cheap housing.

Among the squatters there also were some militant groups, so-called "Streetfighters",

future".

In the autumn of 1980, the alternative scene volcano erupted once more. In spite of a housing shortage, landlords, including some non-profit corporations, had permitted about 20,000 low cost apartments to stand empty. It was more profitable to let them decay and then get permission to tear them down and build new, high-rent apartments. Berlin became a write-off paradise: whole city blocks were marked for demolition.

But now, an army of "squatters" gathered to combat such doubtful enterprise. Within two years, 170 vacant buildings were occu-

who were happy for every opportunity to clash with the police. Again, the Springer press and a few politicians used the violence of these few rowdies to defame the entire squatters movement. Once again an atmosphere of conflict permeated the city, and in September 1981, during a brutal street fight young Klaus-Jürgen Rattay was run over and killed by a bus on Potsdamer Strasse as he fled the club swinging police. The "movement" had another martyr. Major riots soon followed.

After first taking a strong stand against the movement, the conservative Senate abruptly changed its tactics and "legalised" one-third of the buildings, turning them over to their young occupants. They changed from squatters to apartment owners with the total blessing of the Berlin Senate. In addition, Senator Ulf Fink gave 10 million marks to several self-help groups and co-operative businesses a few months after the legalisation decision.

Some conservative politicians realised that the activists actually propagated conservative ideals: protecting the environment, concern for historic buildings, using natural substances to avoid a dependence on technology, and backing away from the "throw-

guides the way through the Berlin alternative jungle. Listing over 1,800 cultural projects, self-help groups, and small businesses. One hundred thousand drop-outs have created their own world. Their stores, bars, newspapers, and theatre-groups transmit a new consciousness in Berlin which no longer relates to the old overweening phrase "*Ich-bin-ein-Berliner*" ("I am a Berliner") which was coined in 1961 by President Kennedy.

Even the so-called "monopoly-press" could no longer cope anymore with such a variety and gave up its efforts to undermine the social and cultural impacts of this sub-culture. On the other hand, the conservative

away" consumer mentality. Anyone could relate to such concepts, whether he wore a tie or a torn T-shirt, short hair or long hippie locks. Again, it was "being happy according to one's own fashion" in Berlin.

Self-help in the asphalt jungle: "All the colours here are so lovely, I just can't decide", Punk singer Nina Hagen wailed into the microphone as early as 1978. Today, the STATTBUCH 3, which weighs over a kilo,

Left, alternative fashion-fair "Off-Line". Right, hooked on hair.

press could not ignore the new culture And so the new—be it children's theatre (GRIPS, "Rote Grütze"); writers and wild young painters; music from punk to jazz; sub-culture films (from Lothar Lambert, Wieland Speck and veteran Rosa von Praunheim); fashion designers (Claudia Skoda, Sylvia Cossa)—spread far beyond Berlin. Metropolitan magazines such as *Zitty* and *Tip* acted as catalysts and attracted new layers of society to the alternative scene and its many new organisations.

Such variety implies difficulty of choice for the curious visitor. Even if equipped with will, tolerance and readiness for "scene-shock", how can he find a way in? The best entré into the third Berlin is the same as into the first–through the famous and crowded "Kneipen", such as those in Mehringhof. Here, the newcomer sits in the middle of the scene; it is here that it is most concentrated. In what earlier was a complex of factories at Gneisenau Strasse 9, one finds 28 businesses from A, "Alternative Energie", to Z, "Zitronenpresse". Cabaret and free groups perform in the evenings in the Mehringhof Theatres. The "Ökodorf" on Kurfürsten Strasse 14 is a gathering place for Berlin's ecological scene.

women and men who are living and working together in a large family characterise themselves. They are all proud of what has been accomplished since the "peaceful take-over"—involved becoming renters of this abandoned film studio and setting up self-help groups and small businesses. The UFA circus is another venture which is popular in Berlin and beyond: 35 commune members work as jugglers, clowns, artists and magicians, with a "desire to make ourselves and others happy .... a childhood dream become reality."

During summer, another good meeting place is the Tempodrom, a permanent circus

Another meeting place is Viktoria Strasse 13 in Tempelhof. This is the site of the "UFA-Fabrik", a centre of alternative culture, sport, and handicraft (subway station Ullstein Strasse, bus 25, 68). The café "Olé", open from 1.00 p.m. onwards, is a good starting-point for a tour of the compound. There are ecologically oriented projects such as a roof garden and a barnyard for children, Berlin's only open-air theatre, dozens of courses and workshops, and a whole-grain bakery which produces 2,500 loaves a week. "No boss, a kitchen, a cash register, and lots of beds," is how the 70 "alternative"

run by a former nurse, Irene Mössinger. In the 1970s she unexpectedly inherited half a million marks and used it to make a childhood dream come true–a circus that did not merely present trained animals but also alternative entertainment with great colour and variety. From April to October, her Tempodrom offers soccer broadcasts on a large screen, a more conventional activity, but also not so conventional, commercially risky enterprises such as a "women's circus festival" or a "Salsa festival", and other happenings for the alternative scene which other venues would not stage. There is no question that bankruptcy is always at hand, even in such joyful ventures. Incidentally, the Tempodrom stands on a historical site just across from the Reichstag in the Tiergarten. It was originally called "In den Zelten" ("In the tents") and already, 150 years ago, was a place to which pleasure-seeking Berliners came on weekends to dance and to drink beer. Sometimes the dancing went on through the night ("bis in the Puppen"), but serious Berliners deny that this is why the nearby Hohenzollern statues are called "Puppen", or "puppets", by the locals.

Minorities : The women's movement and the gay scene also found historical backing

and sexuality (also non-heterosexuality) away from the sphere of the influence of men. Out of these first contact groups there developed a network of counselling projects, bookstores, cafés and handicraft collectives. Women's shelters and SOS telephone services for raped women were organised. The most important gathering-places are the women's bookstores "Labrys", "Lilith" and "Miranda" but, most important of all, is the "Frauennetzwerk Goldrausch e. V.", where a woman can get a "high that is never followed by a hangover."

Drinking as a woman among women, can be enjoyed in (lesbian-oriented) bars such as

in Berlin for their demands and activities. As early as 1908 women united in Berlin to try to legalise abortion. Sixty years later, out of its student's beginnings, the "second women's movement" arose, when feminists started operating the first autonomous kindergartens and set up women's self-encounter groups to investigate their own bodies

Left, breathing space for sexual minorities, Lesbians at St. Christopher's Day parade. **Above**, alternative whole-meal bakery in the UFA-Fabrik.

"die zwei", "Pourelle" and "Paramount". The "Frauensauna" in Steglitz, is where women can have a sweat-session without men gaping, thus fulfilling the desire for a "feminised life-style" and a "rejection of the aggressive, success-oriented attitude, typical of men" (Robert Jungk).

Although 100,000 gays are said to live in Berlin, the conventional bar, bookstore, bistro, and bath scene is uninteresting. Here, the homosexual scene arising out of the gay movement has taken over the terrain completely. The Kreuzberg "Oranienbar" and the café "Flip-flop" offer the best chance for striking up a conversation. The "Andere Ufer" on Haupt Strasse is an excellent mixture of gallery, cafe and friendly beer bar. It is not a "den of vice" but a brightly lit stand-up bar for the "new gays", which is just as sexual pioneer Magnus Hirschfeld would have wanted it. He founded the first "institute of Sexual Science" in Berlin during the Weimar republic, and scientifically freed deviating sexual inclinations scientifically from the stigma of perversity. Although the Nazis persecuted homosexuals after they seized power and deported many of them to concentration camps, an underground homosexual movement continued to exist

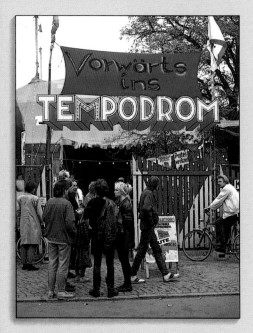

during the Hitler years. A relic of those times is the "Kleist Casino", which seems to change both its owner and its sexual orientation every month or so. The political side of the German gay scene has gained momentum in Berlin during the last 15 years. Films by Rosa von Praunheim, the annual "gay" parade on *Christopher Street Day* at the end of June, information campaigns and many self-help groups which resulted from the AIDS crisis have all contributed to this. The bookstore "Prinz Eisenherz" on Bleibtreu Strasse has a wide selection of literature and sells the monthly information letter of the gay movement *Siegessäule*.

Creative contradictions: A visitor to Berlin probably does not need the services of the carpenter collective "Wilder Hammer", nor is he likely to buy anything at the electronic shop "Wuseltronic". It is also unlikely that he will have his car repaired at the women's garage "Autofeminista". It is likely, however, that he will want to try "alternative sausage" at the "Alt-Berliner Metzgerei" on Mannheimer Strasse or to buy whole-food at the "Naturkosthaus Sesammühle". Five hundred businesses like the printing collective "Agit", deliver everything from early morning milk to a late-evening glass of wine made from organic grapes. Many of them are organised in networks such as the one started in 1978. They act as a sort of bank through which private persons and other projects lend their money to new starters. The bank's logo is a flying "piggy-bank".

In the meantime the Senate has come to appreciate the "scene". The squatters have created new ways for restoration of old houses–roof gardens, solar panels and heat pumps which nowadays are regarded as a standard of ecological and economic restoration. Young engineers who were laughed at when they suggested windmills, today are writing professional articles and appearing as experts on television.

Yesterday's strangely dressed people with brightly coloured hair of yesterday will probably be the intellectual and technological elite of tomorrow. So, the young settlers in the end were right—against all campaigns of the Springer press and some politicians— to stick to the old motto of Fredrich the Great: "Everyone shall be happy here in his own fashion". Perhaps a city must become dilapidated, reactionary and corrupt in order to stimulate new talents, and to create new life-styles.

Or could it be that the metropolitan sophistication which Berlin had developed over the years never really disappeared, even when the overpowered ex-capital was being abused from within and without?

Left, the Tempodrom, the alternative venue in the Tiergarten. **Right**, Berlin is young again.

TRAVEL TIPS

WEST BERLIN

EAST BERLIN

GETTING THERE

BY AIR

There are various ways of getting to Berlin: by air, by bus, by car *via* the transit autobahn or by train. You reach Berlin most quickly, comfortably and avoid eastern checks if you come by air. There are direct airline connections to Berlin Tegel from the following West German airports: Frankfurt, Munich, Nuremberg, Stuttgart, Friedrichshafen, Saarbrücken, Cologne/Bonn, Düsseldorf, Münster/Osnabrück, Hannover, Bremen and Hamburg. There are direct international connections from, among others, New York, London, Paris, Brussels, Amsterdam, Oslo/Copenhagen,

Zurich, Geneva and Basel. They are operated by various airlines of the three protective powers such as Pan American, Trans World Airlines, Air France, British Airways, Dan Air, Euroberlin and Berlin Regional U.K. Visitors from Paderborn, Braunschweig and Dortmund land at Tempelhof with the regional company Tempelhof Airways (Bayernring exit).

The U 6 subway station and the last stop of the A 19 bus route are at Tempelhof airport. From either of these there is transport to the city centre: the journey takes less than 20 minutes.

Tegel airport in the north of Berlin is connected with the inner city by an extensive network of city highways. However, if you arrive or leave at rush hours allow plenty of extra time, to be on the safe side, because of traffic jams. Otherwise, the journey to the city, where most of the hotels are concentrated, takes about 15 minutes. The blue airport bus A 9, departs the Hotel Inter-Continental and the Zoo station every 10 to 15 minutes, and takes the traveller right into the heart of city for the normal public transport fare. The A 8 bus line connects Tegel

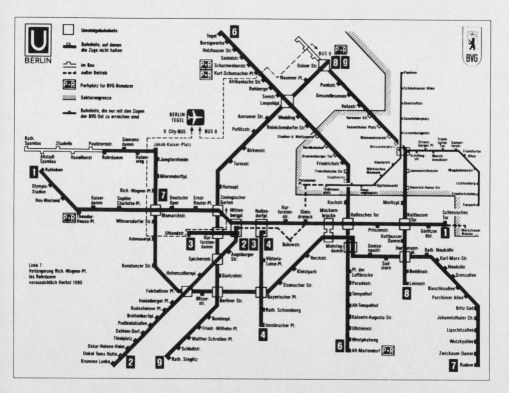

airport to the subway stations Kurt-Schumacher-Platz (U 06/U 09) and Osloer Strasse (U 08/U 09).

Tegel airport's distinguishing feature is its compactness. From the landing gate, which is brought to the door of the plane, one goes straight into the waiting rooms where the baggage is distributed and checked by the customs. From there it is just a few steps to the taxi rank or the bus stop.

On the flight to Berlin the traveller is immediately aware that he/she is over the GDR because the plane drops to an altitude of 10,000 feet (3,000 metres) prior to crossing the border. This is because the three air corridors may only be traversed at this height. Most flights go directly to Tegel; only under particular wind conditions does the plane fly over almost all of Berlin, curving around the East Berlin telecommunications tower ("Telespargel") and sweeping into Tegel from the East. While approaching Berlin Tempelhof, which lies in the centre of the city, one sees much of Berlin before landing.

BY RAIL

The journey takes longest by rail. The Deutsche Reichsbahn of the GDR and the West German Bundesbahn do not exactly choose the most modern trains for the Berlin route. They do not meet Intercity standards in terms of either speed or comfort, but are, however, frequently equipped with GDR Mitropa buffet cars. Stopping in Wannsee or Spandau some 25 trains travel back and forth to Hamburg, Cologne/Hannover, Frankfurt am Main/Bebra and Munich/Nuremberg *via* Hof/Probstzella. The West Berlin terminus is the Zoo station (from here there are good public transport connections to all city districts). Final stop for the trains the Friedrichstrasse station (Berlin-citytrain) in East Berlin. For technical reasons they stop at some stations while travelling through the GDR. Transit passengers are not allowed to leave the train, but you get some insight into everyday life in East Germany from your compartment window.

Deutsche Reichsbahn
(East German Railways)
Friedrichstrasse Station,
Tel: 03 72/4 92 23 40

VIA AUTOBAHN

Four transit routes through the GDR lead to Berlin. From Nuremberg and Munich one takes the Hof autobahn (E 06) toward the border post Rudolph-stein/Hirschberg and reaches Berlin in about three-and-a-half hours. From Frankfurt one must reckon with about a four hour journey from Herleshausen/Wartha (E 63), the autobahn joining the Munich transit route shortly after Jena. From Hannover it takes a good two hours from Helmstedt/Marienborn (E 08) to the West Berlin checkpoint Dreilinden. From Hamburg *via* the northern autobahn from Gudow/ Zarrentin to Berlin-Staaken (from 1988 Stolpe/Heiligensee) a good three hours are required.

You cannot get there any faster. In the GDR there is a 100 km/h speed limit for cars the observance of which is monitored by well hidden radar traps. Those exceeding the speed limit have to pay up a few hundred yards later. The fines are heavy and must be paid in cash or by giro transfer form. Non-payment can result in exclusion from the transit route.

Other traffic regulations should be strictly observed too: absolute prohibition of alcohol, compulsory seat belts, it is forbidden to change lanes to make it easier for other drivers to move onto the autobahn. In addition, visitors are not allowed to leave the designated transit route, to take East German citizens with them or to hand over or receive objects in the GDR. Should all these points be observed there is no problem in travelling through the GDR. As long as you are not travelling at the beginning or end of the holidays, there is scarcely need to wait at the border checkpoints.

The western part of the motorway ring around Berlin between Heilingensee, Nauen, Potsdam and Dreilinden is now open for transit traffic. At the border crossing points into the Federal Republic there are now exits. The exit of Hagenow takes one in the direction of Hamburg, for Helmstedt there is the Eisleben exit and for Herleshausen the Eisenach-West exit. The Schleiz exit is the one for Hof.

Intertank garages, where one pays with West German money are positioned at regular intervals, as are restaurants, some of which are also reserved for bus travellers.

Should you be stranded en route because of a breakdown, summon the breakdown service on the transit phone and be sure to wait by your vehicle until they arrive. If the defect cannot be repaired, you must try to arrange for it to be either towed privately by another transit driver or by the GDR recovery service. However the latter is only allowed to drive as far as the eastern checkpoint. From there defective vehicles are taken over by a West Berlin service. Only two firms have official permits for the GDR and East Berlin:

VMCD Verkehrshilfe
Tel: 3 31 80 08

Peter G. Sutter
Tel: 7 91 76 91/8 01 74 75

You can get to Berlin comfortably by bus. Sixty-four regular buses from all over the federal territory converge on the central Omnibusbahnhof (ZOB) at Charlottenburger Messedamm. Here or at the travel agencies detailed information about routes and times of departure can be obtained.

TRAVEL ESSENTIALS

VISAS & PASSPORTS

Travelling by air avoids hassle. Only direct flights from abroad are subject to passport control when entering West Berlin. Citizens of the Federal Republic of Germany require only their valid identity card, which must be produced when checking in at Berlin Tegel for the return journey. It is however advisable for West Germans to carry their passport in case they decide to visit East Berlin.

All those crossing the GDR by land, assuming they are not West Berlin citizens, require a passport. Children under 16 years of age must either be included on their parent's passport or produce a child's iden-

tity card. There is no longer any need for a visa, instead the transit traveller receives a form to fill in, and foreigners pay 5.00 DM.

MONEY MATTERS

For those wishing to change money or to cash Euro or traveller's cheques after hours money-changers (Wechselstube) can be found in the Zoo station (Mon.-Sat., 8 a.m.-10 p.m.) and Joachimstaler Str. 1 (Mon.-Fri., 7:30 a.m.-9:30 p.m.; Sat., 6 p.m.). Normal opening hours are in operation at: Bank für Handel und Industrie, Kurfürstendamm 26a (Sat., 10 a.m.-1 p.m.); Berliner Commerzbank in the Wertheim department store, Kurfürstendamm 231 (Sat., 10 a.m.-1 p.m.), on "long" Saturdays opening hours till 6 p.m. Bank für Handel und Industrie in the KaDeWe department store at Wittenbergplatz (Sat., 10 a.m.-2 p.m.), on "long" Saturdays till 6 p.m. Cash dispensers are found at banks and savings-banks in all districts.

WHAT TO WEAR

What you wear in Berlin depends primarily on the season and the weather. From October to April it is essential to bring warm clothing; you should have a sweater or a jacket in your luggage as well as a light raincoat. As for fashion, in Berlin just about anything goes: whether one attends the theatre in evening dress or jeans is entirely a matter of taste, and nothing is too way-out for the disco.

ANIMAL QUARANTINE

Those wishing to take dogs, cats or other pets with them need a vaccination certificate against rabies for the animal. If needed you can have a five-day health pass made out at the GDR border. In the train all dogs should wear a muzzle.

CUSTOMS

There is no limit on the amount of Deutschemarks or other western currencies which can be carried while in transit, or on personal baggage and presents. East German Marks or other East European currencies must not be brought in. A transit traveller paying in a GDR restaurant with East German currency is liable to prosecution. Car telephones, CB radios and weapons must be declared at the border, but there is no problem in taking them.

GETTING ACQUAINTED

HISTORY

Berlin (West) is a federal state (land) and/or city at one and the same time. According to German law it belongs to the Federal Republic. However, the three Western Allies suspended the appropriate articles in the Basic Law (constitution of the Federal Republic) and the Berlin constitution of September 1, 1950 with regard to the international agreement on the Four Power Status of the whole of Berlin. Inasmuch as the special rights of the Allies remain untouched, West Berlin is legally fully integrated in the financial and economic system of the Federal Republic. About 40,000 people are employed by the various federal offices of the city, more federal civil servants than in Bonn. The Berlin Senate with its seat in the Schöneberg Rathaus is responsible for both state and district affairs. The chamber of deputies, the highest legislative body, elects the ruling mayor and other members of the Senate, and the state parliament is elected every four years. At present, the CDU (Conservatives), SPD (Social Democrats), FDP (Liberals) and the AL (Alternative List) are represented. Berlin is divided into 12 administrative districts which deal with a welter of local government tasks. The local district offices and their mayors are responsible to district representative assemblies.

The political division of Berlin began in 1948 in the shadow of the Cold War and the Blockade. Since then Berlin has had two administrations and two different currencies. The division of the old imperial capital was made final at least for the time being, with the building of the Wall in 1961. However, the signing of the new Quadripartite Agreement in 1971 saw the end of acute East-West confrontation in and around Berlin. In contrast to the Soviet Union, which officially no longer exercises rights of occupation in East Berlin, the Western powers are of the opinion that the Four Power Status agreed on in 1944-5 is still valid for Berlin as a whole.

The separate celebrations of Jubilee year 1987 were based on a document of October 28th, 1237 in which the trading settlement Cöllin, adjacent to Berlin on the left bank of the Spree river, was mentioned for the first time. In fact the two towns, which united their administration in 1307 and in 1432 thus creating the twin town Berlin-Cöllin, have existed even longer than the documentary evidence. Excavations carried out in the last decades prove that they had already developed in the last third of the 12th century. A time lapse view of Berlin's 750-year history after the merger with Cöllin follows:

1470   Residence of the Electors of Brandenburg.
1709   Prussian Royal Residence City.
1740   Frederick II ascends the throne, Berlin as capital gains European status.
1871   Capital of the (Second) German Reich.
1920   Creation of the united municipality "Greater Berlin" with 20 districts.
1933   Seizure of power of the Nazis.
1944   London Protocol: division of Germany into different occupation zones and a special Berlin area.
1945   Signature of the Unconditional Surrender in Berlin-Karlshorst. Establishment of the Allied Command and Control Council.
1948   The Soviets leave the Interallied Command and the Control Council, eleven months of Blockade begin.
1961   Violent division of the city with the building of the Wall.
1971   Signature of the Four Powers Agreement and the respective Inner German Regulations.
1987   750th Anniversary celebrations in both parts of the city with prominent guests from East and West.
1989   Unrestricted travel without the necessity of visas, and opening of the Wall.

GEOGRAPHY

Berlin lies in the centre of Europe. It is roughly on the same latitude as London and the same longitude as Naples. Before Germany was divided in 1945, Berlin was the capital and the geographical focal point of the German Reich which was founded in 1871. Situated on the great plateau of the North German flat lands West Berlin is the biggest German city and covers a surface area of 341 sq miles (883 sq km) or 54.5 per cent of the total Berlin area. Berlin extends approximately 24 miles (38 km) from north to south; the eastern and western limits of the city are 28 miles (45 km) apart. The highest points in the city are Great Müggelberg in the eastern part (383 feet/115 m) and the 400-foot (120 m)-high Teufelsberg in West Berlin, which was built on the rubble of bombed houses. On average Berlin lies 113 feet (34 metres) above sea level. Two-thirds of its total surface area are made up of water, woods and meadows; in West Berlin lakes, rivers and canals add up to a total length of 203 miles (324 km).

TIME ZONES

Local time in Berlin corresponds in the winter months to Central European Time (MEZ) and from April to September to Central European Summer Time (MESZ). When it is midday in Berlin it is also noon in Paris, Rotterdam, Madrid and Rome. It is:

11 a.m. in London
8 a.m. in Buenos Aires and Sao Paulo
6 a.m. in New York and Montreal
4 a.m. in Denver
1 a.m. in Honolulu and Anchorage
Midnight in the Midway Islands
1 p.m. in Athens
2 p.m. in Moscow
4 p.m. in Karachi
9 p.m. in Sydney

CLIMATE

Berlin's climate is determined by a mixture of sea winds from the Atlantic and continental air. It is rarely extremely cold in winter or extremely hot in summer. In January or February the thermometer frequently drops to minus 20° Celsius; it is often very cool until April. At the height of summer the temperature climbs at times to about 30°C: the cool of autumn returns in mid-October at the latest. Unfortunately, the once proverbial tickling good air of Berlin has almost disappeared. In winter there are frequent meteorological inversions: a layer of cold air high up keeps the warm air down at the ground, and West Berlin's industry and traffic as well as the lignite power stations in the GDR produce high levels of sulphur dioxide. The result is smog, which at alarmingly high levels can lead to the prohibition of the use of cars without exhaust filters.

BUSINESS HOURS

Usually the opening hours of the shops are the same as in the Federal Republic, *i.e.* Mondays to Fridays from 8 a.m. or 9 a.m. to 6 p.m. However, in the city centre some businesses do not open until 10 a.m. or 11 a.m. and close at 6:30 p.m. On Saturdays, shops are open from 9 a.m. till 1 p.m. with larger department stores not closing till 2 p.m. Every first Saturday of the month and the four Saturdays before Christmas are "long" Saturdays and shopping goes on till 6 p.m. The laws governing opening hours are interpreted liberally in the city centre, especially during the summer in the areas around the Gedächtniskirche and the Ku'damm where many of the smaller shops and boutiques stay open until 9 p.m.

Food, wines, spirits etc. can be purchased outside normal opening times, although at slightly higher prices, at the Metro-shops sales points in the U-Bahn stations Kurfürstendamm (5 p.m.-11 p.m., Saturday till midnight), Fehrbelliner Platz (noon-10:30 p.m.) and Schloastrasse (3 p.m.-10 p.m., Saturday 1 p.m.-10 p.m.).

International newspapers, magazines, city maps etc. can be obtained after hours at various shops near the Zoo station, in the "Ku'damm" block and in the Europa-Center (till 11 p.m.). In the evenings you can purchase fresh flowers at the Zoo station.

RELIGIOUS SERVICES

Around 60 percent of the inhabitants of West Berlin are Lutheran-Protestants; next come the Catholics with 12.5 percent. You will find churches all over the city, but most of the time they open only for church services. The Protestant Kaiser-Wilhelm Memorial church in the middle of the town-centre is open all day. Virtually all Christian churches and world religions have parishes and places-of-worship in Berlin. The Jewish Congregation of Berlin with around 6,200 members has synagogues in the Pestalozzstrasse and on the Fraenkelufer. There are two Russian Orthodox churches, dozens of mosques and even a Buddhist monastery.

Evangelisches Konsistorium (Protestant)
Bachstr. 1-2, Berlin 21
Tel: 39 09 13 99

Erzbischöfliches Ordinariat (Catholic)
Wundtstr. 48/50, Berlin 19
Tel: 32 00 61 18

Jewish Community of Berlin
Fasanenstr. 79/80, Berlin 12
Tel: 88 42 03 32/34

COMMUNICATIONS

MEDIA

Newspapers and magazines: In the middle of the 19th century Berlin developed into an important press centre. By 1929 with 147 political publications the metropolis had risen to become the largest newsprint city in the world. At the end of the World War II the Allies distributed the newspaper licences and by 1967 there were 10 papers with a total circulation of 1.1 million. By virtue of shrinking advertising market the number of newspapers then fell drastically. Today, the dailies market is clearly dominated by the Springer Publishing House and its right wing conservative *Berliner Morgenpost* and the two sex and crime papers *BZ* and *Bild*. Among them these three publications capture 73 percent of the market. Apart from these there are only the *Tagesspiegel* and the left-liberal *Volksblatt Berlin*. To this politi-

cal uniformity the alternative green TAZ is adding some new opinions; the SEW, a branch of the eastern SED (East German Communist Party), publishes the *Wahrheit*. The total circulation of all of West Berlin daily newspapers is 850,000.

The Berlin periodicals *Tip* and *Zitty* have an independent position in the media world, each appearing every 14 days in alternating rhythm. Apart from an editorial section dealing chiefly with local political and cultural events, both magazines provide a comprehensive programme guide. All the important public, daily television transmissions including radio, theatre, concerts, films, art exhibitions and public discussions, are listed. In addition, lists of addresses and many interesting small ads appear including *Spirits* and *Lonely Hearts*.

Radio and television: What Berlin has lost in newspapers it has gained in electronic media. With luck one can receive 22 radio stations in West Berlin, assuming one lives in a "cabled" household. Even for others, there is a wide range of choice. The Sender Freies Berlin (SFB) has four stations while the RIAS (Radio in the American sector), which was set up by the Americans in 1946 as a German language radio, has two. It boasts one of Europe's most powerful radio transmitters with four medium wave, one short wave and four FM stations. News bulletins are every hour on the half hour: on SFB they are every hour on the hour. In Berlin you can find out every 30 minutes about the latest events.

All three of the Allies have set up their own programmes, the Americans with AFN, the British with BFBS. In addition, there is a BBC FM service in German and in English. Those who prefer French should listen to the FM programme of the FFB from Paris. There are also four GDR stations on the dial: DDR 1 and 2, Voice of the DDR and Berlin Radio. Then there are two private western stations.

Television also offers a wide range of choice. The local Sender Freies Berlin (SFB) produces eight percent of the West German Channel 1 (ARD, a joint programme of the nine West German and Berlin TV stations). The regional news at 7:20 p.m., "Berliner Abendschau", is watched by most viewers in the city. SFB has a one-quarter share of the North German regional Channel 3, a joint venture with NDR and Radio Bremen. The Federal Channel 2 (ZDF) maintains a large production studio in Berlin. The Western Allies have their own TV stations. AFN-TV and BFBS are run by the army. The French receive their TV from Paris *via* satellite. Relatively complicated extra appliances are needed to receive the Allied programmes in the respective sectors, TV 5 coming *via* cable. In Spandau it is even said that occasionally the Russian troops' programme from the neighbouring camp of Döbenitz flickers on the screens. GDR television can be received without difficulty, with most West Berlin TV sets being able to adapt to the Secam Colour System used in the East. TV GDR has two channels which sometimes show old films which are no longer shown in the West. Finally, *via* cable the popular private and third programmes can also be watched in the Federal Republic.

POSTAL SERVICES

Generally, post offices in Berlin are open from Mondays to Fridays from 8 a.m. to 6 p.m. and on Saturdays from 8 a.m. to noon. The post office at the Zoo station is open around the clock. The Poste Restante is also located here. The post office at Tegel airport is open Mondays to Fridays from 6:30 a.m. to 9 p.m., the one in the International Congress Centre (ICC) Mondays to Fridays from 9 a.m. to 1 p.m. and from 1:45 p.m. to 4 p.m. The code number for the city from outside Berlin is 030, for East Berlin 0372.

WEST BERLIN POSTAL DISTRICTS

Berlin 10	Charlottenburg
Berlin 12	Charlottenburg
Berlin 13	Siemensstadt, Plötzensee
Berlin 15	Wilmersdorf, Halensee, Charlottenburg
Berlin 19	Charlottenburg, Westend, Eichkamp
Berlin 20	Pichelsdorf, Staaken, Hakenfelde
Berlin 21	Moabit, Hansaviertel
Berlin 22	Gatow, Gladow
Berlin 26	Wittenau
Berlin 27	Borsigwalde, Tegel, Tegelort, Konradshöhe, Heiligensee
Berlin 28	Lübars, Hermsdorf, Frohnau

Berlin 30	Schöneberg, Tiergarten-Süd
Berlin 31	Wilmersdorf
Berlin 33	Grunewald, Schmargendorf, Dahlem
Berlin 36	Kreuzberg
Berlin 37	Zehlendorf
Berlin 38	Schlachtensee, Nikolassee
Berlin 39	Wannsee
Berlin 42	Friedenau, Steglitz
Berlin 44	Neukölln
Berlin 45	Lichterfelde
Berlin 46	Lankwitz
Berlin 47	Britz, Buckow, Rudow
Berlin 49	Lichtenrade
Berlin 51	Reinickendorf
Berlin 61	Kreuzberg
Berlin 62	Schöneberg
Berlin 65	Wedding

Post Office
11 Möckernstrasse 135-141, Berlin 61, Tel: 2 68 26 53

EMERGENCIES

Berlin is one of the safest cities in Europe in the evenings and at night as well as during the day. However, one is advised to beware of pickpockets in the hustle and bustle and on public transport: their favourite beat is the town centre.

Medical out-patients departments for accident victims and emergency wards are part of virtually all the bigger hospitals. Emergency telephones, free of charge, are found in the telephone boxes outside the larger post offices and elsewhere. Emergency call posts are mainly in the suburbs. The telephone numbers according to the circumstances are:

Police	110
Fire and Ambulance	112
DRK Rescue Service	85 85
Medical Emergency Service	31 00 31
Emergency Chemists	11 41

Dental Emergency Service	11 41
Toxicological Advice Service	3 02 30 33
Drugs Emergency Service	24 70 33
Aids Telephone	3 02 60 31
Spiritual Counsellor	1 11 01
Women's Crisis Line	65 42 43
Youth Emergency Service	6 10 06-33 33
Society for Protection of Children	4 55 60 70
Veterinary Emergency Service	6 81 97 99/ 11 41
Lankwitz Animal Home (emergency service)	7 72 10 64
Taxi	69 02/ 24 02 02 21 60 60 26 10 26
National Directory Assistance	11 88
International Directory Assistance	0 01 18
Telegrammes	11 31
Wake-up Service	11 41
Weather	11 64
Road Conditions	11 69
Time Announcing Service	11 91
Berlin Tourist Office	2 62 60 31/ 33

POLICE STATIONS
(INNER CITY AREA)

Wilmersdorf	8 91 40 86
Charlottenburg	11 13 98-1
Patrol	39 87 12 42
Zoo station Railway police	3 13 60 41

Lost-property Offices (Fundbüros)
BVG (public transport)
Potsdamer Str. 188,
Tel: 2 16 14 13

Police
Platz der Luftbrücke 6,
Tel: 6 99-1

GETTING AROUND

FLIGHT CONNECTIONS

Tegel (tel: 41 01-23 06), Tempelhof (tel: 69 09-1). The three big airlines Pan Am, British Airways and Air France have their town offices in the Europa-Center. For seat reservations and information, call the following telephone numbers: Pan American (reservations: 26 10 51) and (information: 4 10 43 27). Dan Air (reservations and information: 4 10 27 07). UK Regional (reservations and information: 2 62 50 61) or in Tegel (4 10 28 30). Trans World Airlines (8 82 40 06), reservation office Kurfürstendamm 14-15. German Lufthansa has its town office at Kurfürstendamm 220, 1000 Berlin 15, (8 87 55), at Tegel airport (41 01 27 39).

PUBLIC TRANSPORT

Local public transport in Berlin is so efficient that you will have no difficulty getting around without a car. The Berliner Verkehrsbetriebe (BVG) not only runs the subway (U-Bahn) and fast trains (S-Bahn), but also 81 bus routes, which cover 650 miles (1,040 km), a coordinated network of night buses concentrated around the Zoo station and a ferry over the Havel between Wannsee and Kladow. Sixty-three per cent of all passengers, and that is about 1.7 million daily, are transported by the yellow double-decker buses. The quickest and environmentally least harmful form of transport is the subway with eight different lines, two of which cross East Berlin in a north-south direction. In addition to the U-Bahn which, with 68 miles (109 km) of track is the longest in Germany, there is also the S-Bahn, with three lines covering 45 miles (71 km), which is a quick way to reach to Wannsee, and suburbs in the north and the south. The S-Bahn (S 3) is also the quickest way of getting across the city to the Friedrichstrasse station border crossing. It is possible to change to the S 2 or U 6 in a separate section of the station without going through formalities. Tickets stamped in West Berlin are valid for two hours on the East Berlin system. In addition, one may travel as far as Potsdam, Teltow, Kleinmachnow and Stahnsdorf with this ticket stamped in the West. Monthly tickets and 24-hour tickets are also valid in the Eastern sector. Fares are subject to regular changes on the 1st of May of each year: there are various reductions available for tourists in the form of multiple tickets or tourist tickets. At time of writing, fares are as follows:

One-way ticket, change of transport possible, 2.70 DM
Concessionary ticket for children, unemployed and senior citizens, 1.70 DM
Multiple ticket for 5 journeys, change of transport possible, 11.50 DM
Concessionary multiple ticket, 7.00 DM
Day ticket for 24 hours, 9.00 DM
Younger children accompanied by an adult travel free of charge.

In town, from Wittenbergplatz to Rathenauplatz (or vice versa), the A 19/A 29 bus runs at a special fare of 1.00 DM.

Single tickets and multiple tickets can be bought from machines on all subway stations. Tourist tickets can be bought at the BVG information desk in the ICC, at the BVG Kiosk at the Zoo station, at BVG-Kundendienst at the junction of Potsdamer Strasse and Grunewaldstrasse and at the ticket counters at various stations, at the ZOB bus station and at the theatre ticket counter of the KaDeWe department store. Further inquiries, including queries about night bus routes, are answered around the clock by the BVG customer service under (tel: 2 16 50 88).

DAY TICKETS

The *Schmetterlingslinien,* which are recognizable by a triangle, take you to Berlin's parks and lakes. The price is 1.00 DM, but one is not allowed to change. One route, open from May to August, goes along the Havel *via* Schildhorn and the Grunewald tower. The starting points are the subway stations Theodor-Heuss-Platz (U 1) or the S-

Bahn station Wannsee (S 1/S 3). Moreover, from May to October, there is a special line from Wannsee station to the Pfaueninsel. Two other lines run from the Nikolassee S-Bahn station to the Wannsee bathing area and from Tegel U-Bahn station (U 6) to the Tegel bathing area. A combined day ticket, which also includes the boats on the two routes, costs 14.50 DM for adults and 7.30 DM for children (6-14). Further information at the BVG counters or from customer service tel: 2 16 50 88.

RAIL & BUSES

Information on bus connections to and from Berlin can be obtained at the Zentraler Busbahnhof (ZOB), Messedamm 8, (tel: 3 01 80 28). The transit bus to the East Berlin airport Schönefeld also departs from here. Train information is obtainable at Auskunftsstelle der Deutschen Bundesbahn, Zoo station, Hardenbergstr. 20, tel: 1 94 19. East German Deutsche Reichsbahn has a number of information and sales offices in West Berlin, where onward tickets from East Berlin to Scandinavia, Warsaw, Prague etc. can be purchased. The office at the Zoo station is open daily from 6 a.m.-10 p.m. (tel: 3 13 30 55); offices in Steglitz (tel: 7 92 29 00), at Tegel station (tel: 4 34 20 37) and in Spandau (tel: 3 31 72 26); dial 1 15 31 for recorded announcements of regular services.

TAXIS

West Berlin has about 5,000 taxis. They can be reached by special telephone or at taxi ranks all over the city. Apart from this one can order a taxi by telephone over four different radio headquarters which can be reached under the following numbers:
69 02
26 10 26
21 60 60
24 02 02

Some of the special telephones numbers in the city are:

Fasanenstrasse/ Kurfürstendamm	8 81 52 20
Schlüterstrasse/ Kurfürstendamm	8 81 15 46
Savignyplatz	3 12 11 61
Wittenbergplatz	24 74 24

At present flag drop is 3.40 DM, and the price per kilometre on weekdays between 6 a.m. and midnight is 1.58 DM. At night, at the weekend and on public holidays the kilometre charge is 1.60 DM. A taxi ride from Tegel airport into town costs about 18 DM. No one is permitted to stop an East Berlin taxi in West Berlin to take advantage of the lower rates.

PRIVATE TRANSPORT

Even in its 750th anniversary year Berlin was unable to avoid roadworks in spite of resolutions to the contrary. There is always some part of the network of 3,000 km of road which is being dug up; 850 km of these are officially classified as main roads. At present there are some 600,000 registered private automobiles, which is about one for every third resident. Calculations by the ADAC predict a total of about one million vehicles by the turn of the century, an ecological horror vision for this walled-in city. Even the spacious planning of Berlin as a capital, the benefits of which West Berlin drivers on the broad boulevards and the long arterial roads still enjoy, will not be able to handle such numbers. Other than the rush-hour periods on weekdays, roadworks on the city highways and accidents cause additional traffic congestion, one gets around Berlin much faster than in most other big cities. Signposting of routes to the various parts of town has improved considerably in the last few years. Of late, the borders of the districts have been marked, but the sign Berlin Mitte leads to the historical centre at the other side of the Wall and not to the West Berlin city centre. Upon arrival at both checkpoints automobile drivers can book their hotel and get hold of brochures, including a map of the city's multi-storey car parks at the Verkehrsamt. The ADAC office at Bundesallee 29/30 (on the corner of Güntzelstrasse) also has city maps and other tips. In case of emergency there is a direct line from Dreilinden to the ADAC breakdown service. The no-parking and no-stopping regulations have been strictly enforced of late. On the sides and the strip down the middle of the Kurfürstendamm only short term parking with a disc for 2 hours is tolerated between 9 a.m. and 6 p.m. Persistent parking offenders face, among other things, a fine of 200 DM to get their vehicle back once it has been towed away. In this case it is best to get in touch with the nearest police station, for example at the Zoo station or the Police Headquarters, tel: 110. Otherwise the three automobile associations offer the tourist both advice and support. They can be found under the following addresses:

ADAC
Bundesallee 29/30, Berlin 31
Tel: 86 86
ADAC City Breakdown Service, 1 92 11

AVD
Wittenbergplatz 1, Berlin 30
Tel: 2 13 30 33
AVD City Breakdown Service, 4 62 20 70

ACE
Kleiststr. 19/21, Berlin 20
Tel: 2 11 90 31/32;
ACE City Breakdown Service, 2 11 22 55

24-HR GASOLINE STATIONS

Shell (Kant-Garagen)
Kantstrasse 126, Berlin 12
Tel: 3 13 44 96

Shell (Uhland-Garagen)
Uhlandstrasse 187, Berlin 12
Tel: 8 83 43 78

Shell
Hohenzollerndamm 41/42, Berlin 31
Tel: 87 17 74

Shell
Tiergarten, Reichpietschufer 16/18, Berlin 39
Tel: 2 61 37 80

BAB Tankstelle checkpoint Dreilinden
Dreilinden Westseite, Berlin 39
Tel: 8 03 40 30

Telephone Assistance of the Automobile Insurances
Tel: 1 92 13

BREAKDOWN SERVICES

Heinz Fischbach
Antwerpener Str. 47, Berlin 65
Tel: 4 53 61 56 (day and night).

City Autodienst
Seesener Str. 8, Berlin 31
Tel: 8 92 49 88, weekends
Tel: 8 53 10 25 (also smaller repair work).

RAIL & BUSES

Aral Tankstelle Kurth
Potsdamer Chaussee 6, Berlin 37
Tel: 8 02 70 07

Horstmann Reifennotdienst (tyres)
Sachsendamm 68-70, Berlin 62
Tel: 7 81 44 06.

Pannenhilfe Katens & Warnke
Koloniestr. 8, Berlin 65
Tel: 4 94 25 98. From 10 p.m. tel: 4 32 93 42

AUTHORITIES

Polizeipräsidium (Police Headquarters)
Platz der Luftbrücke 6, Berlin 42,
Tel: 6 99-1

Sichergestellte Fahrzeuge (Impounded Vehicles)
Belzigerstr. 52-58, Berlin 62
Tel: 78 10 71, ext. 1996

BORDER CHECKPOINTS

Police station Dreilinden
Tel: 8 03 60 51

Police station Heerstrasse
Tel: 3 66 10 66

CAR RENTAL AGENCIES

Avis International
Budapester Str. 43, Berlin 3
Tel: 2 61 18 81.
Tegel Airport
Tel: 41 01 31 48

Europa Service Car Rentals Arnim
Kurfürstendamm 65, Berlin 15
Tel: 8 83 50 13, 8 83 89 58

European Car Rental
Kurfürstenstrasse 101-104, Berlin 30
Tel: 2 13 70 97/98

Guse Car Rental
Kantstrasse 155, Berlin 12
Tel: 3 13 90 09

Hertz Car Rental
Budapester Str. 39, Berlin 30
Tel: 2 61 10 53
Tegel Airport
Tel: 41 01 33 15

Inter Rent
Xantener Str. 14, Berlin 15
Tel: 8 82 79 80
Tegel Airport
Tel: 41 01 33 68

WHERE TO STAY

Berlin hotels have a long tradition. The city centre of the old capital of the Reich was crammed with first-class hotels but there have always been houses offering good value in the centre too. Today some 26,000 guest beds are available in the 350 hotels and pensions of West Berlin. Some of them, like the Hotel Berlin and the Hilton (now the Inter-Continental) set standards for planning a new town in the ruins left over by the war; they not only serve an accommodation purpose but also as centres of social life.

According to the "Consumer Products Test Foundation" ("Stiftung Warentest") there are no real first-class hotel in West Berlin, but a number of places offer above average comfort. These include the Bristol Hotel Kempinski, Kurfürstendamm 27 (between 210 DM and 420 DM per night, around 1000 DM for a suite); the Inter-Continental Berlin, Budapester Strasse 2 (between 160 DM and 340 DM per night) as well as the Schweizer Hof, the Hotel Palace and the Steigenberger.

A number of smaller hotels some years ago joined to form the group "Berlin City Hotels" (with prices per night between 50.00 DM and 120.00 DM). Reservations for these hotels may be made through a central office at Marburger Strasse 17, tel: 0 30/ 24 50 84. At other hotels bookings are dealt with individually.

With the slogan "Berlin for less money" ten hotel-pensions in various districts have joined together for joint advertising and reservation. A list is available at the Tourist Information Office. Other hotels advertise as "the individual ten" in a collective pamphlet which can also be obtained from the Tourist Office. For example, the Novotel Berlin Airport is at Tegel airport and a few minutes away by taxi is the Novotel Berlin Siemensstadt. At the border checkpoint Dreilinden stands the Motel Grunewald. Here are three out-of-the-way hotels which are beautifully situated: Hotel Igel on the upper Havel, the Haus Dannenberg am See in Alt-Heiligensee and the elegant Schloss-hotel Gehrhus in Grunewald.

Private bed-and-breakfast guesthouses are particularly good value. The Tourist Office provides addresses of private house-holds offering beds for the night. At the Jebenstrasse exit of the Zoo station a private organization arranging rooms and hotel beds operates a kiosk.

There are also camping sites in Berlin: the site in Kohlhasenbrück, tel: 0 30/8 05 17 37; the site in Kladow, tel: 0 30/3 65 27 97; the camping and caravan site Haselhorst, tel: 0 30/3 34 59 55 and the camping and caravan site Dreilinden, tel: 0 30/8 05 12 01. Charges are 5 DM per tent or dormobile per night plus 6 DM per person; under 16 years, 1.70 DM. It is advisable to book ahead.

FOR THE YOUNG

Young people can find suitable accom-modation in Berlin. Travel groups are ad-vised to get in touch with the Informa-tionszentrum Berlin at Hardenbergstrasse 20, Berlin 12, tel: 0 30/31 00 41 72. You will also find a brochure here "Berlin for young people" with many interesting tips and ad-dresses. The information centre also has the addresses of numerous youth guesthouses in West Berlin. A guest house which has been specially equipped for handicapped young

people is that of the Fürst Donnersmarck Foundation, Wildkanzelweg 28 in Berlin 28, tel: 0 30/40 20 21. Information on youth hostels can be obtained from the Berlin state association of the German Youth Hostels Federation (Deutsches Jugendher-bergswerk), Bayernallee 35 in Berlin 19, tel: 0 30/3 05 30 55.

HOTELS

Alsterhof Ringhotel Berlin
Augsburger Str. 6, Berlin 30
Tel: 21 99 60

Hotel Ambassador Berlin
Bayreuther Str. 42/43, Berlin 30
Tel: 2 19 02-0

Hotel am Zoo
Kurfürstendamm 25, Berlin 15
Tel: 88 30 91

Arosa Aparthotel Berlin
Lietzenburger Str. 79-81, Berlin 15
Tel: 88 00 50

Arosa Sporthotel Berlin
Lietzenburger Str. 82-84, Berlin 15
Tel: 88 28 81

Hotel Berlin
Kurfürstenstr. 62, Berlin 30
Tel: 26 92 91

Berlin Crest Motor Hotel
Güntzelstr. 14, Berlin 12
Tel: 87 02 41

Berlin Excelsior Hotel
Hardenbergstr. 14, Berlin 12
Tel: 31 99-1

Berlin Penta Hotel
Nürnberger Str. 65, Berlin 30
Tel: 24 00 11

Berlin Plaza Hotel
Knesebeckstr. 63, Berlin 15
Tel: 8 84 13-0

Bristol Hotel Kempinski Berlin
Kurfürstendamm 27, Berlin 15
Tel: 88 10 91

CFC City Castle Apartment Hotel
Kurfürstendamm 160, Berlin 31,
Tel: 8 91 80 05

Econtel
Sömmeringstr. 24, Berlin 10,
Tel: 34 40 01

Hotel Hamburg
Landgrafenstr. 4, Berlin 30
Tel: 26 91 61

Hotel Hervis International
Stresemannstr. 97/103, Berlin 61
Tel: 2 61 14 44

Hotel Inter-Continental Berlin
Budapester Str. 2, Berlin 30
Tel: 2 60 20

Hotel Igel
Friederikestr. 33/34, Berlin 27
Tel: 4 33 90 67

Kanthotel Berlin
Kantstr. 111, Berlin 12
Tel: 32 30 26

Hotel Lichtburg
Paderborner Str. 10, Berlin 15
Tel: 8 91 80 41

Hotel Mondial
Kurfürstendamm 47, Berlin 15
Tel: 8 84 11-0

Novotel Berlin-Airport
Kurt-Schumacher-Damm 202, Berlin 51
Tel: 41 06-0

Hotel President
An der Urania 16-18, Berlin 30
Tel: 21 90 30

Motel Raststätte Grunewald
Spanische Allee 177/179, Berlin 38
Tel: 8 03 10 11

Hotel Rheinsberg am See
Finsterwalder Str. 64, Berlin 26
Tel: 4 02 10 92

Hotel Savigny
Brandenburgische Str. 21, Berlin 31
Tel: 8 81 30 01

Savoy Hotel
Fasanenstr. 9, Berlin 12,
Tel: 31 06 54

Schlosshotel Gerhus
Brahmsstr. 4/10, Berlin 33
Tel: 8 26 20 81

Hotel Schweizerhof
Budapester Str. 21-31, Berlin 30
Tel: 26 96-1

Hotel Seehof
Lietzensee-Ufer 11, Berlin 19
Tel: 32 00 20

Hotel Steglitz International
Albrechtstr. 2, Berlin 41
Tel: 79 10 61

Hotel Steigenberger Berlin
Los-Angeles-Platz 1, Berlin 30
Tel: 2 10 80

Hotel Sylter Hof
Kurfürstenstr. 114/116, Berlin 30
Tel: 2 12 00

MODERATELY PRICED

Hotel-Pension Schöneberg
Hauptstr. 135, Berlin 62
Tel: 7 81 88 30

Hotel-Pension Wittelsbach
Wittelsbacherstr. 22, Berlin 31
Tel: 87 63 45

Hotel-Pension Arka-Halensee
Kurfürstendamm 1032, Berlin 31,
Tel: 8 92 98 88

Hotel-Pension Bregenz
Bregenzer Str. 5, Berlin 15
Tel: 8 81 43 07

Hotel-Pension Chilcott
Meineckestr. 17, Berlin 15
Tel: 8 81 12 97

Villa Mirabell
Hammersteinstr. 8, Berlin 33
Tel: 8 23 62 37

Hotel Comet
Kurfürstendamm 175, Berlin 15
Tel: 8 82 70 21

Hotel-Pension Lenz
Xantener Str. 8, Berlin 15
Tel: 8 81 51 58

Hotel Casino Berlin
Königin-Elisabeth-Str. 47a, Berlin 19
Tel: 3 03 09-0

Hotel Riehmers Hofgarten
Yorckstr. 83, Berlin 61
Tel: 78 10 11

FOOD DIGEST

WHAT TO EAT

There is no such thing as "Berlin Cuisine" but there are Berlin specialities. The restaurants where you can enjoy genuine Berlin cooking have become rarer over the last decades: foreign restaurants are far more numerous.

A traditional Berlin restaurant will be fond of serving their guest *Aal grün*, eel from the Havel in herb sauce. Fresh water fish are still caught in local waters too. Thus some pub-restaurants, particularly those near the water also serve pike, perch, roach and catfish. *Wildschweinbraten* (Roast joints of wild boar) can be ordered in the restaurants near the extensive hunting grounds of Grunewald.

At parties, even large affairs, people are no longer embarassed to put on an "Old Berlin Buffet". The guests queue up for *schusterjungs* with dripping, *kartoffelpuffer* (potato pancakes) with apple-sauce, *bouletten* (meat-balls) with mustard, for pancakes (known elsewhere as "Berliner"), rollmops (herring) and sour gherkins. Sometimes pubs have *Katerfrühstück* (hangover breakfast) on offer; it invariably consists of

some dish made with herring. *Matjeshering* (raw herring fillets) is prepared with apples, onions and gherkins in cream. One speciality which at first seems strange but then wins people over is *Matjeshering* with green beans and potatoes boiled in their jackets. The fillets are served on cubes of ice with a lump of butter beside them.

In each "Stampe" (snack-joint) and, as a matter of course, in the better restaurants you will find the Berlin speciality *eisbein* (knuckle of pork). It is traditionally served at topping-out ceremonies, although these days some prefer to have a *schnitzel* (fillet of veal) to avoid eating too much fat.

Eisbein garnished with *sauerkraut* and *erbspüree* (mashed peas) is a favourite with many Berliners, especially in winter. It is claimed that the real connoisseurs leave the fatty bits aside and devote their attention to the lean meat inside. Beer and ice-cold *Schnapps* (white brandy) are drunk with this dish.

You take your chances with potato salad and meat balls. Bad restaurants serve up ready-made potato salad any old how from plastic buckets and there are too many breadcrumbs in the meat-balls. The latter are therefore ridiculed as "bewitched rolls". Best to try both at a friend's place only or at a so-called "Berliner Party".

But now it is time to talk about the *Kasseler*. *Kasseler* is salted spare rib or cutlet of pork, or belly; occasionally it is *Rolle*, that is to say compressed meat. The dish is not named after the German city of Kassel but after the Berlin master butcher Kassel. Fried with a tasty sauce it is a favourite with all at any family-party. Served as a cold cut fried *Kasseler* is also unbeatable. When eaten with potato salad it is dressed with mayonnaise or oil and vinegar, and with an abundance of finely chopped onions.

One item which appears regularly on both the restaurant and domestic menu is *Königsberger Klopse* (meatballs in cream sauce with capers). You use the same amount of meat that you would take for meat-balls and boil (not fry) it; it is best to use half pork and half ground beef. The broth is then made up into a light-coloured caper sauce. You can also leave the meat in loaf form. This is *Falscher Hase* (false hare) which elsewhere in Germany is known as *Hackbraten* and is served with gravy. On

Saturdays the family has *Kartoffelsuppe* (potato soup). It is served with bits of fried bacon or sausage and fresh parsley.

Pellkartoffeln mit Quark (jacket-potatoes with curd cheese) and for those who so desire *Spreewlder Leinöl* (linseed oil from the Spree forest) is said to be a meal which only a native Berliner can stomach. A slight hollow is made in the curd cheese for the oil. Such are the joys which remain incomprehensible to the stranger.

Beer is the most typical of all Berlin drinks. At the turn of the century over 100 breweries produced about 110 million gallons (five million hectolitres) of beer. Today, the number of companies has been reduced to four illustrious names: *Schultheiss, Engelhardt, Berliner Kindl* and *Hochschul-Brauerei*. The *Berliner Weisse mit Schuss* (Berlin wheat-beer with a shot of raspberry syrup), which is also known as the "champagne of the North", dates back to the Huguenots. The local beers were too bitter for their taste and so toward the end of the 17th century they started brewing high fermentation wheat-beer. The "shot" consists of either raspberry syrup or the woodruff variety. This accounts for the taste and the red or green colour.

The best way to enjoy a typical meal is as the guest of a Berlin family. Of course they might present snails and "Mousse au Chocolat", for where have they not been? However it would be more in Berlin style to have a bowl of pea soup with fried breadcrumbs followed by *Königsberger Klopse* with mashed potatoes, rounding off with *Kartoffelpuffer* and apple-sauce with coffee. This is "Berlin Cuisine" or, to be more exact, Berlin specialities.

WHERE TO EAT

In West Berlin there are around 1,300 restaurants and at least as many snack-bars and take-away stalls. The most famous stalls are outside Amtsgericht in Charlottenburg. If you include all the pubs, beer halls and bars then they all add up to a good 5,000 gastronomic businesses. From the "New German Cuisine" and international specialities from Copenhagen to Bombay through solid home-cooking, Berlin buffets to "curry sausage" there is everything you can imagine. Should you wish, a guidebook *Gas-*

tronomischer Wegweiser by the Tourist Office is recommended. The greater part of what is currently on offer is listed, but without any comments on quality. Those wanting more precise information should consult the *Guide Michelin* or the new special issue of *Zitty Essen, Trinken und Tanzen in Berlin*. You will find inexpensive addresses in the guide *Spezialführer Berlin*.

A few names should be mentioned: currently, the most exquisite food is served in the north of Berlin at **Rockendorf**'s in the Düsterhauptstr. 1. That at least is the opinion of those gourmets and lovers of French cuisine who are not put off by the long trek out to Waidmannslust in the Reinickendorf district. Reservations are a must (tel: 4 02 30 99). Also very much in favour with gourmets but at the other end of town is **An der Rehwiese**, Matterhornstr. 101 in Nikolassee (tel: 8 03 27 20). Those who wish to remain closer to the city centre will make for the recommended **Alt Luxemburg** at Pestalozzistr 7a in Charlottenburg (tel: 3 23 87 30) while lovers of fish and shellfish will opt for **Le Poisson**, Westfälische Str. 41 in Wilmersdorf (tel: 8 92 56 91).

Excellent restaurants are also found in the international hotels: in the Bristol-Kempinski, the **Kempinski**, in the **Steigenberger**, the restaurant of the same name, **La Reserve** in the Palace and **Die Hugenotten** in the Inter-Continental. Experts swear by both cuisine and service in the **Berliner Grill** of the Hotel Berlin. The **Conti-Fischstuben** in the Hotel Ambassador in the Bayreuther Strasse is also renowned. The excellent **Pullmann** restaurant in the ICC is not so well-known; the restaurant in the **Berlin Radio tower** is renovated in old style and is popular because of the view over the city roofs.

The best *Kohlroulade* (stuffed cabbage) in the city can be had at **Heinz Holl** in Damaschkestr. 26 in Charlottenburg (tel: 3 23 14 04). Other Berlin specialities like meat-balls, "*schusterjungs*" ("cobbler's apprentice"), pickled eggs, rollmops (rolled up herring) and "*rote grütze*" (red jelly) can be enjoyed during the day in the **Weissbierstube** of the Berlin-Museum at Lindenstr. 14 in Kreuzberg or in the evenings in the **Alt-Berliner Buffet** at Georg-Wilhelm-Str. 20, Halensee. The best knuckle of pork in Berlin is served from 10 a.m. in the rustic decor of **Hardtke** (tel: 8 81 98 27) at Meineckestr. 27. At **Josef Diekmann**, Meineckestr. 7, which is open till midnight, not only is there the pleasure of nouvelle cuisine but also of furnishings which date from the years of the foundation of the Second Reich. In addition to serving refreshments in a "Victorian" atmosphere the restaurant-café also serves as a gallery for young Berlin painters.

The **Tafelrunde** restaurant at Nachodstr. 21 in Wilmersdorf serves a substantial seven-course meal which is prepared in genuine medieval style. You eat with your fingers while a drinking-horn with mead does the rounds. For those wishing to sample food from all over the world without travelling too far or having to look too hard try the Europa-Center. There are so many different restaurants that a week would scarcely be long enough to test them all. The Japanese **Daitokai** is particularly exotic. From **i-Punkt** on the 20th floor you have a beautiful view and **Mövenpick** has an excellent ice cream and salad buffet.

Italian, Greek, Yugoslavian and Asian specialty restaurants can be found all over Berlin: most serve medium-quality food.

Currently the best Italian food is served at **Ponte Vecchio** at Spielhagenstr. 3 (tel: 3 22 35 72) which is in Charlottenburg. In Kreuzberg there are countless Turkish places, but one of the best is in the city centre: **Istanbul** at Knesebeckstr. 77 (tel: 8 83 27 77). The best Indian restaurant is **Kalkutta** at Bleibtreustr. 17 (tel: 8 83 62 93). Fans of vegetarian cooking should try **Hakuin** at Martin-Luther-Str. 1 (corner of Kleiststr.). It is run by a Buddhist community and guests sit in the relaxing surroundings of a Zen garden with fountains and a goldfish pond (tel: 24 20 27): closed on Thursdays.

A number of restaurants for those who visit Berlin's lakes or green areas are also worth mentioning. Excellent German cooking is on offer at the **Alte Dorfkrug** in Lübars, at the **Alte Fischerhütte** on the Schlachtensee and at **Forsthaus Paulsborn** in the centre of the Grunewald. The **Bistro-Café am Kalenderplatz** on the site of the Federal Gardening Show at Massinger Weg is also worth a visit.

Professional Berlin promoters claim "*it*" to be open day and night – there is no closing time. Of course that does not mean that every pub and restaurant is open 24 hours a day, butthat at any time of the day or night there is somewhere to get something to eat and drink. For example **Ça va** at Pariser Strasse 56 still has warm food on offer at 3 a.m., and **Schwarzes Café** at Kantstrasse 148 is where the "Szene" meets – predominantly younger – around the clock (apart from Tuesdays) for breakfast.

DRINKING NOTES

Pubs: The favourite meeting place for Berliners is the traditional *Kneipe* (public house) around the corner. It does not have to be literally around the corner but it must at least have that welcome-back atmosphere.

Different age groups usually frequent different pubs. The so-called Szene-Kneipe ("Szene" covering all people of the wide-range leftist-green-alternative-student spectre) is where a predominantly youthful public congregates which, in contrast to the 1970s, is not only run on Kreuzberg Bohemia-style lines but also as music café, chic New Wave and cocktail bar.

Others prefer the cosy Old Berlin beer halls and bars with pickled eggs, meat balls and fried potatoes and bric-à-brac decor. Whatever, Berlin's pubs are the most important setting for conviviality outside the home: you turn up at the pub regularly, call the publican by his Christian name and have, if needs be, a glass of beer on credit.

Many visitors on the lookout for a really original Berlin pub end up, sooner or later, in **Leydicke** at Mansteinstr. 4, a side street of Yorckstrasse in Schöneberg. This venerable, more than 100-year-old pub with its self-serve counter is as much renowned for its furnishings, which are worthy of a museum, as for its colourful clientele and the unpredictable effects of its home-made fruit-wines and liqueurs. In the city-centre the **Ku'dorf** at Joachimstaler Strasse 15 and **Sperlingsgasse** at Lietzenburger Strasse 82–84 are veritable mazes with one pub after the other. Travel groups spend their free evening here.

Today "in", tomorrow "out" is the rule according to which certain pubs and garden cafés are suddenly thrust into the limelight, become *the* place to be seen at and where anyone who is somebody can be seen. In retrospect it is hard to see why a particular bar or café turns into the meeting point for celebrities, the in-crowd and a whole following of curious ordinary guests. The **Paris Bar** at Kantstr. 152 has kept its place on the list for years because it is frequented by many celebrities of the literature and art worlds. **Chez Alex** on the upper part of Ku'damm in Halensee on the corner of Eisenzahnstrasse is more a piano-bar with an intimate atmosphere where a fashionable clientele gathers, **Fofi's** at Fasanenstr. 70 is regarded as a typical in-crowd spot. **Ax-bax** at Leibnizstr. 34 and **Exil**, Paul-Linke-Ufer 44 in Kreuzberg are both haunts for people from the film and entertainment industry with some Austrian atmosphere provided by their founder Ossi Wiener, incidentally, nobody shows up at these spots before 11 p.m. One of the favourite places for the "cultural mafia" to gather during the day is **Café Einstein** at Kurfürstenstr 58. It is run along the lines of a Vienna coffee-house: in summer you take breakfast outside under the trees and the *Apfelstrudel* (apple-pie) is excellent. The **Galerie Bremer** at Fasanenplatz is an art gallery with a bar which is open in the evenings. Rudi von Laak, one of the veterans of Berlin night-life, caters for his guests with an unwavering friendliness.

Around Nollendorfplatz and on towards Kreuzberg the pubs and hang-outs tend to become less respectable and more punkish. "Underground pubs" are found in the Goltzstrasse (**Slumberland**) at Nollendorfplatz (**Swing**) and in Kreuzberg (**Oranienbar**). These are just three names selected from among dozens. Best ask around but do not forget: what was yesterday's hot spot might welcome you as its only guest.

A category apart is that of the gay pubs. If you don't already know certain names from hearsay, then a stroll along the side-street between Wittenbergplatz and Nollendorfplatz will be sufficient to put you in the picture. Otherwise one can consult the *Siegessäule* (Victory Column), the monthly magazine of the Berlin homosexual community. Around the Eisenacher and Motzstrasse you will also find a variety of "Ladies Only" bars, sporting names like **Pour Elle** and **Ladies Night** which are immediately recognizable for what they are.

THINGS TO DO

AROUND BERLIN

This section briefly describes the districts in Berlin, highlighting the places of interest, events, exhibitions and activities peculiar to each district.

KURFURSTENDAMM

Local public transport centres at Zoologischer Garten station with U 1, U 9 and S 1 connecting. At Hardenbergplatz next door buses A 54/60/73/90/94 and 9/69, also: U 2 (Wittenbergplatz, change for Uhlandstrasse) and U 7 (Adenauerplatz). Between Wittenbergplatz and Rathenauplatz, up and down the Ku'damm, buses A 19/19N and A 29 run at a special reduced fare of 1.00 DM.

For Tourists: Most international airlines have their town offices here; Air France, British Airways and Pan Am are based at the Europa-Center, as is the Berlin Tourist Office (Verkehrsamt). City tours also leave from Europa-Center.

Browsing Around: Antique market and museum in the Ku'damm-Karree, 1st floor, daily 3 p.m.-10 p.m. except Tuesdays; Ziller Hof (second hand), Fasanenstrasse at the S-Bahn bridge.

Exhibitions and Events: Staatliche Kunsthalle, Tues.-Sun., 10 a.m.-6 p.m.; Wed. 10 p.m.; Käthe-Kollwitz-Museum, daily 10 a.m.-6 p.m. except Tuesdays. Nationalgalerie; Kunstforum in der Grundkreditbank, Budapesterstr. 33-35. Aquarium Zoologischer Garten, entrance Budapesterstr. 32, daily 9 a.m.-6 p.m. Regular downtown events are the Kunstmeile ("arts mile" end of June/July) and the Internationales Drehorgelfest (barrel-organ festival) early July.

CHARLOTTENBURG

The U 1 and U 9 *via* Zoologischer Garten. U 7 and S 3 offer quick links to various parts of the district. The following buses take you to the places of interest: A/1 (Deutsche Oper, Schiller-Theater); A4/10/69/94 (ICC Messegelnde/Deutschland Halle); A9/54/74 (Schloss Charlottenburg); A 94 (Olympiastadion).

Rathaus: Otto-Suhr-Allee 100 (tel: 3430-1).

Exhibitions and Events: Graphotek City/Kulturforum in der Villa Oppenheim, Am Parkplatz 6-8, Mon., Tues., Fri., 9 a.m.-3 p.m.; Wed., Thur., 9 a.m.-6 p.m. Kunstamt Charlottenburg (district arts council) in der Orangerie, Schloss Charlottenburg June-Sept. Tues.-Sun., 11 a.m.-6 p.m. (tel: 3005388). Heimatmuseum (local history) Charlottenburg, Schlossstr. 69, daily 10 a.m.-5 p.m. except Fri. (tel: 34303201). Olympiastadion sightseeing 9 a.m. till dusk; Glockenturm daily 10 a.m.-5:30 p.m.; ICC guided tours, 10 or more persons by appointment only (tel: 3038-1).

Also in the District: Kunstbibliothek Berlin with Museum für Architektur, Modebild (fashion photography) and Graphic Design, Jebenstr. 2 (tel: 31011); Amerika Haus, Hardenbergstr. 22/24 (tel: 8197661); British Centre, Hardenbergstr. 20 (tel: 310176); Internationale Kunst (cabaret and satirical reviews), Dahlmannstr. 11 (tel: 313 8201).

WILMERSDORF

The U 2 from Wittenbergplatz stops five times in the district and crosses at Fehrbelliner Platz with the U 7 which in turn joins the U 9 at Berliner Str./Bundesallee; S 3, A 19/29/69/86 go to Grunewald; A 10/50/60 to Schmargendorf; A1/16 to Breitenbachplatz; A 4/74 to Fehrbelliner Platz .

Rathaus: Fehrbelliner Platz 4 (tel: 8689-1).

Exhibitions and Events: Kommunale Galerie Hohenzollerndamm 176, Mon.-Fri., 10 a.m.-6 p.m.; Sun., 10 a.m.-5 p.m. (tel: 8689539); next to it (177) the Kommunales Museum, Mon., Wednesday, Friday, 10 a.m.-2 p.m., Tuesday, Thursday, 2 p.m.-6 p.m.; Freimaurermuseum, Emser Str. 12-13 in the Logenhaus (tel: 877100).

Theatre: Kleines Theater at Südwestkorso 64, (tel: 8212021); in late summer every year, wine festival around the Weinbrunnen at Rüdesheimer Platz.

Off Cinemas: Graffiti, Pariser Str. 44 (tel: 8834335); Eva, Blissestr. 18 (tel: 8228527); Bundesplatz-Studio, Bundesplatz 14 (tel: 8533355).

Sport: Roller and ice skating at Wilmersdorf stadium, Fritz-Wildung-Str. 9 (tel: 8241012, 8234060).

In Summer: Nude sunbathing at Halenseewiese and Teufelssee. Ökowerk at Teufelssee (restored water-works and Berlin's first nature conservation centre with exhibitions and demonstrations).

SCHÖNEBERG

The U4 from Nollendorfplatz to Innsbrucker Platz takes you right across the Bayerische Viertel and to the Rathaus Schöneberg; other subway connections go *via* Wittenbergplatz (U1/2) and Kleistpark/Potsdamer Str. (U7); the U9 and S1 (Wannseebahn) go to Friedenau; the S2 crosses the southern area and stops at Insulaner (Priesterweg station). Bus connections to and through the district area: A 4/16/65/73/74/85 (all lines connect with Rathaus Schöneberg; A 48/83 (Potsdamer Str. and Hauptstr.); A 25/68/76 (Friedenau and Insulaner).

Rathaus: John-F.-Kennedy-Platz (tel: 783-1).

Exhibitions and Events: Kunstamt Schöneberg (district arts council) Haus am Kleistpark, Grunewaldstr. 6/7, Tuesday-Sunday 10 a.m.-7 p.m. (tel: 7833032): in the same building the Heimatmuseum (local history), Monday and Friday, 10 a.m.-1 p.m., Thursday 4 p.m.-7 p.m., Wilhelm-Förster-Sternwarte (observatory) and Zeiss-Planetarium, Munsterdamm 90 (tel: 7962029 for programme information). For the Kulturgemeinschaft Urania, An der Urania, see announcements. Hochbahnhof fleamarket at Nollendorfplatz, daily except Tuesday 11 a.m.-7 p.m. Also at Nollendorfplatz is the "Nolle" (old style Berlin pub with jazz on Sunday morning).

Off Cinemas: Notausgang, Vorbergstr. 1 (tel: 7812682); Xenon, Kolonnenstr. 5-6 (tel: 7828850); Cinema, Bundesallee 111.

TIERGARTEN

U9 (direction Osloer Str.) provides good connections to the district especially to the Hansaviertel (Akademie der Künste, Grips-Theater) and Moabit: also S 3 and A 1. Bus lines to Grosser Tiergarten and Tierpark-Süd: A16/24/69 (Tempodrom, Kongresshalle, Reichstag, Brandenburger Tor) and A29/48/83 (Kulturforum, Potsdamer Platz).

Bezirksrathaus: Turmstr. 35 (tel: 3905-0).

Tourist Cafés, Pubs: Café am Neuen See, Lichtensteinallee; Parkhaus im Englischen Garten.

Exhibitions and Events: Historical exhibition daily in the Reichstag except Monday 10 a.m.-5 p.m.; Gedenksttte Deutscher Widerstand (German Anti-fascism Memorial), Mon.-Fri. 8 a.m.-6 p.m., Sat./Sun. 9 a.m.-1 p.m. (tel: 2604/2204); Kunstamt Tiergarten at Lützowplatz (tel: 3905/2234/2338) and next to it Galerie Poll (tel: 26170891); DAAD-Galerie at Café Einstein, Kurfürstenstr. 58; Verein Berliner Künstler (Berlin artists association), Schöneberger Ufer 57 (tel: 2612399); Akademie der Künste (Arts Academy), Hanseatenweg 10 (tel: 3911031); Landesbildstelle Berlin with photography exhibitions, Wikinger Ufer 57 (tel: 39092-1); Staatsbibliothek Stiftung Preussischer Kulturbesitz with concerts in the Otto-Braun-Saal, Potsdamer Str. 33 (tel: 266-1); Hamburger Bahnhof, Invalidenstr. 50/51.

KREUZBERG

U1 to Schlesisches Tor; U6, U7, U8, cross various areas of the district; S1, S2, S3 to Anhalter Bahnhof (Martin-Gropius-Bau, Deutschland-Haus), if neccessary change at Friedrichstrasse: coming from the City A29, from other directions A24/28/41/95; good transfer possibilities at U-Bahn stations Hallesches Tor and Möckernbrücke.

Rathaus: Yorckstr. 4-11 (tel: 25883300/3301).

District-Festival: Kreuzberger Festliche Tage in Victoria Park (August).

Exhibitions and Events: Kunstamt Kreuzberg (district arts council) (tel: 2588/2506) in Künstlerhaus Bethanien, Mariannenplatz 2 (tel: 6148010); Martin-Gropius-Bau, Stresemannstr. 110 (tel: 2548-6302);

Stiftung Deutschland-Haus (Middle and East German culture), Stresemannstr. 90 (tel: 2611946); culture in the restored U-Bahn station Schlesisches Tor.

Galleries: Elefanten Press, Zossener Str. 32 (tel: 6937036); Neue Gesellschaft für Bildende Kunst, Tempelhofer Ufer 22, Monday-Friday 10 a.m.-5 p.m.

Others: Amerika-Gedenkbibliothek, Blücherplatz 1, Monday 4 p.m.-8 p.m., Thursday-Saturday 11 a.m.-8 p.m.; Concerts in the Passionskirche, Marheinekeplatz; Junges Theater, Friesenstr. 14 (tel: 6928735); Hebbel-Theater, Stresemannstr. 29.

NEUKÖLLN

Direct connection with the U 7 (direction Rudow); good bus connections from the city centre, A 4/25/29/73; A 41 to border crossing point Waltersdorfer Chaussee (transit to Schnefeld airport), A 65/95 to crossing point Sonnenallee for Treptow (only for citizens of West Berlin).

Rathaus: Karl-Marx-Str. 83, (tel: 68091)

Places of Historical Interest: The Böhmisches Dorf and Britzer Mühle. **Leisure-time Attractions:** Badeparadies Blub (swimming), Buschkrugallee 64 (U-Bahn station Grenzallee, A 41); Buga-Park, Sangershauser Weg 1.

Events: Britzer Baumblte (blossom-watching in April-May), Hasenheide open-air theatre, Alt-Rixdorf Christmas market at Richardplatz.

Sport: Roller-skating in Hasenheidestr. 108 (tel: 6211028); skating in the ice-sport stadium, Oderstr. 5a (tel: 68902635).

Exhibitions: Kunstamt Neukölln (district arts council) at the gallery in Körnerpark, Schierker Str. 8 (Tuesday-Sunday 11 a.m.-6 p.m., tel: 68902635); Heimatmuseum (local culture), Ganghoferstr. 3 (Wed. 4 p.m.-8 p.m., Thur., Fri., Sun. noon-4 p.m., Sat. 1 p.m.-6 p.m.

Theatre: Freies Schauspiel, Pflügerstr. 3 (tel: 6924672); children's theatre Klecks, Schinkestr. 8-9 (tel: 6937731).

TEMPELHOF

The U 3 travels in a north-south direction through Tempelhof: from the railhead at Alt-Mariendorf there are bus connections to other parts of the district. Buses A 7/76/78/79 to the Trabrennbahn (trotting race course) whose terrace restaurant is also a social meeting place (tel: 7401128). The areas Mariendorf, Marienfelde and Lichtenrade can be reached directly by S 3 as well as A 11/82/83/96: from the city centre the A 19 and A 24 go to the airport (Tempelhof Airways departures: Monopolies Commission).

At the moment there are no guided tours through the old central airport. However, regularly in May there are: Free Access Days to the US Air Force base with demonstrations and shows. On the Airlift-Memorial-Day (May 12th), there is an official festival at the Luftbrücken-Denkmal. For guided tours of Haus Schulenburgring 2, contact Joachim Dillinger (tel: 7857739) or H.J. Müller (tel: 7863459). Exhibition of local history and the history of Tempelhof in the Heimatmuseum, Alt Mariendorf 43 (tel: 7022465).

Art: Rathausgalerie and Galerie der Abteilung Volksbildung, Bürgermeisterstr. 34.

Rathaus: Tempelhofer Damm 165/69, (tel: 7560-1).

The UFA-Fabrik's reputation as a cultural venue has long since crossed the borders of Tempelhof (U-Bahn Ullsteinstrasse A 25/68, programme information tel: 7528085).

STEGLITZ

The U 9 provides the quickest connection to the shopping centre around Schloss- and Albrechtstrasse. At the railhead Rathaus Steglitz, change to buses A 85/88 for Lichterfelde and to A 30/32 for Südende and Lankwitz. Crossing the district with five stations is the S1 (Wannseebahn); other connections are: A48 (Schlossstr., Schlosspark-Theater, Botanischer Garten), A 17 (Lilienthal-Memorial).

Rathaus: Schlossstr. 80 Bürohochhaus Steglitzer Kreisel, (tel: 790410).

Places of Interest: Botanischer Garten from 9 a.m. to dusk; Botanisches Museum Tuesday-Sunday 10 a.m.-5 p.m., Wednesday 7 p.m.; Lankwitz Tierheim (animal home, buses A 2/11/83/96) has lectures and guided tours (tel: 7721064/65); local history exhibitions at the Heimatverein Steglitz, Drakestr. 64a, Sunday 10 a.m.-noon,

Wednesday 4 p.m.-6 p.m.

Theatre: Schlosspark-Theater (tel: 7911213).

Gastronomy: 167 foot (50-metre) high tower restaurant *"Bierpinsel"*; historical *Wrangelschlösschen* is an elegant restaurant with Schinkel decor.

Architecture: *Titania-Palast*, Schlossstr. 5, built in 1927 as a cinema and now a shopping centre has a facade under preservation order; the country houses in the *Altdeutsches Viertel* settlement are in Renaissance and neo-Gothic-style.

ZEHLENDORF

Zehlendorf is divided into the areas of Zehlendorf-Mitte, Dahlem, Nikolassee, Schlachtensee, Wannsee, Kohlhasenbrück and Steinstücken.

Public transport U 2 direction Krumme Lanke, S 1 and S 3 direction Wannsee; the following buses take you to the sights and other destinations: A1/10/17 (Staatliche Museen Dahlem, Botanischer Garten, Freie Universität), A3/60 (Museumsdorf Düppel, tel: 8026671), A6 (Pfaueninsel, Glienicker Brücke), A18 (Wannsee-Mitte, Steinstücken), A60 (Brücke-Museum).

Rathaus: Kirchstr. 1/3 (tel: 807-1; A 48).

Events: Kunstamt Zehlendorf (district arts council) holds exhibitions and concerts in the *Haus am Waldsee*, Argentinische Allee 30 (tel: 8018935); Heimatmuseum (local history), Clayallee 355, Thursday 2 p.m.-6:30 p.m. Serenade concerts in the Jagdschloss Grunewald (tel: 8133597); German-American fun-fair (July).

Where to go: good places to drop in on are the Alter Krug and the Luise, a rustic student pub with beer garden (both in Dahlem, Königin-Luise-Str.); live music in the Eierschale at U-Bahn station Podbielskiallee and in the *Jazzkeller* at Breitenbachplatz (music on Sunday mornings). Popular pubs in the forest Grunewald are *Forsthaus Paulsborn* and the *Chalet-Suisse*; in Wannsee, *Loretta, Wannseeterrassen and Nikolskoe*.

SPANDAU

Fastest connection to Spandau Rathaus is with the U 7, and from there by bus to the areas Wilhelmstadt, Gatow, Kladow, Gross-Glienicke (A 34), Staaken (A 31/92), Hakenfelde (A 56/97) and Johannisstift (A 54); by U 1 to Ruhleben, from there buses to Kladow (A 35) and Pichelsdorf (A 94); connecting to Siemensstadt, Haselhorst and Gartenfeld are A 10/13/23/72 and others.

Rathaus: Carl-Schurz-Str. 2 (tel: 3303-1).

Places of Interest: Zitadelle, daily except Monday, 9:30 a.m.-4:30 p.m., Sunday 10 a.m.-4:30 p.m., guided tours on weekends. Stadtgeschichtliches (local history) Museum Tuesday-Friday 9 a.m.-4 p.m., Saturday-Sunday 10 a.m.-4 p.m. Information about events and exhibitions at the Zitadelle are available from the Kunstamt (district arts council) (tel: 33033134 or 339129733); historic Burg Festival in September; medieval evening banquets, in the *Küchenmeysterey* (tel: 332106).

Theatre: Open-air theatre at the Zitadelle (Altstadt-Theater, tel: 3318776); Spandau amateur theatricals Varianta, Carl-Schurz-Str. 59.

Others: Spandau locks; weekly markets; "Wild West" town of the "Cowboy Club old Texas"; Kolonie Sonneneck, U-Bahn station Paul-Stern-Str.

Events: Thanksgiving at Johannisstift (tel: 33609-0); Christmas market in the old part of town.

REINICKENDORF

Fastest connections to West Berlin's north vary according to where you wish to go; U 6 to Tegel or S 3 through Wittenau, Waidmannslust, Hermsdorf to Frohnau. Buses from Tegel U-Bahn station to Heiligensee, Märkisches Viertel (A13/14), Lübars (A20), and Frohnau (A15); other bus connections *via* U-Bahn station Osloer Strasse (U 8/9), Kurt-Schumacher-Platz or Seestrasse; to the airport by Citybus A9 or A8 with U-Bahn connections in Tegel and Wedding.

Rathaus: Eichborndamm 215/239 (tel: 4192-1).

Places of Interest: Tegel Airport (tel: 4101-1) with visitor's terrace (April-Oct.) and Airport-Gallery.

Events: The Reinickendorf Kunstamt (district arts council) arranges exhibitions and concerts in the Rathaus, Tegel-Centre, and Fontane-Haus (Information tel: 41926276/90); free Access Day to the Quar-

tier Napoléon French army base (mid- June).

Sights: The Borsig Works (tel: 4301-1); Jugendfarm Lübars (a youth park, children will love it); Russischer Friedhof (Russian cemetery); Buddhistisches Haus (tel: 4105580; A 12/15); Tegel Schloss (tel: 3434156; A 13/14/15/20); Heimatmuseum (local history) Alt-Hermsdorf 35 (Wednesday-Sunday 10 a.m.-6 p.m.).

Excursions: Trip on the steamboat Moby Dick, from Tegel to Wannsee (*ca.* 2 hrs).

Industrial architecture: The Borsigtor built in 1896.

WEDDING

The U 6 goes to Wedding's centre around Müllerstrasse; U 8 and U 9 (direction Osloer Strasse) end in Wedding; direct connection by S 2 North (direction Frohnau) to Gesundbrunnen, the second centre of the district around Brunnen- and Badstrasse (with border crossing point Bornholmer Strasse). The following buses run from the city centre; A 16/23/62/65/70/ 89/90.

Rathaus: Müllerstr. 146/147 (tel: 457-0, U-Bahn station Leopoldplatz).

Events: Wedding Kunstamt (district arts council) has exhibitions in the Rathenausaal of the Rathaus (tel: 4573048); Centre Francais with cultural programmes in French and German, also with library, Müllerstr. 74 (tel: 4181418); open-air theatre Rehberge; German-French fun-fair at Kurt-Schumacher-Damm (June/July).

Places of Interest: Heimatmuseum (local history), Müllerstr. 158/corner Triftstr. (Wednesday 11 a.m.-7 p.m.); Zuckermuseum ("sugar" museum) Amrumer Str. 32 (A 64).

Historical Monuments: Alte Nazareth-Pankstr. in Gesundbrunnen; AEG-Tor (1897) in Brunnenstr.

Art: Rathenau fountain in the Volkspark Rehberge: Ackerstrasse Artist's quarter (former AEG building); Künstlerhaus E 43, Edinburgher Str. 43; Fotogalerie im Wedding, Amsterdamer Str. 24 (tel: 4562918).

UNTER DEN LINDEN

The fastest way to this historic part of East Berlin is *via* the border crossing point Friedrichstrasse Bahnhof, which can be reached by the S 3 (*via* Bahnhof Zoo), S 2 or U 6.

Entry into East Sector from 6 p.m.-8 p.m., exit until midnight for day visitors from West Germany and abroad; for West Berliners until 2 a.m. For information on changing money, formalities and other border crossing points please check "East Berlin section". All places of interest between Brandenburger Tor and Alexanderplatz can be reached on foot from Friedrichstrasse Bahnhof, otherwise change to S- or U-Bahn. There is a taxi rank at Friedrichstrasse Bahnhof. It is compulsory to change 25 Deutschemark at a 1 to 1 rate (normally 1 to 19), but this covers all normal expenses for a one-day trip (such as food, drinks, travel and entrance costs, postcards, maps, etc.). At higher priced Interhotels and restaurants 25 East-Mark is not enough. Information on events in East Berlin can be found beforehand in the magazines *Tip* and *Zitty*; the East Berlin fortnightly *Wohin in Berlin?* can be bought at Berlin Information, Neustädtische Kirchstr. 30, or at kiosks.

ALEXANDERPLATZ

Alexanderplatz is the intersection point of two U-Bahn lines and the S-Bahn going to Ost-Kreuz from where there are other transfer possibilities. It is a good starting point for visits to more distant sights such as the Treptow Memorial (official wreath-laying on May 8 and Nov. 8); May 8, 1945 Memorial in Karlshorst (with historical exhibition); Tierpark Friedrichsfelde (over 5,000 animals in open-air enclosures) and the Alfred-Brehm-Haus, a 53 foot- (16 metre-) high green house; Müggelsee (boating with the "white fleet"); Schloss Köpenick (with arts and crafts museum and the "Köpenick Summer"); Volkspark Friedrichshain (with the fairy-tale fountain and graveyard of the "March martyrs"); Dorotheenstädtischer Friedhof (Chausseestr. 126, graves of famous persons such as Schinkel and Brecht).

Information about travel connections at Alexanderplatz S-Bahnhof at *Service Städt. Nahverkehr* (tel: 2462255), also sale of Tourist Tickets and taxi tours. Information and tourist publications also at *Informationszentrum am Fernsehturm* (tel: 2124675) and at VEB-*Reisebüro der DDR*, Alexanderplatz 6 (tel: 2150); where there is a foreign visitors service from where the guided tours depart.

TOURS & EXCURSIONS

Throughout the year guided tours of the city are organized by various companies at all times of day. The buses are very modern with huge panoramic windows and competent personnel. Departure is from Kurfürstendamm between Ranke- and Fasanenstrasse and at the Zoo palace in the Hardenbergstrasse. For example the "City-Tour" lasts two hours and costs about 17 DM, the three-hour "Super-Tour" 22 DM. A combined bus and ship tour is on offer for about 27 DM. The three-and-a-half hour trip around East Berlin costs 24 DM. A minimum exchange is no longer required at the border. The five-hour "Nightclub-Tour" which includes a visit to the revue theatre "La vie en rose" among others is available at 89 DM per person. The prices given here may differ slightly from company to company. Excursions into the GDR are also possible. A day trip to Potsdam and the castle of Sanssouci costs 99 DM: the half day trip costs 84 DM.

On the ship-excursion along the canals of Berlin the visitor will see many of the city's more than a thousand bridges. The trip begins at 10 a.m. at the Schlossbrücke Charlottenburg and lasts about six hours. Visitors can also hop aboard the regular services of "Stern- und Kreisschiffahrt" on the upper and lower Havel. Boats depart from 16 docking points, including Bahnhof Wannsee, the Halbinsel Schildhorn, Freybrücke and Spandauer Lindenufer; information tel: 81 00 04-0/8 03 87 50.

The Heinz Riedel shipping company runs both daytime round trips and moonlight cruises between May 1 and September 30. Boats cast off down town and at the Havel. Further information under tel: 6 91 37 82 or 6 93 46 46 as well at the Kongresshalle ticket counter (tel: 3 94 21 80) or at their Hansabrücke office (tel: 3 92 40 60).

The cultural and historical guided tours of the city which are run by *Kultur-Kontor* are something special. They review the history of Berlin in conjunction with special themes, such as "Berlin at the Turn of the Century", "Berlin's Light Entertainment" or "Industrialization in Berlin". Information and tickets are obtainable at Savignyplatz 9-10, (tel: 31 08 88). The Berliner Geschichtswerkstatt at Goltzstr. 49 (tel: 2 15 44 50) in Schöneberg organizes historical guided tours of the city by boat on summer weekends (Friday 3 p.m.-6 p.m., Saturday 10 a.m.-noon).

CITY TOURS

The following companies organize daily tours. Tickets can be obtained on the buses.

Bärenrundfahrt (BBS)
Rankestrasse 35, Berlin 30
Tel: 2 13 40 77.
Departure: Rankestr./junction with Kurfürstendamm opposite the Gedächtniskirche.

Berolina Stadtrundfahrten
Berlin 15, Meineckestrasse 3
Tel: 8 83 31 31.
Departure: Meineckestr./junction with Kurfürstendamm.

Busverkehr Berlin (BVB)
Kurfürstendamm 225, Berlin 15
Tel: 8 82 20 63.
Departure: Kurfürstendamm 225, opposite Café Kranzler.

Holiday Sightseeing (HRI) Bustours
Fasanenstrasse 67, Berlin 15
Tel: 88 42 07 11.
Departure: Hardenbergstrasse, directly at the Zoo Palace.

Severin und Kühn Berliner Stadtrundfahrten
Kurfürstendamm 216, Berlin 15
Tel: 8 83 10 15.
Departure: Fasanenstr./junction with Kurfürstendamm.

EXHIBITIONS & CONGRESSES

As a city of international trade fairs and congresses Berlin is of international standard. The Internationale Congress Centrum (ICC) and the adjoining exhibition and trade fair centre at the Funkturm are easily accessible by all means of transport. In addition to the many local and regional events there are a number of regular large international exhibitions and fairs which attract many visitors to the city. These begin at the end of January or in early February with the traditional agricultural show *Grüne Woche*. In March the travel industry organizes the *Internationale Tourismus-Börse (ITB)* for tour operators from all over the world. A big pharmaceutical and medical technology exhibition takes place parallel to the *Kongress für ärztliche Fortbildung* (doctor training) (May–June). The big trade fair event in August-September is held in uneven years. *Internationale Funkausstellung* (TV and Radio media), followed by the Third World Cooperation fair *Partner des Fortschritts*, are in September/October. More information can be obtained from the Berlin Tourist Office or the Berlin Ausstellungs-Messe-Kongress-GmbH at D-1000 Berlin 19, Messedamm 22, (tel: 30 38-1).

FOR THE CHILDREN

There are children's playgrounds everywhere in the city. On the 40 or so adventure playgrounds children are even allowed to build, saw and hammer. The *Lübars Freizeitpark* offers all sorts of play and sport facilities with its youth farm on the Quickbornerstrasse in Berlin-Reinickendorf. The farm also provides an insight into rural arts and crafts. There are also children's farms in the inner city districts, where animals are kept and visitors both small and big are welcome. Some of these are the *Weddinger Kinderfarm*, Luxemburger Str. 25 in Berlin 65; *Kinderbauernhof Görlitzer Park* in Wiener Str. 59, Berlin 36; *Kinderbauernhof Mauerplatz*, Adalbertstrasse/Leuschnerdamm in Berlin 36 and the *Kinderbauernhof in der UFA-Fabrik*, Viktoriastrasse 13–18 in Berlin-Tempelhof. The last of these, the site of the former UFA complex, is where one of Berlin's best known autonomous social projects has developed and where, among other things, theatrical and musical events and – especially for children – circus performances are organized regularly. The "Tempodrome", where the audience can participate, near the Kongresshalle at Tiergarten, is a children's circus.

Several theatres in Berlin perform especially for children. Best-known are the productions of the "Grips"-Theater at Altonaer Strasse 22, Berlin-Tiergarten. Performances at the "Klecks" at Schinkelstrasse 80, Berlin-Neukölln and the Berliner Figuren-Theater at Yorckstrasse 59 in Kreuzberg, Berlin 61 are aimed at smaller children.

There is also much for children to discover in Berlin's museums such as the Museum für Völkerkunde (ethnography) at Lansstrasse 8 in Berlin 33, the Museum für Verkehr und Technik (transport and technology) at Trebbinerstrasse 9, Berlin 61 and the Museum für Deutsche Volkskunde (German folklore), Im Winkel 6/8 in Berlin 33. In the Museumsdorf Düppel, a reconstructed village/settlement of the period around 1200 in the Clauertstrasse in Berlin-Zehlendorf, they can even go for rides in an ox-drawn cart. The site of the Bundesgartenschau (Federal Landscape Show) of 1985 at Massinger Weg in Neukölln is also attractive for children of all ages. Then there is always the zoo and the aquarium in the middle of the city with many open-air enclosures, tropical and nocturnal animal houses, and pony rides and coach trips. It is open each day from 9 a.m. until dusk.

The brochure *Berlin – für die ganze Familie* from the Tourist Office is a mine of information. Up-to-date tips on children's films in the cinemas and travelling circuses are provided by *Tip* and *Zitty*. Two new publications offer extra suggestions: the illustrated guide to the city of Berlin and its 750 years' history for children *Raus in die Stadt!* (Out into Town!), published by Elefanten Press, and the Berlin guide for mothers, fathers and children *Was machen wir heute?* (What shall we do today?) by Nicolai. With the *Ausmalbuch Berlin* (Colouring Berlin) children get to know the city by painting it: it is by Beate Nowak and also published by Nicolai.

A tip for parents who want to experience Berlin without their offspring: the "Heinzelmännchen" at the Freie Universität (tel: 8 31 60 71) and the TUSMA at the Technische Universität (tel: 3 13 40 54) organize babysitters: the hourly fee is about 13 DM.

CULTURE PLUS

MUSEUMS & GALLERIES

Prussian Cultural Heritage Foundation
The museums of the Stiftung Preussischer Kulturbesitz (Prussian Cultural Heritage Foundation) in Charlottenburg, Dahlem and Tiergarten make up the greater part of Berlin's museums and permanent exhibitions. The art library in Charlottenburg and the Preussische Geheime Staatsarchiv (Prussian Secret State Archive) in Dahlem also belong to the foundation. For more on state museums visit Stauffenbergstr. 41, Berlin 30, (tel: 0 30/2 66-6).

Anti-Kriegs-Museum (anti-war)
Genter Str. 9, Berlin 65
Tel: 4 61 78 37

Ägyptisches Museum
Schlossstr. 70, Berlin 19
Tel: 3 20 11

Antikenmuseum
Schlossstr. 1, Berlin 19

Berlin-Museum
Lindenstr. 14, Berlin 61
Tel: 2 51 40 15

Berlinische Galerie
Stresemannstr. 110, Berlin 61
Tel: 25 86-0

Bauhaus-Archiv
Klingelhofer Str. 13-14, Berlin 30
Tel: 2 61 16 18

Botanisches Museum
Königin-Luise-Str. 6-8, Berlin 33

Bröhan-Museum
Schlossstr. 1a, Berlin 19
Tel: 3 21 40 29

Brücke-Museum
Bussardsteig 9, Berlin 33
Tel: 8 31 20 29

Deutsches Rundfunkmuseum (broadcasting)
Hammerskjöldplatz 1, Berlin 19
Tel: 3 02 81 86

Friedensmuseum ("Peace")
Stresemannstr. 27, Berlin 61
Tel: 2 51 01 86

Gemäldegalerie
Arnimallee 23/27, Berlin 33
Tel: 8 30 12 48

Georg-Kolbe-Museum
Sensburger Allee 25, Berlin 19
Tel: 3 04 21 44

Gipsformerei (plaster of Paris mould centre)
Sophie-Charlotten-Str. 17-18, Berlin 19
Tel: 3 22 23 67

Grosse Orangerie
Schloss Charlottenburg, Berlin 19
Tel: 3 20 12 53

Hamburger Bahnhof
Invalidenstr. 50, Berlin 21

Kleine Orangerie
Schloss Charlottenburg, Berlin 19
Tel: 3 00 53 88

Kunstgewerbemuseum (arts and crafts)
Tiergartenstr. 6, Berlin 30
Tel: 2 66 29 02/03

Museen in Dahlem
Lansstr. 8, Berlin 33
Tel: 83 01-4 38

Museum Düppel
Clauertstr. 11, Berlin 37
Tel: 8 02 66 71

Museum für Deutsche Volkskunde (folklore)
Im Winkel 6/8, Berlin 33
Tel: 83 20 31

Museum für Verkehr und Technik (transport and technology)
Trebbiner Str. 9, Berlin 61
Tel: 2 54 84-0

Museum für Vor- und Frühgeschichte (pre- and early history)
Schloss Charlottenburg, Langhansbau, Berlin 19
Tel: 3 20 11

Musikinstrumentenmuseum (musical instruments)
Entlastungsstr. 1, Berlin 30
Tel: 2 54 81-0

Nationalgalerie
Potsdamer Str. 50, Berlin 30
Tel: 2 66 26 62

Post- und Fernmeldemuseum
An der Urania 15, Berlin 30
Tel: 2 12 82 01

Staatliche Kunsthalle
Budapester Str. 42, Berlin 30
Tel: 2 61 70 67

CONCERTS

Although Jazz, Rock and Pop venues in Berlin are continually appearing and disappearing there are some places which have established themselves over the years. Other than the Jazz Festival in November and the annual "Jazz Fest in the Garden" which takes place every summer in the Skulpturengarten of the Nationalgalerie, the most interesting address is **Flöz** at Nassauische Strasse 37 (tel: 8 61 10 00). Organized by Franz de Byl, who is a master of the jazz guitar, this is where Free Jazz musicians of international repute perform. The programme at **Quasimodo** at Kantstr. 12a (tel: 3 12 80 86) boasts not only famous names from the Jazz scene but also those of Rock and Blues. **Quartier Latin** at Potsdamer Str. 96 (tel: 2 61 37 07), a former cinema, has been converted into a music venue with restaurant on the first floor. Now Rock, Pop and Blues are performed here, along with off-theatre productions. The most promising of the new discoveries from the West Berlin cellars and garages, plus British Independent Charts and Psychedelic and Rockabilly Underground from the U.S.A. are presented by Monika Döring in **Loft** at Nollendorfplatz 5 (tel: 2 16 10 20). Then there is **K.O.B.** at Potsdamer Strasse 157 (tel: 2 16 52 96), the meeting point for the so-called "Post-Punk" scene. Fans of Reggae and Funk listen to their favourite music live at the discotheque **Empire** at Hauptstrasse (tel: 30 7 84 85 68), while **Go In** at Bleibtreustrasse (tel: 17 8 81 72 18) remains the sure-fire address for Folk fans. A music programme booklet with a comprehensive list of addresses, *Music Scene Berlin*, is available free of charge in pubs, restaurants and at cinema and theatre box-offices. Regular tips also appear in *Tip* and *Zitty*.

BERLIN PHILHARMONIC ORCHESTRA

Reservations are possible in writing but not by telephone. The annual programme comes out at the end of April and will be sent by the Press office when a stamped, addressed envelope is provided. All enquiries to the Philharmonic, Matthäikirchstr. 1, D-1000 Berlin 30, (tel: 2 54 88-0); general enquiries also under tel: 2 61 43 83. Box-office hours for advance booking are Monday-Friday 3:30 p.m.-6 p.m., Saturday, Sunday and public holidays 11 a.m.-2 p.m. Otherwise there are numerous theatre box-offices which make advance booking for visitors from outside the city.

THEATRES, OPERA & DANCE

Deutsche Oper Berlin
Bismarckstrasse 35
Tel: 3 41 44 49

Schiller-Theater
Bismarckstr. 110
Tel: 3 19 52 36

Schiller-Theater Werkstatt ("experimental")
Bismarckstr. 110
Tel: 3 19 52 36

Schlosspark-Theater
Schlosstr. 48
Tel: 7 91 12 13

Theater der Freien Volksbühne
Schaperstr. 24
Tel: 8 84 20 80

Komödie
Kurfürstendamm 206
Tel: 8 82 78 93

Renaissance-Theater
Knesebeckstr. 100
Tel: 3 12 20 53/54

Tribüne
Otto-Suhr-Allee 18-20
Tel: 3 41 26 00

Hansa-Theater
Alt-Moabit 48
Tel: 3 91 44 60

Berliner Kammerspiele
Alt-Moabit 99
Tel: 3 91 65 31/3 91 55 43

Kleines Theater am Südwestkorso
Südwestkorso 64
Tel: 8 21 20 21

Junges Theater
Friesenstr. 14
Tel: 6 92 87 35

Theatermanufaktur am Halleschen Ufer
Hallesches Ufer 32
Tel: 2 51 09 41

Freie Theateranstalt
Klausener Platz 19
Tel: 3 21 58 89

Grips-Theater
Altonaer Str. 22
Tel:3 91 40 04

Rote Grütze
Mehringdamm 52
Tel: 6 92 66 18

Theater zum Westlichen Stadthirschen
Kreuzbergstr. 37
Tel: 7 86 10 09

Mehringhof-Theater
Gneisenaustr. 2
Tel: 6 91 80 21

Tanzfabrik ("dance factory")
Möckernstr. 68
Tel: 7 86 58 61

Transform-Theater
Hasenheide 54
Tel: 6 92 32 39

Theater 36
Muskauer Str. 43
Tel: 6 12 62 94

Theater am Kurfürstendamm
Kurfürstendamm 206
Tel: 8 82 37 89

Schaubühne am Lehniner Platz
Kurfürstendamm 153
Tel: 89 00 23

Theater des Westens
Kantstr. 12
Tel: 3 12 10 32/ 3 12 50 15

Vaganten-Bühne
Kantstr. 12a
Tel: 3 12 45 29

LITERATURE

The heydays of the "Romanische Café" opposite the Gedächtniskirche have long since gone. Literary Berlin is very different today but the centre of activity has remained in Charlottenburg. A focal point for events concerning books was created in May 1986 at Fasanenstrasse 23 with the opening of the **Literaturhaus** in a tastefully renovated town house. In addition to three lecture-rooms it houses a café with summer garden, a memorial to Kurt Tucholsky and a book shop in the basement. A calendar of upcoming events is also obtainable here. Enquiries under tel: 8 82 65 52.

Some other meeting points and institutions of literary Berlin are the **Akademie der Künste** (Arts Academy Hanseatenweg 10, tel: 3 91 10 31), the **Literarische Kolloquium Berlin** in Wannsee (Am Sandwerder 5, tel: 8 03 56 81) and the **Neue Gesellschaft für Literatur** (Bismarckstr. 17, tel: 3 42 20 59). The off-beat scene includes the **Forum unbekannter Autoren** (unknown authors) at Akazienstr. 19 (tel: 7 84 45 83) in Schöneberg and the **Literaturcafé** at Winter-feldstr. 36. Most bookshops are found in the Charlottenburg district, especially around Savignyplatz in Knesebeckstrasse and Carmerstrasse. The **Buchhändlerskeller** at Carmerstr. 1 (tel: 8 82 11 70) is a well-known venue for readings of writers from East Berlin and the GDR. A few houses further down at the Autorenbuchhandlung, Carmerstr. 10 (tel: 3 10 11 51) an audience assembles every Tuesday in a cosy literary haunt. A curiosity among West Berlin's 250 or so bookshops is to be found at Motzstrasse 30 in Schöneberg. Richard Schikowski's bookstore and antiquarian bookshop is particularly well stocked with books on the esoteric, occultism, astrology and parapsychology (2 p.m.-6 p.m. apart from Wednesdays, Saturdays 9 a.m.-1 p.m.). In the past Rudolf Steiner used to work in the same house. A few blocks further on in the Winterfeldstrasse there are six antiquarian bookshops, one after the other, in which to rummage.

MOVIES

Berlin was and remains a film city par excellence, and not only during the annual International Film Festival in February. Numerous production companies are resident here and the Deutsche Film- und Fernsehakademie Berlin, DFFB (film and television academy), Berlin 19, Pommernallee 1 (tel: 30 36-1) trains budding talents here. The large cinemas are concentrated in the city centre between the Europa-Center and Uhlandstrasse. Many have five or six different shows running simultaneously. In addition, there is a wide range of arts cinemas devoting themselves to avant-garde, political film, experimental work as well as to classic and exotic films. The **Arsenal** at Welserstrasse 25, immediately behind Wittenbergplatz (tel: 24 68 48), is particularly worth mentioning. The programme (changes daily) of the **Freunde der Kinemathek** shows special retrospective themes, and publishes an informative monthly programme. The **Odeon** at Hauptstrasse 116 (tel: 7 81 56 67) screens exclusively English language films in original version. Non-dubbed foreign films are occasionally shown at Amerika Haus, at the British Centre and at the Institut Français. The private Berliner Kinomuseum (cinema museum) in Kreuzberg at Grosseerenstrasse

57 is scarcely larger than a living room and is devoted to the care and preservation of old films and projectors. There are showings every Wednesday, Friday and Saturday at 8:30 p.m. and 10:30 p.m. with an additional Saturday show at 6 p.m. The planned transformation of the former Grand Hotel "Esplanade" at Bellevuestrasse 16 at Tiergarten into the Filmhaus Berlin offers the prospect of a further meeting point for the Berlin film enthusiast.

DIARY OF EVENTS

The best guide, with sections for Theatre, Dance, Music, Film, Cabaret, Fine Arts etc. is to be found in the two Berlin periodicals *Tip and Zitty*. The Berlin-Programme, *Zu Gast in Berlin* (Visiting Berlin) and the weekly calendar in the Wednesday edition of the *Tagesspiegel* are helpful guides through the labyrinth of the daily cultural programme and, last but not least, are the telephone announcements and the good old advertisement pillar, the *Litfasssäule*, with their posters and stickers. Most of the larger theatres open their box-offices in the mornings and accept telephone bookings.

BERLINER FESTSPIELE

Information, tickets, books, posters and brochures for the various events can be obtained at the Information Office, Budapesterstrasse 48 at the Europa-Center (from March 14th to November 22th daily from 10 a.m. to 7 p.m. and for the rest of the year daily from noon to 6 p.m. apart from Mondays, tel: 25 48 92 50). Enquiries either in writing or by telephone to the Kartenbüro der Berliner Festspiele, 1000 Berlin 30, Budapester Str. 50: telephone information Monday-Friday from 10 a.m. to 4 p.m. under 0 30/25 48 91 00.

THEATRE BOX-OFFICES

Centrum
Meineckestr. 25, Berlin 15
Tel: 8 82 76 11

Concert Concept
Hauptstr. 83, Berlin 41
Tel: 8 52 40 80

Theaterkasse im Europa-Center
Tauentzienstr. 9, Berlin 30
Tel: 2 61 70 51

KaDeWe
Tauentzienstr. 21, Berlin 15
Tel: 24 80 36

Ottfried Laur
Hardenbergstr. 7, Berlin 12
Tel: 3 13 70 07

Sasse
Kurfürstendamm 24, Berlin 15
Tel: 8 82 73 60

Wertheim
Kurfürstendamm 231, Berlin 15
Tel: 8 82 25 00

Wildbad Kiosk
Rankestr. 1, Berlin 30
Tel: 8 81 45 07

Advance Booking also for East Berlin Events
Theaterkasse Zehlendorf
Teltower Damm 22, Berlin 37
Tel: 8 01 16 52

CULTURAL VENUES

Akademie der Künste (Arts Academy)
Hanseatenweg 10, Berlin 21
Tel: 3 91 10 31

Alte TU-Mensa (university canteen)
Hardenbergstr. 34, Berlin 12
Tel: 3 11 22 33

Freie Universität Audimax (main lecture hall)
Garystr. junction with Boltzmannstr., Berlin 33

Deutschlandhalle
Messedamm 26, Berlin 19
Tel: 3 03 81

Eissporthalle (ice stadium)
An der Jafféstr., Berlin 19
Tel: 3 03 81

Grosser Sendesaal des SFB (main broadcasting studio)
Masurenallee 8-14, Berlin 19
Tel: 3 02 72 43

Haus der Kirche
Goethestr. 27, Berlin 12
Tel: 31 91-1

Hebbel-Theater
Stresemannstr. 29, Berlin 61
Tel: 2 51 27 73

Hochschule der Künste (small concert hall and theatre)
Fasanenstr. 1, Berlin 12.
Concert hall: Hardenbergstr. 33, Berlin 12
Tel: 3 18 50/31 85 23 74

ICC
Messedamm, Berlin 15
Tel: 8 81 35 38

Jüdisches Gemeindehaus
Fasanenstr. 79-80, Berlin 12
Tel: 8 81 35 58

Konzertsaal Bundesallee
Bundesallee 1-12, Berlin 15
Tel: 31 03 31

Kreuzberg Markt
Kreuzbergstr. 37/38, Berlin 61
Tel: 7 86 10 09

Künstlerhaus Bethanien
Mariannenplatz 2, Berlin 36
Tel: 6 14 80 10

Literaturhaus
Fasanenstr. 23, Berlin 12
Tel: 4 65 66 04

Messehallen (trade fair halls)
Am Funkturm, Berlin 19
Tel: 3 03 81

Metropol
Nollendorfplatz 5, Berlin 30,
Tel: 2 16 41 22

Olympiastadion
Berlin 19
Tel: 3 04 74 72

Philharmonic
Matthäikirchstr. 1, Berlin 30
Tel: 2 54 88-0

Staatsbibliothek
Potsdamer Str. 33, Berlin 30
Tel: 26 61

Tempodrom
An der Kongresshalle, In den Zelten, Berlin 21
Tel: 3 94 40 45

UFA-Fabrik
Viktoriastr. 13, Berlin 42
Tel: 7 52 80 85

Urania
Kleiststr. 13-14, Berlin 30
Tel: 24 90/91

FOREIGN CULTURAL CENTRES

Amerika Haus Berlin
Hardenbergstr. 22/24, Berlin 12
Tel: 8 19 76 61

Aspen Institut Berlin
Inselstr. 10, Berlin 38
Tel: 8 03 90 41

The British Council – The British Centre Berlin
Hardenbergstr. 20, Berlin 12
Tel:31 01 76

Institut Franais de Berlin
Kurfürstendamm 211, Berlin 15
Tel: 8 81 87 02/8 81 76 20

NIGHTLIFE

Berlin being open around the clock, pubbing and night life do not exclude one another, and the visitor can spontaneously decide whether to visit the disco or the cabaret and follow this by dining in an all-night restaurant. However, it is only fair to state that Berlin's night clubs and shows are not among the world's best: the city still lives off the myth of the "Golden Twenties".

If a Berliner wants to take his/her guests out for the evening then the first place which comes to mind is **Die Stachelschweine** ("porcupines") in the basement of the Europa-Center, the cabaret troupe having virtually become an institution in Berlin's world of wit and satire. Run under the name of a cabaret group no longer in existence, **Die Wühlmäuse** ("the voles"), the cabaret club at Nürnberger Str. 33 (tel: 2 13 70 47) stages a varied programme with literary-satirical solo cabaret artists as well as quick-change artists and comedians. **La vie en rose**, the international revue theatre in the Europa-Center, is also a good place for an entertaining evening out (except Mondays). There are shows at 10 p.m. and midnight, Saturdays also at 8 p.m., featuring Brazilian carnival and an occasional Paris revue group (tel: 3 23 60 06). Those looking for the unclad and striptease will perhaps get their money's worth (and a worthy bill) from the erotic dancing-girls in the barely lit **New Eden** at Kurfürstendamm 70 (tel: 3 23 58 49). Since the heyday of the legendary **Eldorado** in the Martin-Luther-Strasse Travesty-Shows have been a much-celebrated feature of the Berlin night life.

The most risque show in town is running at **Chez Nous** at Marburger Str. 14 for which table reservations are definitely recommended (tel: 2 13 18 10). There is good parody-cabaret a few streets further on at **Dollywood**, Welserstr. 24 (tel: 24 89 50), and if you prefer a touch of burlesque there is **Straps-Harry** starring at the "**Crazy Theater Dreamboy's Lachbühne**" at Bundesallee 194b (tel: 2 11 85 64). The "**Lützower Lampe**" at Witzlebenstrasse 38 in Charlottenburg specializes in the same brand of entertainment (tel: 3 21 20 97). You will have to spend some 50 DM on weekdays for this kind of amusement and more on weekends.

While there is no international superdisco like New York's "*Palladium*" in Berlin, there is no end to the places at which to dance, with something for every taste and age group. The laser-disco "**Metropol**" at Nollendorfplatz is spacious yet is invariably crammed full at the weekends.

The **Metropol** is also the setting for live concerts. On Fridays and Saturdays the "**Tango bar**", in the style of the 1920s, is open for custom in the same building. Although tiny in comparison the **Cha Cha** in the Nürnberger Strasse is just as busy. A few yards away is the **Dschungel** which for years has been the favourite disco of those who consider themselves "in" and "really cool". The new star among the top discos is **First** at Joachimstaler Str. 26. **Far out** run by Bhagwan followers at Lehniner Platz continues to be popular as is **Abraxas** in the Kantstrasse, which is stronghold of Funk and Soul. For those around 30 **Annabelle's** at Fasanenstrasse 64 can be recommended. The chic Ku'damm clientele frequent **Coupe 77** at Ku'damm 177 as well as the **Ciro-Bar**, Rankestr. 32. People of all ages meet on the roof-garden of the **Hotel Inter-Continental** to dance. **VIP** is the name of the not exactly modestly priced disco on the first floor of the Europa-Center with its view of the Kurfürstendamm by night. This is where singles are guaranteed the romance of the big city. In **Café Keese** at Bismarckstrasse 108 it is up to the women to ask the men if they would care to dance (apart from Mondays). The establishment prides itself on having been the matchmaker of many a solid marriage. The **Tanz-Café Huthmacher** at Hardenbergstr. 29 is where the more mature gather in search of a partner.

A guide to the disco and amusement scene can be found in the Berlin-Programm and the *Zitty-Sonderheft* (special issue). The brochure *Berlin für junge Leute* (for the young) (obtainable free of charge at the Berlin Information Centre) contains the names of the youth discos. Those gentlemen travelling alone with money to spend are catered for by a large number of so-called private clubs, film bars and associated establishments advertising the merits of their live shows, private rooms, nudist conviviality, sauna and similar amusements. In plain English this is commercial sex. The *Stadtplan für Männer* (city-map for men), obtainable at virtually every kiosk in the city centre, provides a guide to the market and the street-walker network with pretty precise descriptions and prices. Similar ads are also found in the BZ and occasionally in *Clipper Magazine* for Pan Am passengers. Various escort agencies also offer their services.

SHOPPING

SHOPPING AREAS

One rule applies when on a shopping spree in Berlin: there is nothing which cannot be found here. An absolute must when shopping is the **KaDeWe** at Wittenbergplatz, the biggest department store on the continent. Spread over seven floors it contains a huge selection of elegant fashion, furnishings and culinary specialties from all over the world. With the transformation of the ground floor into a shop-within-a-shop it is even more stylish. Boutiques like Fendi for leather, Davidoff for tobacco products and Charles Jourdan for shoes are grouped here around the cosmetic department and the jewellery and watch-clock areas. However, the fashionable nucleus of the KaDeWe is the second floor where the finest *haute couture* from Paris for the ladies and everything from Boss and Burberry to Daniel Hechter for the men can be purchased. The food department on the 6th floor with its overwhelming variety of goods on offer and the diverse sampling stands are as much an attraction for the sightseer as the serious shopper.

Great places for a shopping expedition especially when the weather is bad are the "Ku'damm-Eck" (junction of Kurfürstendamm and Joachimstaler Strasse), the "Ku'damm Block" near the Uhlandstrasse and the Europa-Center which has already been mentioned. Regardless of the season one can wander from shop to shop with dry feet and without a coat; spacious multistorey car parks are located very near each complex.

Berlin also sets fashion trends: convince yourself of this by noting the many boutiques in the city. Not only is the Kurfürstendamm recommended in this respect but above all its more intimate side-streets. In the Bleibtreustrasse it is young people's fashion which abounds and the Uhlandstrasse is just as interesting while, the Fasanenstrasse has a particularly classy flavour. In the Nürnbergerstrasse at Tauentzien the stylish boutiques are lined up one after the other. **Chrome** with two outlets, in the Kant- and the Motzstrasse, offers out-of-the-ordinary import and designer fashion goods at reasonable prices. Those interested in second-hand fashion will find that the **Garage** in the Ahornstrasse at Nollendorfplatz has a huge selection of often original clothing which they sell by the kilo.

For lovers of antiques in every price category Berlin has a comprehensive range on offer. Good antique shops, which are also very expensive, are found mainly in the Keithstrasse and surrounding area, in and between Eisenacher- and Motzstrasse and in the Fasanenstrasse and on the Kurfürstendamm. Another place where they may be found is the Suarezstrasse in Charlottenburg. The bric-à-brac shops next to one another in the Nollendorfstrasse, in Kreuzberg around the Bergmannstrasse, and in the Flughafenstrasse in Neukölln are less exclusive but are less expensive. Three **flea markets** are worth mentioning here: the flea market located in the disused surface station at the **Nollendorfplatz subway station** is open every day (except Tuesdays) from 10 a.m. till 7 p.m.; the bric-à-brac market on the **Strasse des 17. Juni** is open on Saturdays and Sundays from 8 a.m. to 3 p.m. as is the **Kreuzberger market** on the Reichpietschufer.

Arts and crafts products are sold throughout the city centre. The area around the pedestrian zone in Wilmersdorfer Strasse is particularly recommended. Experts will undoubtedly be interested in the **Berliner Zinnfiguren-Kabinett** at Knesebeckstrasse 88. It is renowned well beyond the bounds of Berlin for its production of hand-painted tin soldiers. Augsburger Strasse, immediately behind the Kurfürstendamm, is Berlin's shopping centre for inexpensive photographic equipment. The main branch of **Wegert**, Berlin's biggest specialist in film and photography, is located on the corner of Potsdamer- and Kurfürstenstrasse.

For those with money left and who are looking for something special, Berlin's jewellers can be recommended; **Hülse** for example at Kurfürstendamm; in Schlüterstrasse while **Krischke** specializes in Art deco and jewellery and silver from old Russia. The Tourist Office has a shopping guide free of charge, *Shopping in Berlin*.

SPORTS

Berlin undoubtedly keeps its visitors on the move but those seeking physical activity beyond this will find something to suit their tastes. A good beginning is perhaps a jog around the Grunewaldsee, where one meets hordes of like-minded people. There are many open-air tennis courts and, according to the season, you can swim in open-air or indoor pools. International hotels have their own pools. The Neuköllner club, one of the largest swimming and leisure complexes in Europe, is particularly attractive. The recently opened Kreuzberg wave pool at Spreewaldplatz is also very popular. In winter ice-skaters glide around the artificial rinks of the ice stadia of Lankwitz, Neukölln, Wedding and Wilmersdorf, to say nothing of the Berlin Skating Club in the Glockenturmstrasse and the Eissporthalle in the Jaffestrasse. When it is very cold the Berlin Lakes are frozen. The largest of these lakes is ideal for sailing in summer. There are several schools for those who wish to learn. Contact the Havel Segelschule, Alt-Pichelsdorf 19c, in Berlin 20; the Surf-Segel-Schule Preuss at Holsteinische Strasse 44, Berlin 41; the Appelt, Am Rupenhorn 7d in Berlin 19.

"Keep-fit-trails" can be found in the Tiergarten, at the Grunewaldsee, in the Volkspark Mariendorf, in the Gemeindepark Lankwitz and near the Ruppiner Chaussee in Tegel. There are also ski- and sledging slopes, but Berlin is by no means certain to have snow. More exact information on Berlin as a sporting city is provided by the Landessportbund Berlin e.V., Jesse-Owens-Allee 1/2 in Berlin 19 (tel: 30 00 20).

Berlin has become well-known beyond the city limits for its marathon which is run every year in September. In 1986 more than 13,000 runners took part. In addition, at the beginning of May, there is a street-race over 25 kilometres which is organized by the Berlin Athletics Association and the French Garrison. Anyone feeling fit enough can take part. Of greater interest for the spectator are the Internationale Hallen-Fussball-Turnier (indoor soccer) which is held at the beginning of January and the Wasserball-Städte-Turnier (water-polo) which is held at the end of January. At the end of February an international ice-speedway rally follows on. In the middle of May there is the Internationale Tennis-Meisterschaften der Damen (Ladies' Grandprix) and the ADAC Avus car race. In August there is the International track and field event ISTAF; in October the legendary Six-Day-cycling race in the Deutschlandhalle; and in November the Internationale Reit- und Springturnier (Berlin Horseshow).

USEFUL ADDRESSES

TOURIST INFORMATION

The Verkehrsamt (Tourist Information Office) provides information of every kind. It helps with preparations for the journey, sends brochures on request, lists of hotels, shopping guides and the cultural calendar *Berlin tut gut*. The Tourist Information Office also arranges hotel rooms; written reservations should be sent with details of wishes at least two weeks in advance. The office can be reached under the address D-1000 Berlin 30, Euro-Center, Telex 1-83356 vber d. The central information desk at the Budapester Strasse entrance opposite the Zoo is open daily from 7:30 a.m. to 10:30 p.m., (tel: 2 62 60 31-22). Other information counters are found in the main hall of the Zoo station, the main hall of Tegel airport and at the Dreilinden- and Heerstrasse checkpoints. Information, leaflets and brochures on the political situation in Berlin and about East Berlin are to be had at the Informationszentrum Berlin at Hardenbergstrasse 20, not far from the Zoo station (Monday-Friday 8 a.m.-7 p.m., Saturday 8 a.m.-4 p.m., tel: 31 00 40).

American Express International
Kurfürstendamm 11, Berlin 15
Tel: 8 82 75 75

Deutsches Reisebüro (DER)
Kurfürstendamm 17, Berlin 15
Tel: 8 82 10 94
Theodor-Heuss-Platz 2, Berlin 19
Tel: 3 02 50 01
Augsburger Strasse 27, Berlin 20
Tel: 24 01 21
Teltower Damm 22-24, Berlin 37
Tel: 8 01 60 91
Albrechtstr. 3, Berlin 41
Tel: 7 91 20 11

Hansa Reise und Verkehr
Platz der Luftbürcke, Berlin 42
Tel: 78 00 08 10
Tegel Airport, Berlin 51
Tel: 41 01 33 65 and 41 01 33 66
Tempelhofer Damm 152, Berlin 42
Tel: 7 52 60 58
Kurfürstendamm 56, Berlin 15
Tel: 3 23 70 41/ 3 23 70 43

Hapag-Lloyd
Kurfürstendamm 199, Berlin 15
Tel: 8 82 71 24
Rheinstr. 11, Berlin 41
Tel: 8 52 20 96
Tegel Airport, Haupthalle
Tel: 4 13 50 61/ 41 01 33 60

Reisebro Globus
Uhlandstrasse 121, Berlin 31
Tel: 87 36 60/87 46 60

Wagon-Lits
Kurfürstendamm 42, Berlin 15
Tel: 8 81 66 83/8 81 80 39

OFFICES, ASSOCIATIONS AND INFORMATION BUREAUS

Bundeshaus
Bundesallee 216-218, Berlin 45
Tel: 21 26-1

Deutscher Bundestag (West German parliament)
Berlin administration, Reichstagsgebäude, Platz der Republik, Berlin 21
Tel: 3 97 71

Umweltbundesamt (Federal environment agency)
Bismarckplatz 1, Berlin 33,
Tel: 8 90 31

Senat von Berlin
John-F.-Kennedy-Platz, Berlin 62
Tel: 7 83-1

Der Senator für Wirtschaft und Verkehr (economy and transport affairs)
Martin-Luther-Strasse 105, Berlin 62
Tel: 7 83-1

Wirtschaftsförderung Berlin GmbH
(investment promotion)
Budapester Str. 1, Berlin 30
Tel: 23 36-1

Industrie- und Handelskammer, Berliner Absatzorganisation (chamber of commerce) (**BAO**)
Hardenbergstr. 16, Berlin 12
Tel: 31 80-1

Handwerkskammer Berlin (craftsmen's association)
Blücherstr. 68/Mehringdamm 15, Berlin 61
Tel: 2 51 09 31

Informations- und Beratungsdienst für zuwandernde Arbeitnehmer (immigrant workers)
An der Urania 4-10, Berlin 30
Tel: 21 22 24 41/42

Auskunfts- und Beratungs-Center (abc), Informationsdienst für "Neu-Berliner" (new residents service)
Hohenzollerndamm 125; Berlin 33
Tel: 82 00 82 60/61

Landeszentrale für politische Bildungsarbeit (political education)
(Rathaus Schöneberg), John-F.-Kennedy-Platz, Berlin 62
Tel: 7 83-1

Landesarchiv Berlin
Kalckreuthstr. 1-2, Berlin 30
Tel: 7 83 85 86

Stiftung Warentest (consumer goods testing)
Lützowplatz 11, Berlin 30
Tel: 2 62 30 14

Verbraucherzentrale Berlin (consumers organisation)
Bayreuther Str. 40, Berlin 30
Tel: 21 90 70

Deutscher Gewerkschaftsbund (Federal trade unions)
Keithstrasse, Berlin 30
Tel: 2 19 10

Deutsche Angestelltengewerkschaft (civil servants union)
Blissestr. 2, Berlin 31
Tel: 82 96-1

Sender Freies Berlin (SFB)
Masurenallee 8-14, Berlin 19
Tel: 30 81

RIAS Berlin
Kufsteiner Str. 69, Berlin 62
Tel: 85 03-0

INTERNATIONAL AIRLINES

Aeroflot (SU)
Budapester Strasse 50, Berlin 30
Tel: 2 61 82 50/51

Air Berlin (AB)
Tegel Airport, Berlin 51
Tel: 41 01 27 81

Air France
Tegel Airport, Berlin 51
Tel: 2 50 25

ALIA Royal Jordanian Airlines (RJ)
Budapester Strasse 14a, Berlin 30
Tel: 2 61 70 57/58

Alitalia (AZ)
Tauentzienstrasse 16, Berlin 30
Tel: 2 11 01 29/95

Austrian Airlines (OS)
Tauentzienstrasse 16, Berlin 30
Tel: 24 50 24

AVIANCA-Airline of Colombia (AV)
Kurfürstendamm 178, Berlin 515
Tel: 8 82 62 76/77

British Airways (BA)
Tegel Airport, Berlin 51
Tel: 69 10 21

Finnair (AY)
Budapester Straae 26a, Berlin 30
Tel: 2 61 80 55/56

Iberia (IB)
Reservations
Tel: 2 61 70 01

Japan Air Lines (JL)
Budapester Strasse 18a, Berlin 30
Tel: 2 61 12 74/75

Yugoslav Airlines (JU)
Kurfürstendamm 50a, Berlin 15
Tel: 8 83 65 22

KLM (KL)
Kurfürstendamm 17, Berlin 30
Tel: 8 81 10 81

LOT (LO)
Budapester Strasse 14a, Berlin 30
Tel: 2 61 15 05

Lufthansa (LH)
Kurfürstendamm 220, Berlin 15
Seat reservation and Information, tel: 8 87 55
Flughafen Tegel Passagebüro, tel: 8 87 58

Malev (MA)
Budapester Strasse 14a, Berlin 30
Tel: 2 61 48 67/2 61 51 55

Pan Am
Tegel Airport
Tel: 88 10 11

Sabena (SN)
Kurfürstendamm 209 (Ku'damm Block), Berlin 15
Tel: 8 81 70 11

Singapore Airlines (SQ)
Reservations, tel: 3 24 30 56
Tel: (0 69) 7 24 02 04

Swissair (SR)
Kurfürstendamm 209 (Ku'damm Block), Berlin 15
Tel: 8 83 90 01

Turkish Airlines (TK)
Berlin Management, Budapester Strasse 18b, Berlin 30
Tel: 2 62 40 33/34

VIASA (VA)
Kurfürstendamm 179, Berlin 15
Tel: 8 82 78 07

EMBASSIES & CONSULATES

In Berlin the United States, Great Britain and France have embassies and cultural institutions. There are also numerous military missions, consulates general, consulates and delegations of other states, some of which are represented by German honorary consuls. The armed forces of the three Western Allies maintain garrisons with their own housing estates, shops, schools, leisure centres, local press, radio and T.V. stations. The Commission of the European Community is represented by a Press and Information Office in West Berlin.

Commission of the European Economic Community
Press and Information Office
Kurfürstendamm 102, Berlin 31,
Tel: 8 92 40 28

American Consulate General
Clayallee 170, Berlin 33
Tel: 8 32 40 87/8 19 74 50

British Consulate General
Uhlandstr. 7/8
Berlin 12, Tel: 3 02 43 50

French Consulate General
Kurfürstendamm 211, Berlin 15
Tel: 8 81 80 28/29

GETTING THERE

ARRIVING IN EAST BERLIN

West Berlin ends at the Wall. But now the city of Berlin continues, and the Wall is no longer a barrier. Since the events of 1989, crossing over to the eastern part of the city has become almost as easy as visiting areas in the west. The 1,215-foot (365-metre) high silhouette of the television tower in Alexanderplatz can be seen for miles around, and points the way to the centre of the eastern part of what is officially known as "Berlin GDR" or "Berlin, Capital of the German Democratic Republic". A visit to this part of the city completes the picture of the divided metropolis. This applies to the present, determined as it is by proximity of East and West and their gradual coming together, as well as to the 750-or-so years of Berlin's history. It is possible to visit the East at any time, and different conditions apply for the West Berliners, Federal German citizens and foreigners.

East Berlin can be entered on foot, by car, in one of the West Berlin sightseeing buses, on the S-Bahn (fast train) or the U-Bahn (underground), or by bicycle, moped, motor-cycle, but not by boat. Of the present 29 crossing points, 17 lead directly into the eastern part of the city. The crossings at Checkpoint Charlie and Friedrichstrasse (Kochstrasse U-Bahn station) are reserved for foreigners. All the other crossing points

Crossing Point	Local Transport	Type of Vehicle
Heiligensee	Bus 98/E (also transit)	car/motorcycle/bus
Ruppiner Chausee	Bus 14	pedestrian/bicycle
Falkenseer Chauss	Bus 5, 5N, 92, E	all
Heerstrasse	Bus 13N, 92, 94, E (also transit)	all
Potsdamer Chausee	Bus 34	pedestrian/bicycle
Glienicker Bruecke	Bus 6	all
Griebnitzsee	S-Bahn	S-Bahn/bicycle
Dreilinden	Bus 99 (also transit)	car/motorcycle/bicycle
Benschallee	Bus 50, 3	pedestrian/bicycle
Ostpreussendamm	Bus 1N, 10, 68, 85, 96, E	all
Kirchhainer Damm	Bus 75	car/motorcycle
Buckower Damm	Bus 91, 91N	pedestrian/bicycle
Waltersdorfer Chaussee	Bus 41, 73N/E	all
Stubenrauchstrasse	Bus 52, 57, U7	pedestrian/bicycle
Sonnenallee	Bus 15, 19N, 65, 77N	all
Schlesische Strasse	Bus 28, 29N, U1	pedestrian/bicycle
Oberbaumbruecke	Bus 28, 29N, U1	pedestrian/bicycle
Jannowitzbruecke	U8	U-Bahn/bicycle
Prinzenstrasse	Bus 29, 29N, 41, 91N, U8	all
Checkpoint Charlie	Bus 29, 29N, U6	all
Potsdamer Platz	Bus 48, 83, 83N	all
Brandenburger Tor (Brandenburg Gate)	Bus 83, 69, 48, 83N	all
Friedrichstrasse	S2, S3, U6	U-Bahn, S-Bahn, bicycle only S-Bahn
Rosenthaler Platz	U8	U-Bahn/bicycle
Invalidenstrasse	Bus 83, 83N, 90, S3	all
Chausseestrasse	Bus 12, 70, 71, 72, 83, 83N, 90, U6	all
Bernauer Strasse	Bus 16N, 64, 71, U8	pedestrian/bicycle
Bornholmer Strasse	Bus 16N, 61, 70, 89	all
Wollankstrasse	Bus 61, 64N, 70, S2	all

may be used by West Berliners and citizens of the Federal Republic.

There are no restrictions on the number of visits or the amount of time spent in East Berlin or in the GDR. It is only necessary to register with the police if you intend to stay for more than 30 days.

Travel Essentials

VISAS & PASSPORTS

Berliners need to show their identity cards, citizens of the Federal Republic their passports. Children should carry their identification papers. Substitute papers may however be obtained at the border. For this, proof of identity is necessary, e.g. a driving licence. These papers cost 10 DM. Foreigners have to pay visa charges, and are required to observe the compulsory exchange.

MONEY MATTERS

The previous compulsory exchange no longer applies. The official exchange rate is 1 DM West to 3 GDR Marks. Money may be exchanged in banks and moneychangers in the GDR, but it is not necessary. It is, however, forbidden to change GDR Marks in West Berlin and then take them into the GDR. Money changed in the GDR may be brought back over the border, provided one has an exchange receipt.

CUSTOMS

Visitors from the West are allowed to take almost anything into the GDR duty-free. Even newspapers and books are allowed. However, firearms, drugs and right-wing radical literature are forbidden.

On leaving the GDR, various requirements apply. It is forbidden to take almost any article for everyday use, e.g. shoes, children's clothing, curtains and many kinds of groceries out of the country. Taking optical instruments, certain porcelain wares, works of art and precious metals is also not permitted. In case of doubt, enquire at the Office for Internal German Relations.

Goods without restrictions may be taken out of the country duty-free. However, the value taken by visitors who have stayed only one day must not exceed 100 Marks, and for visitors remaining several days, 200 Marks is the limit. For goods exceeding those values, payment of up to 200 percent of the retail value must be paid.

Transit travellers are not allowed to buy and take out any GDR wares, apart from travel necessities.

Getting Acquainted

GEOGRAPHY & ADMINISTRATION

East Berlin extends for over 156 sq miles (403 sq km), one quarter of which are woods and water. The eight districts from the old days of the Imperial capital were made 10 when, in the course of reorganization, the newly-constructed district of Marzahn was added. A territorial extension of East Berlin by way of inclusion of surrounding GDR territory is not permitted by the provisions of the Four Power Status of Greater Berlin and, until now, the GDR has adhered strictly to these regulations.

East Berlin has 1.19 million inhabitants. The city administration is the Magistrat (municipal council). It is headed by the City Mayor who also is a member of the GDR Council of Ministers. The Municipal Council is selected from the City Assembly of Representatives which is elected every five years following the principle of the one-party-list. Its resolutions must be passed unanimously. The individual city districts are run by district councils chaired by the district mayor.

East Berlin is the biggest industrial city in

East Germany, being a centre of the electro-technical and electronic industry and, a scientific and cultural centre as well as being an important junction of the Central European traffic network. Schönefeld international airport, which lies about two-and-a-half miles (four km) southeast of the city limits can be reached from West Berlin *via* the transit route through the Waltersdorfer Chaussee checkpoint. There are flights to Eastern and Western Europe, Africa, Asia and Cuba and, as of late, to Beijing.

Berlin Information: The counterpart of the Verkehrsamt in the West is Berlin-Information in the East. It runs a Visitors Centre in the buildings round Television Tower (Panoramastr. 1), which is open on Monday from 1 p.m. to 6 p.m., Tuesday to Friday from 8 a.m. to 6 p.m. and Saturday/Sunday from 10 a.m. to 6 p.m. A wide range of information is available here, brochures, city-maps etc. In addition the Centre also organizes film shows, talks and guided tours of the city (tel: 2 12 46 75).

VEB Reisebüro der GDR: Another place to head for is the official travel agency Reisebüro der DDR, at Alexanderplatz 5, tel: 21 50, which also runs a foreign visitors service, (tel: 2 15 44 02/03). Both are open from Monday-Friday 8 a.m. to 8 p.m., Saturday/Sunday from 9 a.m. to 7 p.m. The branch at Friedrichstrasse station which is open Monday-Friday 7 a.m. to 6 p.m.

DIPLOMATIC MISSIONS

The GDR maintains diplomatic relations with 120 governments, many of which are represented in East Berlin by embassies or missions. The embassies of the three Western Allies are officially termed as "Embassies with the GDR" (and not in), the USA, Great Britain and France not recognizing the status of East Berlin as a capital city or the "GDR State border" through the city. The Federal Republic maintains a permanent mission in East Berlin as does the East German government in Bonn.

Ständige Vertretung der BR Deutschland, Hannoversche Str. 30, tel: 2 82 52 61

HOLIDAYS

These differ somewhat from those in West Berlin: Official holidays on both sides of the border are: January 1, Good Friday, May 1, X'mas Day and Boxing Day. In addition, there is the special GDR holiday on October 7 (Republic Day). On the other hand, Easter Monday, Ascension Day and the Protestant Buss- und Bettag in November are normal working days.

COMMUNICATIONS

MEDIA

East Berlin is the GDR's publishing centre. In addition to publishing houses, newspapers and magazines, radio and television have their headquarters here. There are nine daily newspapers whose political uniformity is rather obvious. The Berliner Zeitung and BZ am Abend provide an insight into local affairs.

POST & TELEPHONE

The Hauptpostamt (central post office) in the Strasse der Pariser Kommune (central district) is open around the clock (tel: 5 80 08 71). Outside regular hours the post offices at Friedrichstrasse station and the Palast der Republik are open between 10 a.m. and 10 p.m. Calls to the West can be made from telephone boxes with a special sign marked on them.

Dialling Code from West Berlin to East Berlin: 03 72
Dialling Code from East Berlin to West Berlin: 849
Dialling code from Federal Republic to East Berlin: 00372

EMERGENCIES

Some important telephone numbers are:

Police Emergency Line 110
Fire Brigade 112
Rescue Service Emergency
Line 115
Rescue Service 2 82 05 61
Medical Emergency Service 12 59
Pharmacy Emergency Service 160

LOSS

Zentrales Fundbüro
Wilhelm-Pieck-Str. 174,
Tel: 2 82 61 35/2 82 34 72/2 82 34 73

Fundbüro der Deutschen Reichsbahn
S-Bahn station, Marx-Engels-Platz,
Tel: 4 92 16

Federal citizens or West Berlin citizens who get into difficulties while in East Berlin should contact the **Ständige Vertretung der Bundesrepublik Deutschland** at Hannoversche Strasse 30 not far from Friedrichstrasse station (tel: 2 8 52 61: code number from the GDR 002: from West Berlin 03 72: and from the Federal Republic 0 03 72). It functions as a consulate in the GDR and organizes legal aid in cases of arrest or court trials.

When appropriate, non-Germans should contact their own consulates or embassies. The American Embassy is at Neustädtische Kirchstrasse, 1080 Berlin (tel: 2 20 27 41); the British Embassy is in 1080 Berlin, Unter den Linden 32-34 (tel: 2 20 24 31). Australians need to contact their embassy in Warsaw, Gl. Estouska 3-5, tel: 17 60 84 Poland; New Zealanders the Vienna Embassy in 1010 Vienna, Lugeck 1-2 (tel: 52 66 36), Austria; and Irish from the Republic, 2514 BA Den Haag, Dr. Kuyperstraat 9 (tel: 63 09 93), Netherlands.

GETTING AROUND

INNER-CITY TRANSPORT

Information on the inner-city transport network is obtainable from the Service Städtischer Nahverkehr at the Alexanderplatz S-Bahn station. Call 4 92 24 89 for information on S-Bahn and 2 46 22 55 for information on other transport and excursions. The information desk in Alexanderplatz S-Bahn station is open Monday-Friday from 9 a.m.-6 p.m., Saturday from 9 a.m.-1 p.m.

PUBLIC TRANSPORT

East Berlin has an extensive and reasonably priced public transport network. The most important method of transport is the S-Bahn. In addition to the U-Bahn (subway) and the buses, there is also the good old tram. The cheapest fare on any of the transport systems, without changing, is the fixed sum of 20 pfennigs. Fares on the S-Bahn depend on the distance travelled: top fare is 1.30 marks: children up to six travel free of charge. On other forms of transport 6 to 14 year-olds pay 10 pfennigs. There is no tariff connection between the U-Bahn and the S-Bahn, which means that the commuter must pay again when changing from one system to the other. Any ticket stamped in West Berlin is also valid in the East.

TAXIS

Taxis are available at various taxi ranks or by telephone 36 46. Bookings up to seven days in advance can be arranged by calling 3 65 41 76. The flag-drop is 50 pfennigs and, according to the time of day, fares range between 80 pfennigs and one mark per kilometre. Taxis are rare and long queues of waiting people can be seen at the Friedrichstrasse S-Bahn station.

PRIVATE TRANSPORT

Drivers require vehicle documents and, if they come from abroad, a green insurance certificate. In addition, must have a national identity sticker. Drivers must abstain from alcohol. Trams have the right of way.

Breakdown Service (day and night)
Tel: 5 59 25 00
Central Vehicle Emergency Service
Tel: 116
Automobile Assistance (6 a.m.-10 p.m.)
Tel: 5 24 35 65

WHERE TO STAY

HOTELS

There are now no more restrictions on accommodation. For visitors staying for several days, the following possibilities are available for "currency foreigners" in the centre of East Berlin. They offer the international standard of five-star hotels and are accordingly expensive. The best way to obtain a visa is to contact the Reisebüro der DDR, Generaldirektion, DDR 1026 Berlin, Alexanderplatz 5, Postfach 77, tel: 21 50.

Palasthotel
Karl-Liebknecht-Str. 5
Tel: 24 10

Metropol
Friedrichstr. 150-153
Tel: 2 20 40

Stadt Berlin
Alexanderplatz
Tel: 21 90

Unter den Linden
Unter den Linden 14
Tel: 2 20 03 11

Berolina
Karl-Marx-Allee 31
Tel: 2 10 95 41

Newa
Invalidenstr. 115
Tel: 2 82 54 61

Mitropa-Flughafenhotel
Berlin-Schönefeld
Tel: 6 72 39 50

FOOD DIGEST

During the last few years the cuisine on offer has become more attractive. The many Eastern European specialty restaurants contribute to a different culinary spectre than that found in West Berlin. Three of them, **Moskau**, **Haus Warschau** and **Haus Budapest** are in the Karl-Marx-Allee. The Moskau restaurant is a three-time winner of a readers' poll conducted by the *Neues Deutschland* newspaper and, the **HO-Bierstube** was elected the best beer hall. In **La Habana** in the Hotel Metropol Cuban cuisine is the house speciality.

The historical centre around the Spree isle and Alexanderplatz is dominated by German cuisine with solid home-cooking and beer as, for example at the **Alt-Cöllner Schankstuben**, Friedrichsgracht 50. In the renovated **Ermelerhaus**, Märkisches Ufer 10–12, there is a wine restaurant and a Biedermeier style café. **"Zur letzten Instanz"**, one of the oldest inns in Berlin, is well worth seeing on account of its interior, Waisenstrasse 14/16. The theatre restaurant **Ganymed** at Schiffbauerdamm 5 has for long been East Berlin's number one gourmet address. Reservations are definitely necessary at all of the better addresses. The central restaurant service in the "Alextreff", Rathausstrasse, (tel: 2 12 31 69) (Monday-Friday 10 a.m.-7 p.m., Saturday. 9 a.m.-1 p.m.) will be of assistance.

THINGS TO DO

CULTURE PLUS

GUIDED TOURS & EXCURSIONS

There is a choice of 10 different tours starting at 3.00 GDR marks. Some include visits to museums as well as excursions with lunch or a coffee-break. Bookings are possible at short notice: departures are from Alexanderplatz. You can also go on a guided tour by taxi in a small group, as the drivers are trained "cityscape-narrators". There are various routes ranging from 16.5 to 55 GDR marks for up to four passengers. Bookings at the Service Städtischer Nahverkehr at the Alexanderplatz S-Bahn station at (tel: 2 46 22 55). Interhotels also accept reservations.

In season the day trip steamers of the *Weisse Flotte* depart from their harbour at Treptower Park S-Bahn station. For information and advance booking visit the Service Städtischer Nahverkehr or phone the harbour office (tel: 2 71 23 27). Some of the traditional tourist cafés are also located near the water. The **Zenner** is situated directly on the banks of the Spree at Alt Treptow 14/17 and the **New Helgoland** is on the bank of the Kleine Müggelsee.

Daytrips to Potsdam: The same travel requirements for trips to Potsdam and Sanssouci Castle apply as for the rest of the GDR. Thus there are no special formalities. Various travel agents in West Berlin offer tours, among them the Severin & Kuehn, Berolina and Berliner Bäeren Stadtrundfahrt. There are various tours on the programme which include lunch. Severin & Kühn offer an exclusive tour with a serenade concert in the Potsdam castle gardens. The addresses of the operators are **Severin & Kühn**, 1000 Berlin 15, Kurfürstendamm 206 (tel: 8 983 10 15). **Berolina Sightseeing Tours**, 1000 Berlin 15, Meineckestr. 3 (tel: 8 83 31 31). **Berliner Bären Stadtrundfahrt**, 1000 Berlin 30, Rankestr. 35 (tel: 2 13 40 77).

MUSEUMS & EXHIBITIONS

Ausstellungszentrum am Funkturm
Am Alex
Tel: 2 10 32 93

Staatliche Museen zu Berlin (on the Museumsinsel)
Bodestr. 1-3
Tel: 2 20 03 81

Märkisches Museum
Am Köllnischen Park 5
Tel: 2 75 49 02/24

Museum für Naturkunde (Botanics)
Invalidenstr. 43
Tel: 2 89 70

Museum für Deutsche Geschichte
Unter den Linden 2
Tel: 2 00 05 91

Neuer Marstall
Marx-Engels-Platz 7
Tel: 2 38 32 87/2 38 33 11

Otto-Wagner-Haus
Märkisches Ufer 16-18
Tel: 2 79 14 02

Hugenotten-Museum (in the French church)
Platz der Akademie, entrance Charlottenstr.
Tel: 2 29 17 60

Kunstgewerbemuseum (Arts and crafts) in Schloss Köpenick, Schlossinsel (castle isle)
Tel: 6 57 26 51/6 57 15 04

Deutsche Staatsbibliothek
Unter den Linden 8
Tel: 2 07 80

Only a small selection of the 20 or so theatres can be mentioned here. Firstly, there is the excellent **Deutsche Staatsoper** and the celebrated **Komische Oper** in the Behrensstrasse for those who enjoy opera. **The Berliner Ensemble** at Bertolt-Brecht-Platz performs modern theatre: Brecht productions are especially popular. Both classical and modern plays are on the repertory of the **Deutsche Theater, Kammerspiele, Maxim-Gorki-Theater** and the **Volks-bühne**. Operettas are the order of the day at the **Metropol-Theater**. The **Puppen-theater** at Greifswalder Str. 81/84 provides amusement for younger visitors and the new **Friedrichstadt-Palast** with its 1900 seats presents music hall and revue entertainment of international standard. The old **Schaus-pielhaus**, built by Schinkel and once renowned the world over as a dramatic stage, was reopened after reconstruction as a prestigious new concert hall. **Die Distel** in the Metropol-Theater just opposite Friedrich-strasse S-Bahn station is East Berlin's most interesting cabaret. Of the approximate 20 cinemas showing international movies from East and West, the **Colloseum** in the Schön-hauser Allee and the **International** and **Kosmos** both in the Karl-Marx-Allee are worthy of mention. The **Babylon** at Rosa-Luxemburg-Str. 30 shows old German and also silent movies from the Filmarchiv der D.D.R. on Tuesdays and Fridays (7:30 a.m. to 8 p.m.). Information and tickets for theatres, concerts and other cultural events can be obtained in advance at the theatre box-offices in the Palast Hotel, Spandauer Strasse (tel: 2 12 52 58 or 2 12 59 02) Monday 1 p.m.-7 p.m., Tuesday-Friday 10 a.m.-1 p.m. and 2 p.m.-7 p.m., Saturday 10 a.m.-1 p.m.). Recently the Reisebüro der DDR has opened a branch office in the transit area of Friedrichstrasse station where western visitors can buy tickets in advance with their Deutschemarks. The coupons obtained (with 10 percent surcharge) are then exchanged for tickets at the respective box-office half an hour before the perform-ance. Opening hours: Monday-Friday 8 a.m.-noon and 1 p.m.-9 p.m., Saturday/Sunday 9 a.m.-noon and 1 p.m.-5 p.m. (tel: 03 72/2 29 17 50). Otherwise, advance bookings are possible at the box-offices of the respective theatre or by telephone. The West Berlin magazine *Zitty* has a current events calendar for East Berlin under the heading VEB Berlin. Other hints are in *Tip, Berlin-Programm* and in the *Tagesspiegel.* In East Berlin the more comprehensive guide *Wohin in Berlin?* is available at kiosks.

Berliner Ensemble
Bertolt-Brecht-Platz
Tel: 2 82 31 60

Deutsche Staatsoper
Unter den Linden 7
Tel: 2 05 45 56

Deutsches Theater und Kammerspiele
Schumannstr. 13a
Tel: 2 87 12 25/26

Komische Oper
Behrensstr. 55-57
Tel: 2 29 25 55

Maxim-Gorki-Theater
Am Festungsgraben 2
Tel: 2 07 17 90

Metropol-Theater
Friedrichstr. 100-102
Tel: 2 07 17 39

Puppentheater
Greifswalder Str. 81/84
Tel: 4 36 13 43

Schauspielhaus Berlin (in use only as con-cert hall)
Platz der Akademie.
Box-office for the Grosser Konzertsaal
Tel: 2 27 21 29

Box-office for the Kammermusiksaal/Mu-sikklub
Tel: 2 27 21 22

Theater der Freundschaft
H.-Rodenberg-Platz/ Parkaue 25
Tel: 5 57 03 06

Theater im Palast
Marx-Engels-Platz,
Tel: 2 38 23/54

Volksbühne
Rosa-Luxemburg-Platz
Tel: 2 82 96 07

Friedrichstadt-Palast
Friedrichstr. 107, Grosse und Kleine Revue
Tel: 2 83 64 74.
Das Ei in der Spielstätte
Tel: 2 83 64 36

Die Distel (this cabaret group has two venues)
Friedrichstrasse 101
Tel: 2 07 12 91
Degenerstr. 9
Tel: 3 87 51 74

FOREIGN CULTURAL CENTRES

Bulgarisches Kultur- und Informationszentrum
Unter den Linden 10
Tel: 2 00 02 61/2 07 15 05

Haus der Ungarischen Kultur
Karl-Liebknecht-Str. 9
Tel: 2 10 91 46

Kultur- und Informationszentrum der CSSR
Leipziger Str. 60
Tel: 200 02 31

Polnisches Informations- und Kulturzentrum
Karl-Liebknecht-Str. 7
Tel: 2 12 32 68

Französisches Kulturzentrum
Unter den Linden 37
Tel: 2 29 10 20

Zentrales Haus der Deutsch-Sowjetischen Freundschaft
Am Festungsgraben 1
Tel: 2 00 10

Haus der Sowjetischen Wissenschaft und Kultur
Friedrichstr. 176-179
Tel: 2 21 73 20

SHOPPING

A shopping expedition is limited by export restrictions. Apart from the up-market restaurants, which are still well frequented, the prices in pubs and cafes are very reasonable. The normal costs of refreshments, tickets for museums, postcards, brochures, a guided tour and lunch are easily covered because of the favourable exchange rate. Theatre tickets cost between three and twelve Marks.

It is worth buying a guide book or a map of the city. Books and records can also be recommended. A wide selection is on offer at **Das gute Buch** in Spandauer Strasse 2 or at **Karl-Marx-Buchhandlung**, Karl-Marx-Allee 78/84. Theatre enthusiasts could try the bookshop in the **Brecht-Haus Berlin**, Chausseestr. 125. All around music is found at **Musikhaus Carl Friedrich Zelter**, Spandauer Strasse and in the **Kunstsalon**, Unter den Linden 37/45.

In the *Intershops* western money will buy tax-free cigarettes, spirits, jeans, cosmetics, food and other western products as gifts for East Berlin friends and relatives. Some of these shops are situated immediately behind the Weidendammbürcke. Western money is also accepted at the Intertank petrol-stations and in the big "foreign currency only" hotels like the Palast-Hotel, Hotel Metropol and Grand Hotel. Western credit cards are, as of late, accepted by the Reisebüro der DDR and *Interhotels*. The credit card organizations have lists of the names of contract partners: Eurocard alone has more than 300.

PHOTOGRAPHY

A camera or movie-camera with equipment is allowed along with an appropriate amount of film. When walking around town certain photographic bans must be observed. They apply to the railroad, bridges and other elements of the transport system, the border security network along the Wall as well as military objects or military exercises of any kind. Exceptions are the guard-of-honour and the large-scale trooping of the guard at the Unter den Linden Memorial and official parades.

CREDITS

INDEX

S

T

U - V

W

B
C
D
E
F
G
H
I
J
a
b
c
d
f
g
h
i
j
k
l